MEMORIES
OF A
MISSIONARY DOCTOR

MEMORIES
OF A
MISSIONARY DOCTOR

WALTER C. THOMPSON, M.D.

ISBN # 978-0-9841821-0-7

First year of publication - 2009

His Image Publications
PO Box 1102
Williams Bay, WI 53191
walttmd@wi.rr.com
http://aplaceofhealing.info

Dedication

I dedicate this account of my memories as a missionary doctor to the members of my family, all of whom in their own way have contributed to my life and, thereby, to the success of these experiences.

Foremost among these is my wife, Avonne, who has sacrificed over and over again, foregoing many of the blessings, joys, and much of the support anticipated in the marriage relationship so that I could follow the Spirit leading me.

I wish, too, to acknowledge my sister, Myrtle, who inspired me to place my scattered notes and unfathomable memories into writing. Without her encouragement, it is likely my notes would still be scribbled on various papers among my personal effects.

Table of Contents

Introduction

"Someday, you will be a missionary doctor!"

The visiting pastor was in the driver's seat of the car, with me at his side, as we waited for the rest of my family; we were on our way to have dinner with friends after church. As we talked, the pastor reached over, placed his hand on my knee and predicted: "Someday, you will be a missionary doctor!"

I was not much more than six or seven years old when I began to hear stories of missionary doctors in foreign lands. Those were the days of World War II, and mission stories from New Guinea and from the islands of the South Pacific; stories that told of primitive people who still feasted on human flesh, and of *Fuzzie-Wuzzies* (converted cannibals who had come to know Jesus as their loving Savior) who rescued allied soldiers along the jungle trails among the island nations of the South Pacific. I was intrigued!

A few years later, a missionary came to our church and showed movies from Africa. Again, I was inspired by the urge to spend my life ministering in a place like that. Deep within my heart, there grew a desire to become a missionary doctor and to minister to the depressed and superstitious people of foreign lands.

But it seemed to be an impossible dream. I was the seventh of nine children struggling to make a living on a small dairy farm following the untimely death of my dad from tuberculosis. How does one even dream *big* dreams in situations like that?

My mother wanted us to have a Christian education so, after my second year of public high school, my younger brother, Joe, and I left to go to Wisconsin Academy, a boarding academy with a work program. There I was able to work my way through the remainder of my high school education, while my older brothers (to whom I owe a deep debt of gratitude) maintained the family farm.

Following graduation, I went back home to help on the farm. I had no other plans—and certainly no hopes of seeing my dreams fulfilled. I had been home just a few days, when I received a phone call from Ed Gammon, my academy principal. "There is a job waiting for you at the

College Wood Products in Berrien Springs, Michigan," he said. "They are expecting you soon!"

Needless to say, I was excited! Before the end of the day, my mother had given me her grocery money for the week (seventeen dollars), and I was out the door with my few possessions and my *thumb out* to hitch a ride to college—nearly 300 miles away through two major cities (I was a naïve farm boy)!

At college I was handed a hammer and assigned the job of assembling drawers for wooden chests and desks—my wages would be determined by the number of drawers I assembled. I learned to work fast and earned my way through school that first year, but I could not *get* freshman math and ended up with a *D* the first semester and a *C* the next—not a good beginning for application to a highly competitive, medical school. Were that not sufficient to dampen my dreams, I was called home to care for the farm since I was next in line and since all of my older brothers had moved on to other lines of work. I enjoyed the farm. Had it not been for that childhood dream, it is likely I would have settled down on the farm for life. But that dream was still calling! During that year I fixed up the buildings of the farm, readied it for sale and, come September, I was back in school—still in financial straits—but with a wealth of experience that would be most beneficial in days and years to come.

Thanks to my faithful wife, Avonne, who sacrificed completing her own education to support mine; and to Walter B. Clark, Dean of Admissions at The College of Medical Evangelists (now Loma Linda University School of Medicine) who, thankfully, looked at my heart rather than my grades, I was accepted into medical school.

As I neared the end of my first year, Avonne and I learned that we had been accepted, along with classmates Ben and Mona Leduc, to take part in an experimental student-missionary project in Montemorelos, Mexico, working in a small mission hospital there. In addition to sorting sample medicines and making daily hospital rounds, we assisted Dr. Gordon Hackett in surgery. On occasion, Mr. Herbert Fleener, Administrator of Montemorelos, took us high into small mountain villages in the small mission plane to hold clinics. This often meant buzzing the *airstrips* along riverbeds or fields (where cows, pigs and chickens roamed) before coming in for a landing. It was an enjoyable summer that further convinced us that God was calling us into medical ministry.

During the following school year, Avonne and I were invited by dear friends, Elden and Gerry Keeney, to accompany them and their young

The mission plane that took us into the small mountain villages to hold clinics.

family on a weekend camping and mission trip to San Felipi, on the Gulf of Mexico. That day the Santa Ana winds nearly blew our camper off the road, and that night we camped under a star-studded sky at the water's edge—an unforgettable experience! The following morning, we traveled up a steep, gravel road into a small mountain village. There we held clinics and cared for the sick who flocked to see us. It was dark by the time we headed back down the mountain road, only to discover that huge, black tarantulas also traveled there! In constructing the road, loose sand and gravel had been graded into high banks on both sides of the road. The tarantulas could get down onto the road but could not get back up the bank! We stopped, teased a few of the creatures into plastic bags, and put them into a cooler on the floor of the back seats where we thought they might hibernate! They didn't! Our wives spent the remainder of the trip with their legs curled up under them on the back seat. But mission life was growing on us!

The day I received my MD, and Avonne, her PHT (putting hubby through) was undoubtedly one of the happiest of our lives—an *impossible* dream come true! A one-year rotating internship at the Hinsdale Sanitarium and Hospital (now Adventist Hinsdale Hospital), and we were on our way to our first mission appointment—the Island of Guam.

Sometimes God seems to let us dream our dreams while He is preparing other things for us. As it turned out, after a couple of years serving the Seventh-day Adventist Church on the Island of Guam; a few years at the old Battle Creek Sanitarium; and after a surgical residency at Loma Linda, God arranged for me to practice my surgical skills in Chicago's Inner City as well as its western suburbs. There, He provided a base from which I could also participate in a number of short-term missions as an ambassador for the Seventh-day Adventist Church to various locations around the world. It is from these experiences (recovered from my diary) that I now give this account as an example to others—so that they, too, might dream dreams and wait upon the Lord to fulfill them in far more spectacular ways than they might ever imagine possible.

In the pages to follow, you will read of the harrowing experiences of running with the Cambodian refugees while fleeing from enemy mortars; of delivering (and rescuing) babies during record-breaking typhoon winds; of performing complicated surgical procedures under almost impossible circumstances, as well as sharing principles of healthful living with thousands of hurting people looking for a better way of life! You will read stories of miraculous interventions that testify of an ever-loving God who is preoccupied with saving the sick and hurting people of this world—where evil often seems to trump all that is good.

It was into a very sick and hurting world that God sent His son, Jesus. In the Book of Luke, Jesus quotes the prophecy in Isaiah describing His mission, "The Spirit of the LORD is upon Me, because He has anointed Me to preach the gospel to the poor; He has sent Me to heal the broken-hearted, to proclaim liberty to the captives and recovery of sight to the blind, to set at liberty those who are oppressed; to proclaim the acceptable year of the LORD …," Luke 4:18, 19 (NKJV). But it is interesting that Jesus did not quote the entire prophecy of Isaiah! That prophecy continues with these words … "To proclaim the acceptable year of the LORD, and the day of vengeance (alienation) of our God; to comfort all who mourn …," Isaiah 61:2 (NKJV).

It is into this sick world, in fulfillment of this prophecy of Isaiah, that God sends His missionaries today to share the *Everlasting Gospel* as they await the return of Jesus, not as a baby in a manger this time *to make the sacrifice for sin*, but as Lord of Lords, and King of Kings *to bring an end to sin*—the cause of the alienation that has separated us from God for the past 6,000 years—and to restore the fellowship that existed between us and our Creator in the Garden of Eden before the fall—a fellowship that will never end!

As John the Baptist was commissioned to prepare the world for that first advent of our Lord, I believe we have been commissioned to prepare it for this final event. Accordingly, in the pages that follow, and in addition to stories of ministry to those who were sick and suffering with physical maladies, you will read of public evangelism and mass baptisms—stories of healing—not only of the body, but healing in the truest sense of the word—the sharing of Biblical truths that alone can restore oneness with Jesus, the lack of which has for so long led to alienation from Him!

It is important for the reader to understand that neither I, nor the movement that I represent—the Seventh-day Adventist Church—is in competition with any other religious organization or movement. In fact; I believe that God has His true followers among all peoples. The stories, the lessons and the messages shared in this book are for all, and the invitation is for people of all faiths—and those of no faith—to return to the truths divinely revealed in the Holy Bible and find the healing thereby provided.

My thoughts, expressed from time to time throughout these pages, were recorded in private with no intent of later publication. But, as I have relived the events while preparing this book of memories, it has occurred to me that, in this world, all people search and sometimes struggle in their search for God and the truths that govern His vast universe. It is my hope that by sharing some of my own thoughts and experiences, your faith, too, might be enhanced. My prayer is that the reader will interpret these comments in the spirit with which they are here presented—the desire to share that which has given meaning to my life. Jesus said, "... I have come that they might have life ... and have it more abundantly" (John 10:10). That, too, is the desire of my heart for you as you read.

I have had a lifelong burden to share the Everlasting Gospel with the entire world, and I plead with God daily to hasten the day when the terrible experiences in this world, under the usurped dominion of the devil, will be over—when sickness, poverty, famine, war, broken homes, broken people and violent societies will all be a thing of the past. Whatever experiences I have had in life, I owe to the goodness of God who—so much more than I could ever know—longs for that glad day when the last curtain is pulled on the theater of this earth, and sin and evil will be no more—forever!

Chapter I

Guam

"At the very moment the last baby was in the arms of safety, the plate-glass windows of the nursery popped out!"

The highest wind velocities ever recorded had already blown out the windows of most of the hospital as Typhoon Karen barreled across the Island. Only the windows in the 4th floor newborn nursery, and labor room remained intact when we arrived to evacuate the babies and the maternity mothers. Seeing the immediate danger, we quickly took each baby from its bassinet, handed it to one of the mothers, and told them to *run* to the elevator and down to safety. At the very moment the last baby was in the arms of safety, the plate-glass windows of the nursery popped out! As the last lady left the labor room, those windows floated off into the wind. At the very moment all arrived safely on the ground floor, the elevator stopped working. No one present could question divine protection and perfect timing for each of those events on that November night.

But we are getting ahead of our story. As I previously mentioned, I had dreamed of becoming a missionary doctor since I was a child. Now, beyond all reasonable odds, I had graduated from the College of Medical Evangelists (now Loma Linda University) in California and was nearing completion of my rotating internship at Hinsdale Hospital in the western suburbs of Chicago. In keeping with our plans from the beginning, Avonne (my devoted wife who had worked selflessly during the long educational process) and I offered our services as foreign missionaries to the Missions Department of the General Conference of Seventh–day Adventists. In due time, application forms arrived inviting us to serve at the Far Eastern Island Mission on the Island of Guam. This was *not* the place I had dreamed of; why not some place where our services are really needed—some primitive place where there is no other health care available and where the gospel has not yet been preached, I asked myself! I was not happy with the call but, trusting the Lord had heard and was answering our prayers, we reluctantly completed the application process and began our preparations for travel.

The Seventh-day Adventist General Conference Quadrennial Session was held in San Francisco that year. We were invited to take part in the mission pageant before boarding ship for the trip to Guam. Though most missionaries at the time were traveling by plane to the remote corners of the earth, we were told by our sponsors that they wanted us to have the experience of traveling by sea. Accordingly, following the pageant, family members living in the area graciously took us to the port where we were welcomed aboard the cargo liner, *The President Madison*. Just as the sun was setting in the western sky, Avonne and I and our six-month-old son, Greg, found ourselves sailing out under the Golden Gate Bridge and off into the great Pacific. We were finally on our way! What does the Lord have in mind for us, I wondered!

Avonne and our son, Greg, on board *The President Madison*—on the way to Guam.

On board with us were George and Martha Floro (a college anthropologist professor who would be teaching at the College of Guam) and their two children; a retired pastor from another Christian church (going to Guam to fill a vacancy); Amy Messenger, an Adventist school teacher, on her way to teach in the Palau Islands; and Lois Foster, a recent college graduate who would be serving as secretary to the mission. Traveling as we were on a merchant vessel, we were guests of the crew under the care of the First Mate—and fine hosts they were; in fact, he assured us that he knew the eating practices of Adventists and was well prepared to meet our needs and desires. Sometimes during the trip we were sorry for that! Never before—or since—have we eaten so many eggs and so much cheese! It was his sincere desire to supply our protein needs! There was nothing we could want or need that he wasn't willing to supply!

The evening was serene and the waters quiet as we bid adieu to our homeland, watching the Golden Gate Bridge grow fainter and fainter and finally fade off into the distance. We awakened in the morning refreshed and ready to enjoy our first full day at sea. It was while I was in the shower that I began to notice my stomach *turning* a bit and, by the time I had completed my bath, I was so sick I could hardly stand. For the next few days, I found my only comfort was to be flat on my back in bed, while the ship rolled and tossed in the choppy waters off the west coast of the U.S.—much to the amusement of my seaworthy wife.

Eventually, the weather cleared and the sea calmed. Before long, I found my sea-legs and began to enjoy the beauty of the great Pacific. Our days were occupied by lounging on deck, fellowshipping with our shipmates (friendships that have lasted all through the years—until even today), filling our plates and stomachs in the galley, and just standing by the railing and watching the glassy-smooth waters of the deep-blue sea. Often we were entertained by flying fish, breaking water near at hand and then gliding off into the distance with unimaginable grace and ease. At night, as we gazed up into the velvety-black sky, we marveled at the beauty of innumerable sparkling diamonds, or watched as our hosts demonstrated the use of the sextant and determined our progress toward our destination (before the days of the GPS instruments). Sometimes, I found myself sitting alone on the ship's bridge—looking out into those vast heavens and musing about God. Was He real? I could not refute the claim—how else could such vast beauty exist? Was it really He who had called us, and was this really the mission field for us? And, why Guam? I could not understand. During those hours I struggled as I sought to speak with a God I could not hear nor see—yet, at times, seemed so close I could almost reach out and touch Him—His presence seemed so near! I wish that He would just speak to me in an audible voice or that He might show himself in some visible way. Yet, even as I pled with Him, I knew in my heart that—even should He respond to my request—I would still find some way to doubt, to question, to rationalize that perhaps I was hearing voices or having dreams. My experience—though not like that of Jacob who centuries ago wrestled with God—refusing to let go of Him until He had blessed him; or Job, from whom Satan took almost everything he owned—including his health—was nevertheless much the same. For, like them, I needed to know my God; that He existed and that He was with me. But God is good, and before our hosts could point far off into the distance and try to convince us that the little speck in the west was our destination, He and I had found each other and covenanted to be faithful one to the other—so long as life might last.

That speck in the west gradually became bigger and clearer as the day wore on and, by evening, we found ourselves being carefully guided into the spacious Apra Harbor on Guam. Even as we disembarked, many were on hand to give us a royal welcome and to encircle our necks with beautiful, sweet-smelling leis of orchids and plumeria. Only later did we learn that Dr. Robert Gloor and his family—whom we were replacing—had hoped and planned for us to arrive by plane long before this. They, especially, were glad to see us! But—as I reflect back—I am most grateful for the foresight of the one who made our travel arrangements—for those nights on the ship's bridge were a necessary part of my preparation for the work we had been called to do.

Doctor Gloor was already late for his appointments back in the States and was anxious to be on his way. In short order, we met with government officials and arranged for my license to practice my profession on the Island. Then, too, I needed to purchase a car for transportation to and from the hospital. We found a used Volkswagen *bug* for—what I was assured—was a reasonable price on the Island. Then it was off to the hospital to be introduced to the staff and to make rounds on our inpatients. Back at the clinic I met our staff, was given a brief overview of the operations of the clinic, instructed how to order supplies and medications to keep our pharmacy supplied—and then he was gone! I was on my own. The next day, my first full day in the clinic—with the able help of two secretaries and three nurses—we saw nearly one hundred patients; a pattern that was never to let up!

The offices of the Far Eastern Island Mission and Clinic were situated in Agana Heights, a beautiful site overlooking the government buildings and the beautiful Agana Bay. In addition to the mission office and clinic building, the mission compound consisted of the Agana Heights Seventh-day Adventist Church, located just behind the mission office; and, not far away, our home—a one-story cement-block house with a corrugated metal roof and louvered glass windows. In addition, there was a small, wooden-frame house near ours and, down the grade a bit, a duplex of similar construction as our house. Across the street and down the hill a short distance, were two more wooden-frame homes and a couple of World War II metal quonsets serving as church school buildings. About five miles to the east, the Guam Memorial Hospital (where we admitted our inpatients) sat on another point overlooking Tumon Bay. It was a long, narrow reinforced-concrete building positioned so as to catch the gentle breezes coming off the ocean. The U.S. Naval Hospital and Naval Base were located a couple of miles to the west of our mission compound.

Our clinic consisted of a waiting room; a reception area, which included our medical records; a fully-supplied pharmacy; three examining rooms, one of which had a large picture window with a view of Agana Bay; a room for minor surgery, and my office—which doubled as a storage area and from which I ordered our pharmaceutical and clinical supplies. Clinic hours began when I finished my morning hospital rounds, though patients began arriving in the early morning hours to assure a good place in line. Hours ended when the last patient had been seen—sometimes late in the evening. I was on call 24/7 for emergencies, with patients who needed to be cared for often knocking on our door in the middle of the night.

Besides the Mission Clinic, there were two other outpatient clinics available for civilians on the Island; the Catholic Medical Center; and the Outpatient Department of the government-run, Guam Memorial Hospital.

One of the patients in the hospital, when I arrived, was a lady in her early twenties with end-stage pneumonia. Everything possible had been done for her, but she was beyond help and died soon after my arrival. Another, a young man with nephrotic syndrome—a form of kidney failure—died a few days later with overwhelming sepsis due to pneumococcus peritonitis, an infection of the belly—not a real good record upon which to begin a medical mission! A third patient that Dr. Gloor introduced me to in the hospital was a young lady who had recently experienced an uncomplicated delivery of a baby, but who ended up paralyzed below the waist. His conclusion, after evaluating the situation carefully, was that she was suffering what was then known as a conversion reaction. Her problem was not in her spine but, rather, in her head. Unfortunately, she was not responding to the therapy he had prescribed. By the time I arrived on the scene, she was tired of lying in a hospital bed and requested that I release her to go home and be cared for there. Somewhat reluctantly and urging her to keep in touch with me, I wrote the discharge order. I made a house call, sometime later, to see how she was doing and discovered that she was being treated by a local traditional healer. I wasn't impressed with her choice of caregiver, but I had to admit that we hadn't helped her. A few weeks later, she came to see me in the clinic—now cured and walking normally. Though we suspected that some of the patients who came to the clinic had been made even sicker by the treatment of the traditional healers, I learned to respect this one and, during my time on the Island, enjoyed a very good working relationship with her.

During medical school, we had studied about intestinal parasites and visualized prepared slides of them under the microscope. One day I had opportunity to test my educational achievement. She was a lady, perhaps in her late '20s, who was pregnant and had severe, bloody diarrhea. In the process of checking things out, I obtained a swab of bloody mucus from her lower bowel and placed it on a slide under the lens of the microscope. I could hardly believe my eyes. It was virtually swarming with live ameboid forms of E. histolitica (a frequent cause of severe bowel and liver disease in many places around the world) such as I had never seen before, but that I recognized at once. Since she was pregnant, I was somewhat limited in what medications I might prescribe to eliminate the parasites. Fortunately it is amazing what one can do, sometimes, with something as simple as a retention enema!

My typical day went something like this: I was up and out of bed by 5:30 a.m. Following a shower, a shave, and a brushing of teeth it was time for personal devotions—a time to read God's Word and share with Him my thanks, my needs and my desires for the day. Then it was off to the hospital for morning rounds, often arriving there by about 7:00 a.m. The time of my arrival home for a quick breakfast with Avonne and Greg was dependent upon the number of patients and the seriousness of their ills. From there, it was to the clinic to begin seeing patients—some who had already been waiting for hours. Thanks to the pleasant and efficient staff—patients were registered, placed in a room, and prepared for consultation before my arrival. Thus, my whole attention could be given to hearing them describe their problem, give them a thorough examination, and make recommendations for them. Any medications that were indicated were dispensed from the pharmacy by our staff. At the conclusion of the visit, a brief note was placed in the medical record for future reference. Thus working, we could minister to the needs of many, many patients while giving them the attention and care they had come to expect. On those days when an emergency surgery or a lady in labor was ready to deliver and it was necessary for me to return to the hospital, the patients waited for my return. Sometimes this occurred several times daily; I learned to admire the patience of my patients.

Colds, flu, high fevers and fever-related convulsions were common, everyday illnesses that needed care. Other frequent problems included rashes of many kinds; especially, infected rash of the feet arising from the thongs held in place by the great toe. Diarrhea and various kinds of intestinal worms were also common. Many patients suffered from gouty arthritis and often came in with excruciating pain. Pneumonia and meningitis (infections of the brain) were all too common, often leading to death or serious brain injury. Food poisoning, from the ingestion of seafood during certain seasons, was quite common—as were injuries incurred while fishing or swimming among the coral reef. On one occasion, we experienced an epidemic of meningitis caused by a parasite obtained from eating fresh-water shrimp gathered from local streams and pools of water.

There was an unwritten law on the Island governing emergencies. It was this: When it is necessary to get somewhere in a hurry, you turn on the lights, lay on the horn and *go*! At the time, Guam had one of the highest birthrates of anywhere in the world. Many of these were my patients and, many times, it was necessary to exercise the unwritten law regarding emergencies. Only once did an officer seem to forget the law. It was a Sunday afternoon and traffic along the coastal highway to the hospital was very heavy. I had spent the morning at the hospital trying to induce a lady to deliver her baby under controlled conditions. Her previous baby had been born in the car on the way to the hospital, and she was terribly afraid of a repeat of that experience. As the day arrived for her due date, we made the necessary arrangements to do things right. The trouble was—though she had good contractions while the medicine was running into her veins—nothing was happening as a result. And, as soon as I turned off the medication drip, all contractions stopped. We decided to call it off and to try again another day. I returned home. Just as I arrived home and began to open the door, the phone rang. It was the hospital; my patient was having contractions. I knew what I had to do. I got back into my Volkswagen *bug*, turned on the lights, placed one hand on the horn and was off to the hospital. Before I had reached the bottom of the hill, red lights were flashing and a siren screaming behind me. What to do? I kept going—in and out of traffic as fast as I could safely go—rushing to the hospital to meet my obligation; the squad car sometimes nearly catching up. Arriving at the hospital, I pulled up to the curb, ran into the hospital, got into the elevator and arrived in the delivery room just in time to attend to the birth—much to the relief of the mother. Meanwhile, the officer whose squad car lights were flashing and whose siren was screaming, ran up to the administration desk and asked where I had gone. When later I spoke with those behind the desk, I was told that the officer was as pale as a ghost when he arrived. After hearing of the emergent nature of my call, he turned around and walked back to his car and left! I heard no more from him—nor was the law changed. But how I might have wished he had chosen, rather, to serve as my escort than as my pursuer!

One morning as I arrived at the hospital to make my rounds, I stopped at the Emergency Department to see a baby who was now a couple of months old but was not thriving, and who was experiencing repeated *convulsions.* Various formulas and feeding schedules had been tried, but to no avail. In examining the baby and speaking with the mother, it dawned on me that there could be only one explanation for this baby's trouble. He had to be vomiting because of an obstruction of the gut, and he was *convulsing* from salt imbalance and low calcium as a consequence of repeated vomiting. I knew, at once, that the baby needed to be seen and cared for by a surgeon. There was none available among civilian caregivers. Fortunately, the U.S. Naval Hospital had an understanding with the Government of Guam to help out on such occasions. Upon discovering this, arrangements were made to refer the baby to the surgeon there. I called a few days later to find out what had happened to the baby and to learn how he was doing, and the surgeon came on the line. He had indeed operated on the baby, found a birth defect almost completely blocking the outlet from the stomach, corrected the defect and the baby was now doing well. At his kind invitation, I went to meet him and to see the baby. While there, he gave me a tour of the hospital, introduced me to some of his colleagues, and finally took me down to the main floor and introduced me to Captain Miller, the Chief Operating Officer of the hospital. They seemed to be impressed with my diagnosis, and I was equally impressed with their kind assistance.

Though busy, I knew that all work and no play was about as bad for one's health as no work and all play! Therefore, when Tommy Cruz, the husband of Violet Cruz—one of the clinic nurses—invited me to go snorkeling with him one night, I jumped at the opportunity. That evening, swimming around the coral reef in search of shells and observing the many beautiful fish and sea creatures with Tommy, was just the beginning of a long and lasting friendship with this native islander. Thanks to him, Guam became—not only a place of service—but a virtual natural paradise, as well.

One of the creatures I saw that night was a sea slug—no, not just one—but hundreds of them! Varying from a foot or two in length and two or three inches in diameter, these creatures crawl around on the floor of the reef. As a child in school, I had read about how the American Indians used to catch fish and place them in the ground under the seeds when planting their gardens. Therefore, I wasn't too surprised when, upon visiting with George and Martha Floro one day (our transoceanic travel companions), I found that George had gone out and gathered these large slugs to use as fertilizer around his papaya trees and in his sweet potato patch. By all appearances, he was on to something good for the garden—though I am not so sure the same was true for the sea!

Meanwhile, back at the clinic there was no letup. Let me share just a few examples: A car salesman at the Ford dealership on the Island who loved his smokes came to me with far-advanced lung disease. Sitting in the chair in my examining room, Don (all patient names are fictional) always found it necessary to lean forward with lips pursed, as he struggled to breathe. Even then, his lips were often more blue than pink, and his fingernails curiously shaped like spoons. It was not an easy battle for him to give up the tobacco, but with frequent encouragement and many prayers on my part, he was eventually able to be content just holding his unlit cigar between his lips! We rejoiced together with that victory.

One day a little girl, about five years of age, was brought to me covered with boils. Job had nothing over on her! Never had I lanced so many boils on the same person (nor have I since). Much time was spent in instructing her parents regarding her diet and in keeping her clean so as to prevent a recurrence.

Another day it was a little girl, about the same age, who arrived with black and blue patches all over her body. It was immediately evident to me that something was awry with her blood coagulation system. I placed her in the hospital where lab tests confirmed my diagnosis of idiopathic thrombocytopenia (insufficient platelets in her blood to prevent bleeding). After a day or two—and long before we had opportunity to do a full evaluation and begin treatment—her family decided to take her home. They were convinced that the problem was the result of being pinched by the *spirits* that dwelt in the banyan trees, as she disobediently went outside at night to play. They did not return to the clinic for follow-up, and I never knew what finally happened to her.

Ruthie was in her late teens when she came to me for a second opinion. She had missed a period and was told by another doctor that she was pregnant. She was from a *good* family with high Christian standards and knew that it was impossible for her to be pregnant. She needed reassurance. My examination confirmed the previous doctor's diagnosis—*not* what Ruthie wanted to hear—nor did she believe me either. She would consult with yet another doctor.

Tony was about 20 years old when I first saw him with advanced heart disease. Some time earlier, he had had rheumatic fever that affected the valves of his heart. Already, at this young age, he was in serious trouble with a heart so large it filled much of his chest. One could almost hear the rumble made by rushing blood through leaking valves—even without the aid of a stethoscope. There was little I could do for him, other than to try to control some of the symptoms and encourage him along the way. Surgical correction was not an option for Tony.

One of the banes of the diabetic is infection leading to gangrene of the feet. When, one day, an old farmer arrived at the clinic with a large, black, ulcerated foot, I immediately hospitalized him and placed him on a regimen to remove the dead tissue and encourage healing. After a few days, he went home with instructions to continue the outlined program. I saw him a time or two after that, but the foot was not doing well; then I didn't see him again for several months when, suddenly, there he was again. This time the foot appeared completely healed. Of course, I wanted to know what he had been doing. I shouldn't have asked, for the story he told me was almost unbelievable! Tiring of the wound care I had advised, the man began putting herbs that he found around his home on the ulcerated foot, all the while continuing to walk with his feet uncovered through the barnyard mud and manure. What was I to say to him? Quite obviously, he knew something I didn't know! Unfortunately—though there were a few weeks of exultation—the infection returned, and my farmer friend sadly ended up with an amputation.

Parkinsonian dementia (Parkinson's Disease accompanied by loss of mental functions) and Amyotrophic Lateral Sclerosis (Lou Gehrig's disease) were two diseases of the nervous system that occurred in epidemic proportions on the Island. In fact, because of their high incidence, a permanent research institute was established on Guam just to study them to try to determine the cause and find effective treatment options. It didn't take me long to learn to look for uncontrolled muscle twitching in every patient complaining of weakness or other unusual symptoms. Most patients with these diseases had a rapid downhill course to death, but there was one man I was asked to see at his home in the village of Umatic who was in his 17th year with the disease. Unfortunately, he was totally bedridden and fully dependent upon the care of others during many of those years.

While on the ship on our way to Guam, we were told by our Captain and First Mate that, though typhoons were common in the Pacific, for some reason they usually went around the Island of Guam as they stormed north and west. Thus reassured, it was one less concern for us to worry about upon our arrival on this tropical paradise. So, when in early November—just a couple of months after we arrived—we heard weather reports describing a storm brewing far to the south, we noted it with interest but with little concern.

All this began to change when, each day, the newscaster reported that the storm—now a full-fledged typhoon—was remaining on course for a direct hit on our Island. By week's end, we could no longer ignore the warning. There was no longer any question; we were on target to be hit late on Sunday afternoon. We began to make plans. Continuous radio updates instructed us in our preparations, while I continued caring for my patients in the clinic and at the hospital. On Sabbath morning, a very sick baby that I had just delivered a few days earlier was brought to the clinic for care. The baby was hot and lethargic. The soft spot on its head was firmer than it should have been, and I noted that its skin was covered with very small, red dots. I sent the family to the hospital immediately and followed them there. A needle was placed in the spinal canal for a sample of fluid for exam, and the baby was immediately started on antibiotics. Unfortunately, it was all too little, too late. The baby died that very afternoon from meningitis. I was saddened by the loss of life. Death of a child is never a pleasant thing, but for a newborn to die was heart-rending; my heart ached for the family. What words can one speak at such a time?

By the next morning, one sensed a silent, eerie feeling in the air. There was no sun visible in the sky—only a strange sort of darkness that enveloped the land. My clinic that morning was quiet. Only a patient or two who needed to be seen ventured out. Likewise, things were quiet at the hospital with my patients doing very well; some were anxious to go home before the storm. I arrived back home early to the pleasant aroma of beans baking in the oven. Our bathtub had already been filled with water, and other precautions taken in preparation for what was now inevitable. This was going to be a major storm, and everyone was urged to seek safe shelter. Because the Naval Hospital was deemed to be a safe place we, along with others of the mission staff, planned to go there to weather out the storm.

It was about 5:00 p.m. when I received a phone call from the hospital. A lady was in active labor and I was needed there at once. What was I to do? I responded to the call. Already my Volkswagen *bug* was being buffeted by the wind as I drove along the coastal highway toward the hospital; palm trees lining the beach were performing a hideous dance in the wind. Arriving at the hospital, I discovered that I had not arrived a minute too soon. The patient was already on the delivery table and ready for my assistance. Just then, the lights of the hospital flickered and went out. The delivery was completed with the aid of a flashlight! Electricity was back on by the time I finished my work. I phoned home to tell Avonne I didn't think it wise to try to return home, and she assured me that she and our son, Greg, and Martha, the Palauan student who lived with us, would soon be joining the mission president and his wife at the Naval Hospital so I need not worry. Sometimes it is true that families pay a higher price for service than does the servant himself; such was surely the case this night.

Upon completing my work in the delivery room, I took a walk through the hospital. I was already concerned when I walked through the Pediatric Department. Gusts of wind were rattling the windows with frightening intensity, and we were still only on the very edge of the storm. I knew we must evacuate the kids to a safer place. That begun, I walked through the orthopedic ward. There I saw a young man lying in his bed strung up in traction, all four extremities badly broken as a result of a motorcycle accident. He could not move. Panic filled his eyes and reflected throughout his entire being, as he looked up at the windows beside him and saw them yielding further and further toward collapse with each new gust of wind.

The bottom floor of the hospital was partially below ground level; it was the safest place to take the many patients. The business office soon became our all-purpose ward, but we had not yet evacuated the nursery or labor room on the 4th floor. Upon our arrival there, the wind had already blown out all of the windows on both sides of the hospital between the stairs (and elevator) and the patients needing rescue. To reach them, it was necessary to walk through a virtual wind tunnel. Plaster walls were already crumbling; the nursing center and equipment had already been torn apart and were blowing away.

Entering the nursery and sensing the urgency of the situation, two of the administrative staff and I, quickly lifted each one of the 31 babies from their bassinets and handed them to the ladies who had been seeking shelter in the labor room just across the hall. With baby in hand, we told them to *run* for safety. At the very moment the last baby was in the arms of safety, the plate-glass windows of the nursery popped out! Then—just as the last person left the labor room—those windows, too, disappeared into the wind! When, at last, we arrived at the ground floor, all electrical power ceased—including power to the elevator. We thanked God that all had been brought down to safety.

Fortunately, though the windows around us bowed and shook, they held firm throughout the storm. We could only imagine what destruction must be occurring outside. To add to the excitement of it all, one more women from the labor room decided that the time had come. We delivered her baby by the light of a flashlight—before a whole room of witnesses!

Meanwhile, with the winds blowing and the very foundations of the building shaking, I wondered what was happening at home to my family and to the clinic building. I knew the hospital was being destroyed, and I hoped and prayed that my family would be safe and that the mission would be saved to minister to the needs that would surely follow. There was nothing more I could do but wait and pray.

By midnight the worst of the storm had passed. A couple of us went upstairs to assess the damage; everything was a mess. Only a few of the windows in the Tuberculosis Wing remained—all others were gone. Walls had weakened and begun to disintegrate by the force of the wind-driven salty water. We found almost nothing that was salvageable. Oh yes! There WAS one thing! Stashed away in the linen closet at the end of the hallway next to the nursery, we found another baby—sleeping contentedly in the blanket in which it had been wrapped when removed from the bassinet. Evidently, one of the ladies panicked and, rather than to risk carrying the baby with her as she ran to safety, she, instead, placed it on a shelf in the closet!

Only a few of the windows in the Tuberculosis Wing remained—all others were gone.

Upon awakening from a couple of hours of very restless sleep at the dawning of another day, I wandered by the business office to check on things. All there were safe and sound. There was just one little problem! Three of the baby girls had the same names—both first and last. We could only hope their mothers would be able to identify their own!

I walked out of the main entrance to go home. My car had been blown firmly up against another and was immovable. It was pocked with hundreds of dents, apparently due to the pea gravel from the roof of the hospital. Fortunately, at just that moment, an ambulance arrived from the Naval Hospital. Since our mission compound was on the way back, I was able to catch a ride home in it. By then heavy equipment had opened up a path through sand and debris along the coast, allowing traffic to go through. On the way we passed Shipwreck Charley's place. His whole store was gone but, already, Charlie had carefully displayed his remaining wares on the sidewalk in front of the place where his store had once been, and he was ready for business! I marveled at his optimistic enthusiasm.

No! God had not answered my prayers to save the mission complex—at least not in the way I had wished. The roof was gone! Windows were gone! Only the concrete walls remained. I walked back to our home, and it, too, was in ruins. I opened the door and was met by my wife inside. The roof was gone—except over the room where my family and friends had gone during the storm. The windows were gone. The cupboards were empty. Only a lonely pot of baked beans, with the cover still on, sat firmly on the kitchen counter—apparently undisturbed! The floor was cluttered with broken glass, shattered timbers and all manner of debris. Avonne had, just moments before, sustained a deep gash on her leg where she had caught it on a protruding nail. She had ripped off the bottom of her slacks and bound the wound to stop the bleeding. I took her over to what remained of the clinic. In one drawer in the minor surgery room, I found a single, dry suture set. With it, I repaired the wound on her leg while she rehearsed the events of the past 15 hours.

The roof of our house was gone! Windows were gone! Only the concrete walls remained.

At the last minute, she and the family with whom she was planning to go to the Naval Hospital, decided to stay in our house instead. As the storm grew in intensity, they all ran into the back bedroom where they placed mattresses up against the windows and waited and prayed. At one point, when Avonne and one of the students were lying across the twin bed with their heads against the wall resting, they both—suddenly and simultaneously—sat up, only to have a heavy picture that had been hanging on the wall above their heads fall violently to the floor. They will never be convinced that angels do not exist and "encamp round about us!" Miraculously, though all of the rest of the house was ruined, the windows and roof of that one room remained firm and dry throughout the storm.

Upon completing the repair of my wife's leg, I *hitched* a ride back to the hospital where I expected to find many injured patients waiting. To my surprise, there were no serious, life-threatening injuries. A long line of people who had stepped on dirty nails were waiting to receive tetanus shots but, apart from that, things were mostly quiet. While there, I was told that Captain Miller had come by to invite me to join with his staff at the Naval Hospital, to care for the sick and wounded until such a time in the future that our clinic and the government hospital might be rehabilitated. (While the Naval Hospital had lost a few windows, it suffered no major damage.) Then I knew that divine providence had been at work, when months before I had referred the convulsing baby to that facility for care and had opportunity to meet the captain and his staff. For the next couple of months, I worked side by side with his staff sharing medications and supplies; sharing obstetrical call; seeing one another's patients and, in every way, complimenting the efforts of the other. Only God knows why I was so honored, for no other civilian physician on the Island was given that privilege. I give God all of the praise!

As if the damage were not enough, a rumor began spreading around the Island, later in the day, indicating that Typhoon Karen was changing direction and heading back toward Guam. Fortunately, it was only a rumor. Reports appearing in many newspapers stateside—describing Typhoon Karen as a giant steamroller crossing the little Island—were pretty accurate.

Witnessing the power of the storm and seeing the damage it had inflicted, I had anticipated hundreds of dead and injured; thankfully, I was wrong. The final death toll from the storm was 29. There were few other major injuries—a fact many attributed to divine protection. This was most evident when, the following Sabbath, we met at the Telafofo

Church for worship (this church, located at the southern portion of the Island away from the main impact of the storm, was not badly damaged). If ever there was a day of true gratitude and praise in worship to God, we witnessed it that day. The church was packed. Everyone had a testimony to share of how they had been kept safe through very dangerous and frightening experiences. Nor was there any sense of urgency to conclude the service as so often occurs.

Many, many people with whom I spoke during the following weeks and months told of similar, harrowing experiences and of miraculous protection. I found it most interesting that God seemed not to have been any respecter of persons in giving out his blessings—further convincing me that, though the devil seeks to devour and destroy, a loving God has no such desire. The Bible says, "God so loved the world that He gave His only begotten Son that whoever believes in Him should not perish but have everlasting life. For God did not send His Son into the world to condemn the world, but that through Him, the world might be saved," John 3:16, 17. (NKJV)

Though the wood-frame houses in which our mission officers lived suffered some damage they, unlike our own *of more sturdy construction,* remained livable. For the next couple of months Gideon (our president) and Avonelle Haas shared their home with us. I thought it interesting that the wooden houses built on stilts survived the storm better than houses like ours—even better than the metal quonsets that appeared so indestructible (residuals from World War II). Obviously the Chamorro natives had learned some valuable lessons about home construction through the years.

Only later—though we knew the storm had been bad—were we told that the barometric pressure in the eye of the storm had reached an all-time low (at least 934 mbars), and that unprecedented wind velocities had carried away the International Weather Station tower, designed to withstand winds of 225 Knots. (Typhoon Karen still holds the record for wind velocity with sustained winds estimated at 155 - 190 mph with gusts to 207 mph.)

Indeed, it was a different Guam to which we awakened the next morning after Karen played her *trick* on our little Island. Essentially, all communication with the outside world had been cut off. Entire communities along the coast had been completely wiped out, and most others seriously damaged. People were forced to find shelter wherever they could. Often this meant that relatives, friends, and *sometimes* enemies, must share shelter and facilities. I was, especially, made aware of this when—one evening some days later—a man came to the house to get me to see his father who had been shot and was dying at home. Upon arrival at his home, the victim was already dead—shot during an altercation over a coveted, prize-fighting cock (cock-fighting was illegal at the time). I comforted the family as best I could.

One might naturally expect the medical needs of people to increase following such a devastating experience—I did; but they did not! While pregnant mothers continued to have babies, and while nail punctures knew no favorites; my clinics at the Naval Hospital were much, much lighter than had been the case previously. Only as supplies arrived by ship from the outside world and people began to get their lives together again, did my work load begin to pick up.

During the weeks it took for building materials and other supplies to begin to arrive, we were well cared for. Our Palauan students were very adept at preparing food over an open fire—our electrical appliances being worthless. Without air-conditioning or screens on the windows, we discovered other means to reduce the mosquito burden—though sometimes they did keep us awake with their threatening, monotone, high-pitched whine around our beds. Without phone service, I had no need to fret over emergency calls—though I was required to rotate in-house call at the Naval Hospital on nights and weekends.

By Christmastime, we were back in our house. A new roof had been built on it and on our clinic building. Windows had been replaced, and things were reasonably back to normal. By then, too, as other Islanders became settled in their homes, the numbers of patients swelled. For weeks—while people were busy putting their lives back together—they had no time to get sick. As a deer, running from the claws of a tiger, receives a boost of adrenalin to make its escape, so I discovered similar behavior among human beings during periods of high stress. Often, it is only when the attack is over, that the symptoms of stress become evident.

Lillie was one such example. We have often heard that cold hands are an indication of a warm heart. Lillie must have had an awfully warm heart—for when holding her hands out for me to see—drops of perspiration dripped visibly from the tips of her cool, moist fingers.

Andy had a different problem. At the most unexpected times, he became disabled by shortness of breath and pain in his chest. Sometimes his lips became *numb* and his fingers cramped up. Though his symptoms could be rapidly improved by breathing into a brown, paper bag for a few minutes; and though physical findings, X-rays, and electrocardiograms were normal, I had a difficult time convincing Andy that he was suffering from the results of anxiety, and his life was not in danger.

But symptoms were not the only illnesses on the increase. Blood pressures began to rise. Diabetics were more difficult to control. I was, again, seeing patients with colds and flu and complications of these. Asthmatic patients, too, found their attacks more severe and of increased frequency. Rose was one such patient. She was not a new patient, but I began to see her more frequently in the clinic and, almost as frequently, at my door in the middle of the night seeking help with her breathing. Fortunately, she usually responded well to the medications and was able to return home to carry on her family responsibilities. On one occasion, she appeared during clinic hours in severe distress. No sooner had we administered the usual medications, than she passed out and fell to the floor. Giving mouth-to-mouth resuscitation is not usually a pleasant experience, but on this occasion, it paid off well! I admitted Rose to the hospital for a couple of days but, fortunately, there were no long-term, adverse effects from the experience. And, yes, I was reminded, again, that one can effectively send up a prayer to heaven while blowing the breath of life into another person!

In time, too, the windows at the Guam Memorial Hospital were boarded up and the doors opened, again, for service. One of the doctors, hired by the Government of Guam to fill vacancies created when others left the Island after the storm, was an obstetrician. He was a lifesaver for me for—during the few months he was there—he taught me how to do emergency C-sections. Sometime earlier, I had had a young lady in labor with her first pregnancy that was not progressing well. Though she was having good contractions, nothing was happening with the movement of the baby. Unfortunately, at the time, there were no obstetricians at the hospital for consultation, and I knew I needed help. I called the Naval Hospital hoping to either transfer her there or have someone from there come to help me—only to be told to be patient and to wait longer! When, at that point, I knew it was past-time and they were not available, I called the operating room staff to prepare for an emergency section; I dared wait no longer. By the time the crew arrived and was ready, the baby's buttocks began to show at the outlet. In short order, the body was delivered and, with a little help from a very experienced midwife, the head followed. The baby and mother were OK but, from that point on, I knew I needed to be prepared to do my own C-sections. As a result of this new obstetrician's kind help and excellent instructions, I had many opportunities to successfully use those new skills.

I must tell of a couple of other pregnant mothers I was privileged to minister to! One was a lady, pregnant and in labor, with her 28th pregnancy. At age 48, I concluded that she hadn't taken too many *vacations* through the years! At any rate, she was now in labor and scared to death. Her labor was not complicated, and the delivery easy enough. Unfortunately—in spite of all of our best efforts—she could not stop bleeding. Her womb was too old and worn out to contract properly. Only after what seemed much longer than the clock admitted, did the bleeding finally slow down and stop. When at last she realized she was going to live, she was ecstatic. When making rounds the next morning, she expressed her gratitude—honoring me by giving her new little boy my name.

Earlier, I related the experience of the young lady who had come to the clinic seeking proof that she was not pregnant. Because the next doctor she had gone to see had left the Island following Typhoon Karen, Ruthie ended back under my care. And, yes, she was pregnant and finally believed it herself; in due time, she delivered a beautiful baby girl!

Another patient that I admitted to the hospital about that time was a little girl with a hernia of the umbilical area and who was scheduled for surgery the following morning. I had seen her late the night before surgery and made all of the necessary preparations for early morning surgery. She was the picture of health. I walked back into the Pediatric Ward in the morning, at the time of shift change for the nurses, to check on her before completing my rounds—only to find her lifeless in her crib. There was no evidence of foul play. Nor did we find any explanation for this terrible turn of events during the postmortem exam of the body. How does one share such news with the family? No! Life is not always fair.

As usual, waiting time at the clinic often lasted for hours. One of those patients had just been seen by me and had returned home to her daily duties—only to find her two children missing. After a prolonged search, they were found in an abandoned refrigerator where a house had stood before the storm. Rigor mortis had already set in. Some days one wonders why such tragic things happen to innocent people. I did that day!

Mr. Lee, a Chinese businessman living on the Island, began to rebuild the facilities Karen had stolen from him. Lee adhered to the philosophy that length of life was related to building and growing. He had owned many properties before the typhoon and wasted no time in resuming his work in its aftermath. His wife and two darling, little girls were frequent patients at the clinic, coming for recommended immunizations as well as symptomatic care for even minor ills. He would have nothing but the best for his children, but I seldom saw Lee. Then, one day, he appeared—complaining that he was having difficulty sleeping because of a roaring sound in his right ear. Sure enough, when I placed a stethoscope over the adjacent neck area, I, too, could hear the aggravating noise. Recognizing the sound as coming from a partially-blocked artery in the neck, I urged him to go to Hawaii for further evaluation and probable surgery. He wasn't so sure and, as far as I know, never did follow that advice. One day he invited my wife and myself to a celebration he was having at his home. It was a magnanimous affair with many of the rich and famous of the Island attending. Yet, we were made to feel that we were the guests of honor; such a spread of food we have never seen! And his home! It was built near the edge of a very high cliff overlooking the beautiful Agana Bay. I should not have been surprised when, in spite of what appeared to be a spacious home, I saw other unfinished rooms still under construction. How I wished Lee could catch a vision of the coming heaven and new earth that Jesus has gone to prepare and to focus his attention on that life that will never come to an end.

Few people have the opportunity to experience the excitement of the birth of a new life—or the anguish of unexpected death—as often or as intensely as a busy physician. Both of these events soon became very frequent occurrences in my life on the Island of Guam, but none hit me with such force as the experience with Lourdes. During her pregnancy, Lourdes had kept her prenatal appointments regularly. Her labor and delivery were uneventful. It seemed that she—and her equally young and enthusiastic husband—had the world on a string in their hands when a beautiful baby girl was born to them. It was a time of true rejoicing for their family. But, on the morning before I was planning to discharge Lourdes and her baby girl from the hospital, I noted that she looked pale. Totally unexpected, it turned out that Lourdes had acute Leukemia. In no time, her life had ebbed away. Though the day was bright and sunny when I attended the wake, my heart knew only pain and sorrow for this loving husband and his now-orphaned little girl. Some men get angry with God when confronted with such unfair disasters—whether large or small—but I know that tears are flowing from the eyes of God even, sometimes, when I must hide mine inside. No! It is not our God who is responsible for such sad experiences, but the enemy of all life—the devil himself!

In early February, Guam was hit by another major typhoon—not as bad as Karen by any stretch of the imagination—but neither was it a minor affair. It, essentially, completed taking down the few things Karen had left and firmly convinced us that the assurances given to us on board the President Madison were no longer true! As that storm headed off to sea, we took a walk near the ocean where the waves met the reef and watched as waves 30 feet high or more crashed at our feet—scary, and most impressive.

Long hours and heavy responsibilities gradually take their toll on anyone. I was no exception. First it was *walking pneumonia—walking* because there was no one else to care for the patients! For weeks I coughed until I thought it would never stop. When, eventually, that resolved, I developed a most uncomfortable infection in my sinuses. I was grateful for the gentle warmth of the mid-day sun; the one thing that gave me relief. Perhaps this helps to explain why I was pleased when, one day, I was told that another doctor and his family would be joining us come summer. I was glad to see Tom and Dee Gibson when they arrived to help carry the load.

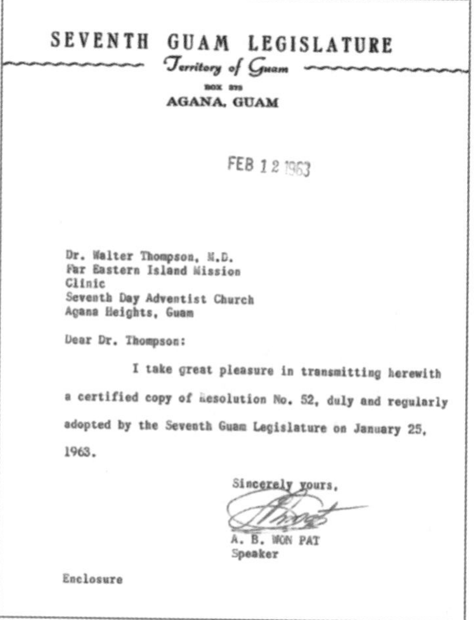

SEVENTH GUAM LEGISLATURE
Territory of Guam
BOX 373
AGANA, GUAM

FEB 12 1963

Dr. Walter Thompson, M.D.
Far Eastern Island Mission Clinic
Seventh Day Adventist Church
Agana Heights, Guam

Dear Dr. Thompson:

I take great pleasure in transmitting herewith a certified copy of Resolution No. 52, duly and regularly adopted by the Seventh Guam Legislature on January 25, 1963.

Sincerely yours,

A. B. WON PAT
Speaker

Enclosure

A letter from the Government of Guam Legislature, recognizing the benefits provided by the clinic.

About that time, I received a special resolution from the Government of Guam Legislature, recognizing the benefits provided by the clinic to the people of Guam; and, more specifically, for my work at the Guam Memorial Hospital during that night when Typhoon Karen played her games. Though to me, my efforts that night were nothing more or less than what any conscientious person would have done given the same circumstances. I was indeed honored by the recognition—a copy of which follows.

SEVENTH GUAM LEGISLATURE
1963 (FIRST) Regular Session

Resolution No. 52

Introduced by __________
J. T.H. Toves

Relative to commending Dr. Walter Thompson, M. D., of the Far Eastern Island Mission Clinic of the Seventh Day Adventist Church, for his heroism at the Guam Memorial Hospital during the night of Typhoon Karen.

BE IT RESOLVED BY THE LEGISLATURE OF THE TERRITORY OF GUAM:

WHEREAS, Dr. Walter Thompson, M. D., of the Far Eastern Island Mission Clinic of the Seventh Day Adventist Church, Agana Heights, Guam, although not on the staff of the Guam Memorial Hospital, nevertheless took it upon himself to be at the hospital at its hours of greatest need, that is, during the long night of Typhoon Karen; and

WHEREAS, while at his post as volunteer doctor on the Maternity Ward of said hospital on that night, Dr. Thompson by his courage, calmness and fortitude prevented panic from breaking out among the mothers, fathers, nurses and other hospital employees, who all eventually were forced to take refuge in the delivery room on the fourth floor of the hospital when the typhoon essentially destroyed the remainder of said Maternity Ward; and

WHEREAS, when it later became necessary to evacuate the babies and mothers and others on the ward, Dr. Thompson remained to the end, assisting other volunteers in carrying out the babies and in helping the mothers out and was one of the last persons to leave the ward; as a result of his heroism along with that of his assistants, miraculously, not one life was lost nor one baby even slightly injured; now therefore be it

RESOLVED, that the Seventh Guam Legislature does hereby on behalf of the people of Guam express to Dr. Walter Thompson, M. D., of the Far Eastern Island Mission Clinic of the Seventh Day Adventist Church, warm commendation and sincere praise for his heroism at the Guam Memorial Hospital during the night of Typhoon Karen; and be it further

RESOLVED, that this resolution do also serve as an expression of commendation to the said Seventh Day Adventist Church for its operation of Dr. Thompson's Clinic which has over the years done much in the way of providing low cost medical assistance to all in the territory needing the same, without regard for race, color or creed, all of which is in the highest traditions of the American missionary movement; and be it further

RESOLVED, that the Speaker certify to and the Legislative Secretary attest the adoption hereof and that copies of the same be thereafter transmitted to the Director, Far Eastern Island Mission, Seventh Day Adventist Church, to Dr. Walter Thompson, M. D., and to the Governor of Guam.

DULY ADOPTED ON THE 25TH DAY OF JANUARY, 1963.

V. B. BAMBA
Legislative Secretary

A. B. WON PAT
Speaker

An expression of praise by the Guam government for the Dr. Thompson's heroism during Typhoon Karen.

With the arrival of a partner, I was freed up to enjoy some of the beauties of our Island home: snorkeling, searching for rare shells, observing beautiful fish of every brilliant color and shape, watching little octopi *scoot* away before our eyes, and examining the many kinds and colors of living coral on the coral reef was always interesting.

If it weren't snorkeling, it was strolling along the beach looking for shells and other interesting objects that had washed up on shore. Avonne and I were amused when, one late afternoon, we were walking along the beach at Telafofo Bay finding shells for our son, Greg, who was then about two years old. He was thrilled with the *little* shells and promptly tucked them, carefully, inside of his swimsuit. Fortunately, the little hermit crabs that inhabited many of those shells were not able to inflict serious injury with their pincers—but they really made him squirm!

Some of our most pleasant occasions occurred along the beach in front of the little cemetery where the local saints lay awaiting resurrection morning. There, in addition to little hermit crabs, we sometimes found giant coconut crabs, jellyfish and many other creatures of the sea. That was, also, where we sometimes met with fellow believers for sunset worship, or a bonfire and picnic on the beach. On other occasions, we met for Sabbath evening worship at Fort Santa Aqueda (Apugan) and, from our view overlooking Agana Bay, we often enjoyed the afterglow of the setting sun. *The Fort,* built in 1800, was located across the highway from the mission compound adjacent to the Governor's Mansion. This, too, was a favorite site from which fireworks displays originated for those special occasions and memorials.

Just down the road a bit farther is Latte Park. Here, huge limestone pillars, capped with coral heads, provided us much opportunity for speculation regarding their origin and purpose. Some theorized they were of the same nature as the findings at Stonehenge in England, with perhaps some religious significance. Others suggested they formed the supporting pillars for their ancient longhouses (which is the predominant current thought).

Two Lovers' Point is so named for two young Chamorro lovers who—according to legend—jumped to their death 378 feet below when their parents refused consent for marriage. It provides a beautiful, bird's-eye view of white, sandy beaches and a deep, blue sea. Standing cliffside and looking straight down to the swirling shark and barracuda-infested waters below, was not for one fearful of heights!

Ancient hieroglyphic writings in Gadao's cave near the village of Inarajan, and the monument to Ferdinand Magellan at water's edge in the village of Umatic, were sure to trigger one's imagination of past times and peoples who traveled these seas. Whether true or a mere story, we were told that had Magellan not happened upon the Island while circumnavigating the globe in 1551, it is likely the whole crew would have died from starvation and disease. As it was, they lived—but not before they allegedly killed the Chamorro men and raped the women.

Sunrises and sunsets were gorgeous on whatever beach one might happen upon but, especially spectacular, when punctuated by the silhouette of fishermen throwing their nets upon the golden waters. Thanks to Tommy Cruz, we were taken to places to see and do things we never would have been able to experience without his enthusiastic guidance.

The owners of the filling station where I purchased my fuel kept a cute little fruit bat for a pet. It was about the size of a crow and looked a bit like a dainty little teddy bear with long, brown fur and neatly folded wings. Though Tommy took us on a search for fruit bats in the wild, we never did find any. It seems they are considered a gourmet delight by the native Chamorros—not good for those who would conserve the little creatures!

These excursions around the Island were nice, but the previous year had taken its toll on our strength and we needed some time away. For this, we chose to travel south to the Palau Islands to spend some time with our friends Ed and Janice Higgins and their family. The Palau Islands were gorgeous, and the fellowship with our friends and fellow believers pleasurable and relaxing. Among the hundreds of emerald-green islands; vast reefs of living coral; and sandy, white beaches scattered about in a sapphire ocean, we found a most friendly people. With them we visited their traditional longhouses, feasted on tapioca (a staple food fixed in a myriad of interesting ways), snorkeled among their pristine coral reefs and enjoyed a day touring the area with the high school kids—our guide for the day being the same person who had guided *National Geographic* photographers before us. When time to leave, I decided to travel by copra ship, via the Yap Islands, while Avonne and our son, Greg, took the quick way home by seaplane.

Expecting to spend a day or so on Yap taking on a load of copra (dried coconut), I must say I became rather restless when, after four days, they had hardly begun to load the cargo. Obviously, this was a culture for which time was not important. Though some were well educated in the best schools of the world; upon returning home, they often returned, as well, to the ancient customs of dress and behavior. Grass skirts for the women and G-strings for the men remained standard attire for most occasions. And, whereas, modern Guamanian people seemed fearful of venturing too far out into the sea, no such hesitancy existed among the people of Yap. In fact, they were known to board their dugout canoes loaded with coconuts and take off for distant places hundreds of miles away. For this, they were respected as spiritual leaders by other island nations far and wide. (It should be noted that in past times the Chamorros had gained mastery of the oceans—guided by the stars in the sky with the help of a sidereal compass—their canoes are believed to have been some of the fastest in the ancient world.) Since one of the reasons I had chosen to travel this way was to check out the potential for establishing a mission outreach, I made a point to visit a Christian (German Lutheran, I believe) school. My hosts were very gracious but confessed frustration over the difficulty of creating significant behavioral change among the students.

Although, at the market, my dollars were accepted as a medium exchange, the traditional wealth of the Islands of Yap consists of stone cartwheels. Lining the streets or in backyards of its residents, one may see round, stone pieces (with a central hole) varying in size from less than a foot to nearly six feet in diameter. Their value is apparently related to the price of obtaining them—having mined them from a small island in Palau, nearly 400 miles away, and transported by dugout canoe—a seemingly impossible task; just one more evidence of their adventurous spirit!

Not long after we were finally loaded and our ship launched out to sea, I discovered that we were sailing in the tail of a typhoon. I didn't become too alarmed until my on-deck abode began rising and falling like a giant teeter-totter with each oncoming wave! This was my first experience riding waves taller than the ship itself—and looking up at them from the troughs between! Then I realized—just a little bit—of what the Biblical characters, Jonah and the Apostle Paul, must have experienced on their travels on the Mediterranean Sea; and, I hadn't even learned yet, that we had lost radio contact with the outside world and were lost at sea! Eventually, the storm passed; our ship was still in one piece and still carrying our full cargo. It was good to be home again on Guam!

We had found many dear friends on Guam. This became even more evident when it was announced that we would be leaving. Many expressed their love and gratitude, but none showed it in such a grandiose way as one Chamorro couple for whom I had cared and who invited us to their humble home for a Sunday brunch. When, at first, Mary extended the invitation, I reminded her that we preferred vegetarian food; she assured me that would be no problem. We could not believe our eyes when we saw—upon entering their home as the only guests—the table filled with bowls and bowls of the very choicest of Guamanian dishes and delicacies, including a large bowl of Heart of Palm salad. To say the least, my family hardly made a dent in the scrumptious fare.

Why Guam? Why not some other needy or exotic mission field? Only God knows, but He had proven to me, once again, that He leads His children only along those paths that—if they could see the end from the beginning—they would choose to go. Such was the case with our experience on this mission for Him.

Chapter II

Haiti

"... all to the frenzied, hypnotic beat of the voodoo drums."

It was a very nice building, solidly constructed and in a nice location—but a real mess! Plaster, broken construction materials and other debris cluttered the whole building site, inside and out. Our work for the next ten days was clearly cut out for us.

The place was just outside the city of Port-au-Prince, Haiti; the building, a new clinic that had been mostly completed before money ran out, leaving it vacant and useless. I was one of a group consisting of a number

The new "Polyclinique Adventiste," located just outside Port-au-Prince, Haiti.

of high school students, a dentist, an optometrist, myself, (a physician) and a couple of nurses who had volunteered to spend Christmas vacation ministering to the people of Haiti, one of the poorest nations in the Western Hemisphere.

We had chartered an old 1943 DC-3 airplane for the trip, not realizing that it came without heat or air conditioning—or oxygen! At boarding time that December morning in Battle Creek, Michigan, the thermometer read: minus 10 degrees F! We shivered as we loaded our supplies into the back of the plane and settled ourselves on the floor or in the few available seats. Recognizing our plight, the pilot stopped at the airport in Indianapolis so that we could warm up a bit. Later in the day, as we began our voyage out across the Atlantic, dense fog (clouds) obscured our vision—leaving us to wonder if even the pilot knew where he was going! By the time we arrived over Haiti, the sky had cleared, giving us a bird's-eye view of the land we were to call home for the next ten days.

In addition to cleaning up the new clinic building and readying it for service, we would be holding clinics in Port-au-Prince and other sites around the nation. In preparation, we had collected and brought with us hundreds of pairs of used glasses, dental supplies and boxes full of medicine and vitamins, etc.

That evening as our hosts took us on a tour of the city, my mind was filled with images I would never forget—a view of Papa Doc's spacious home on the hillside while, nearby, rows and rows of people lay—side by side—asleep along filthy, storefront sidewalks overrun with rats. Try as I might, I could not imagine living under such sordid circumstances.

We set up clinics the next morning near our dormitory. Long lines of waiting people soon formed around the eye doctor, each person anxiously hoping to find a pair of glasses. The line for the dentist, too, was long. My line, by contrast, was easily manageable—giving us a quick view of what the people deemed most important.

During breaks we often wandered down to the shops along the water's edge, dickering with the craftsmen for the best price on paintings, carvings and other interesting creations. By all appearances, the merchants enjoyed our visits as much as we did; I still treasure a painting purchased there for a *reasonable* price!

Early one morning I, along with some members of our team, boarded four-wheel-drive vehicles for an all-day trip into the mountains to hold clinics near the border with the Dominican Republic. Going was slow; hampered first by police blockades and, later, by narrow, winding, mountain roads and frequent streams to ford. Little homes (shacks) along the way reflected the poverty pervading an otherwise gorgeous land.

It was early evening when we arrived at our destination—a quaint little town situated along the side of a wide, shallow river. Our hosts graciously opened up their humble home for us and shared their meager bounties with us. Of these, I remember only the boiled eggs. Their bright colors and home-grown flavors will be etched in my memory forever!

The nearby river served as the local laundry, bathhouse and drinking fountain for man and beast alike.

The next morning, we opened clinics in the town square. For me—on this day—there was no shortage of patients. Nearly everyone had bellyaches. Almost everyone was pale and anemic. Some had boils, eye infections, rashes and other maladies. We did the best we could with what we had, and the people appreciated our efforts. In fact, by mid-afternoon, our supplies had almost been exhausted—even while long lines of patients still stood waiting. When word got out that we were running low on supplies, the people began to riot and rush the center. Seeing the urgency of the situation, the police quickly urged us into our vehicles and out of town—much to the disappointment of the waiting throngs.

The rivers in Haiti serve as the local laundry and bathhouse, as well as providing water for cooking and drinking.

Back in Port-au-Prince, our hosts offered to take us to witness a voodoo ceremony. The ceremony was already well in progress when we arrived, and we were ushered to our seats. The room was dark, lit only by a few coals near the alter. A pole stood in the center of the tent. There we watched as one after another, the people (mostly ladies) came, calling the spirits with singing and vulgar dancing around and around the pole—all to the frenzied, hypnotic beat of the voodoo drums. As they were overtaken by the spirits, they fell staggering or convulsing to the floor, at which time they were picked up and carried out by strong, young men. They were immediately replaced by others, or by those who had recovered from a fall and were ready to go at it all over again. This, we were told, would continue all night.

At that time, voodoo ceremonies were permitted during certain holidays; Christmas was one of those permissible times. From our sleeping quarters, we could hear the sound of the beating drums coming from all directions and, yes, all through the night—the beat, rapid at first, but by the wee morning hours, at a much slower pace.

It was a beautiful day as we left our *Haitian vacation.* Scattered, fluffy, white clouds filled the bright, blue sky. Children, flying their colorful, home-made kites reminded us that—even amidst such impoverished conditions—life was still worth living. Our time in Haiti had been short, but already we had learned to love these people. They would long remain in our thoughts and prayers.

Chapter III

Cambodia

"That guy borned today, only one day old!"

Bangkok was warm and humid at 2:00 a.m., but an air-conditioned commuter ushered us to the terminal and the disembarkation procedure. Finally, my turn came to present my previously *completed* form and passport, etc., to the Thai officer sitting behind the window. He looked at my form, threw it back through the window and advised me—in broken English—to fill in the blank I had overlooked. Upon completing this simple procedure, I handed it back to him. In a couple of seconds, the card was again on the counter in front of me. "Were you borned today?" In my stupor from the long, sleepless trip, I had placed the current date in the space asking for my birth date. Quickly, I crossed out the incorrect date and placed the date of my birth there. He took it again, reviewed it carefully, stamped a number of forms and waved me on. As the next person stepped up to the counter, I overheard the officer say, "That guy borned today, only one day old!" No change of expression crossed his sober face! Such was my welcome to the *Storyland of Siam* on my way to Cambodia to serve the refugees living in refugee camps along the border.

Everyone had heard of the terrible atrocities occurring in Cambodia, as the Khmer Rouge—under the cruel rule of Pol Pot—turned Cambodia's rice bowl of the Orient into a killing field. When the *Seventh-day Adventist World Services* (SAWS) contacted Hinsdale Hospital (where I was serving as Surgical Teaching Chief for the Family Practice Residency program), seeking volunteers to spend a month in Thailand serving the refugees, I could not refuse to accompany a couple of residents on the mission.

United Airlines gratuitously and graciously flew us to Los Angeles where, after a brief orientation and introduction to the members of our team at Loma Linda, we were bound for Thailand on Pan Am Airlines—also first-class and free—as a gift of charity to the hurting people of Cambodia.

During the 20-hour flight to Bangkok, I tried to write but could not do so. Finally, after struggling, I was able to spend an hour or two recording some of my thoughts. It was poorly done, somewhat incoherent and far short of my expectations. It was a very long flight, and I was tired—yet unable to sleep—and now going into the third night. I blamed my blank mind onto my tiredness.

For the next month, I was unable to think or write constructively. I found it impossible to fulfill my plans to write a daily evaluation. By force of will, I was able to record the events of each day in a brief note but found that my mind was almost completely unable to do abstract thinking. It is from those brief, nearly-daily notes—many quoted directly—that this account is derived.

In Bangkok, the talk was all about the terrible atrocities occurring in Cambodia. Hand-drawn pictures of mass graves, and huge piles of skulls and personal testimonies of survivors were seen and heard everywhere. What had been happening in Cambodia was indeed beyond imagination—beyond human dignity and civility.

Our headquarters in the town of Aran Pra Thet, near the Khao I Dang refugee camp, was a nice house on stilts, rented by SAWS for its workers at the camp. The bathroom consisted of the usual Oriental toilet over which one squatted to do one's business, and a large, wooden tub of water from which one could dip water to pour over oneself to bathe. A small stream of water running under the house carried away any refuse left by the pigs and chickens. A large central room and two smaller rooms off to the side provided floor space for all of us to roll out our blankets to sleep. Perhaps 100 yards away, a large speaker blasted traditional music day and night.

Soon after our arrival, we were taken to Camp Khao I Dang, given a bit of orientation, shown around the camp and the hospital complex and assigned our place of duty. I was assigned to the medical ward of the SAWS hospital. Camp Khao I Dang was a very well-planned and organized camp holding more than 120,000 refugees. It was located a few hundred yards from the Cambodian border and encircled by a carefully guarded fence. Live ammunition helped to reduce the numbers of refugees crossing from Cambodia into Thailand in the zone between the camp and the Cambodian border. The hospital was located within the camp. It consisted of a number of separate units constructed of split-bamboo walls and thatch roofs. Each hospital unit served a particular specialty area, and each was operated by a charity organization—one run by the German Government, one by the Japanese Government and the others by Christian Charities. The SAWS unit to which I was assigned was a general medical unit. Simple cots were lined up in rows along the sides of the long buildings, with a walkway down the middle.

I now quote from notes made at the time. "Military planes circled overhead that first morning in Khao I Dang as we made medical rounds. As I would now be in charge of this unit, I was instructed regarding the procedures for admission and referrals, etc. We had patients with pneumonia, gastroenteritis, cancer, leukemia, tuberculosis, parasitic infestations and malaria, etc. One lady was jaundiced and had a very large liver. Another lady, with cancer of the uterus, had five children who would soon be orphaned. As I was getting acquainted, I received word that a patient with diarrhea was on her way to our unit from the Emergency Department. Due to some procedural uncertainties, it took a while for her to arrive; when she did, I stopped by to evaluate her. Understanding that she came in with diarrhea, I asked her how frequently she was moving her bowels. The answer I received—through the translation process—was that she had none. Diarrhea without loose bowels! I was puzzled! In pursuing the questioning, I noted that, as she turned, a steady stream of liquid was running from her anal area, across the bed and onto the floor.

"I had studied about cholera in medical school, but I had never seen anyone with it; yet, I was sure that this must be the lady's problem. In checking around, I was told that cholera had not been reported in the camps; so, since there had been none in the camps, and since none of us had been exposed to it before, we didn't know exactly how to treat it most effectively. While I got IVs started and began pumping large volumes of fluid into her veins, my colleagues were on the international telephone checking to see what kind of antibiotics we should be administering to her. Since we were giving such large amounts of fluid by IV and by mouth, we needed some way to assure that we were replacing the loss—but how were we to measure the loss! After some discussion, we decided to cut a hole in her bed and place a plastic bag under it to collect the drainage. (The bed was made of heavy, rough, sawn lumber and cutting a hole was, itself, a challenge.) It worked well. Since we knew that cholera was spread primarily through the water, we weren't too concerned about isolating her, but we were not certain that the many flies might not spread it to other patients; so, we surrounded her bed with mosquito netting! During the next 24 hours we gave the lady 66 liters (quarts) of fluid—to which she responded fantastically—to full recovery. I learned later that a second cholera patient did not fare so well and lost her life. Fortunately, a cholera epidemic was avoided.

"Things were not going as well at Sac San, a camp within Cambodia farther to the south, where the two residents from Hinsdale Hospital had been assigned. Active fighting in the area called for someone with surgical experience, so bright and early the next morning I was on my way with Pastor Hall to my new assignment. As we traveled he told me a little about Sac San Village—how when the Khmer Seri Ka (one of the non-communistic democratic parties) had been squeezed out of their Cambodian homeland by the Vietnamese liberators, they found refuge in this mountain hideout near the Thai border. (Note: When one of Pol Pot's generals realized where the activities of the Khmer Rouge were heading, he called on neighboring Vietnam to join him in stopping the atrocities of Pol Pot's forces. Unfortunately, the actions of the Vietnamese army appeared to be as bad to the Cambodians as were the Khmer Rouge. These Vietnamese *liberators* were the ones against whom the Khmer Seri Ka were resisting here at Sac San.) I was told there were about 5,000 people—mostly between the ages of 15 and 35—living here. When SAWS first came into the camp, people were starving. Kids were sitting around, listless, sad and quiet. People were dying like flies. But that was a couple of months ago; things were different now since the International Community had arrived. Medical help was being provided by SAWS and a team of French doctors from Monaco. Unicef, CAMA (Christian and Missionary Alliance), Red Cross and others supplied food, medications and other supplies.

"It was the Khmer New Year. Celebrations were occurring all along the way. We arrived at the secondary-supply warehouse at the Thai-Cambodian border by late afternoon. Camp Sac San was at the top of the mountain—a little over a mile away—accessible only by a steep, jungle trail. At the camp, I was introduced to Colonel Prom (in charge of the army, the village and, of course, the volunteers); the Scales (a young couple from Australia who headed up the SAWS work there); Rayone, our Cambodian translator (the only known survivor of her family), and the rest of the SAWS team and the nurses and medics.

"It was now late afternoon, and the hospital was getting low on IV solutions and other supplies. Since I wanted to get acquainted and learn how things worked, I volunteered to go with our student missionary, a young college student, down to the warehouse at the Thai border to pick them up. The trip down the mountain was easy. We loaded our backpacks with liter bottles of IV solutions and other medicines and began the journey back to camp. What I hadn't counted on, was the fact that my companion had been walking these trails for weeks and was in top condition! By contrast, I was not well-conditioned and had not yet recovered my reserve from nearly a week of traveling. I kept up with him quite well—until we reached the place where the trail got really steep where one sometimes had to hang on to the brush along the side to help pull oneself up the red-clay grades. Meanwhile, the sun was getting low in the sky, and we had a long way to go. I could tell that my companion was getting restless waiting for me, so I told him to go on ahead. I would come at my own pace. He did, and I did! Dusk was settling in. I could hear the monkeys chattering in the trees. Every now and then, I heard the sound of sticks cracking—as if something were walking there. I had just seen a skin from a tiger that had been killed by a mine, and I knew they were in the area. I had no idea where we were in respect to the enemy lines. My backpack was heavy, and my legs could hardly lift me from one step to the next. If you've ever been in such a situation, you know there are a hundred eyes out in the darkness watching—just ready to pounce the moment the victim drops! I walked on as the shadows lengthened and the trail grew dim. By the time I reached the village outskirts, I found my companions coming to help me. My dwelling was the last green tent in a long line along a low ridge—my bed was made of split bamboo. I slept well!

"I awakened early the next morning to the lovely song of a thousand birds. In celebration of the Khmer New Year we were invited, as special guests of the village, to their program. There were speeches, folk-songs, dances and a band playing traditional string instruments. It was a joyous affair. We were honored to be there. The afternoon was quiet, as was the night.

Without labs, X-rays and other modern equipment, there was a limit—even to what *we* could do—to say nothing about *them*. Everyone had malaria.

"Until now, the Cambodian *medics,* who had been trained on the job, had depended upon foreign doctors to diagnose and prescribe the necessary care at the hospital and in the sector clinics. In order to prepare them to be self-sufficient, we (Steve and Keith, the residents from Hinsdale, and I) began on-the-job training—teaching the medics how to do exams, evaluate symptoms and findings and administer proper treatment. Accordingly, mornings were spent making rounds in the hospital and teaching the medics. In the afternoons, we went with them into the various sectors of the village where we taught them to examine ears, eyes, mouths, chests and bellies. Of course, without labs, X-rays and other modern equipment, there was a limit—even to what we could do—to say nothing about them. Everyone had malaria—either in a chronic stage or in acute exacerbation. Everyone—especially the kids—had huge spleens and enlarged livers, and most of them were anemic. Fevers of unknown origin were common—generally assumed to be due to malaria and treated as such. Malnutrition was still common. I even saw—my first ever—*magenta tongue* (a vitamin deficiency) and, of course, there were injuries to deal with.

"Our hospital was new. It consisted of upright poles (which also served as our IV poles) cut from the surrounding jungle; split-bamboo walls (extending from about three feet from the red-clay ground to the palm-thatch roof), and beds of split bamboo (or hammocks strung between the poles). There was a toilet *pot,* but the jungle was more appealing to those who were able to hobble outside. There were no screens or mosquito nets.

"As Pastor Hall had shared with me, the people looked quite healthy. The kids were happy and playful; some skinny; some pale and anemic, but none who appeared really bad. I saw only one pregnant lady. She was seven months along, but the fetus was very small for its age, and she—pale, malnourished and with a high fever—presumably from malaria. Until very recently, because of the extent of malnutrition and stress, etc., women were not menstruating, and pregnancy was not much of a problem. By orders of Colonel Prom, marriage was not allowed. The men were needed on the front lines to protect the village from the threatening Vietnamese army.

"Sac San village is composed of a number of sectors scattered about in the mountaintop jungle. Each has its elder who is responsible for the people living there—making sure they get their fair share of food, etc. One sector is reserved for the Khmer Rouge. They have no arms or ammunition and serve as laborers to the camp. All of the other men serve in the army under Colonel Prom, protecting the perimeter of the village from the Vietnamese army. An orphanage cares for more than 50 kids. Homes are made of split bamboo with thatch roofs.

"The food supply appeared adequate as far as calories were concerned, though probably deficient in some of the B vitamins. What they had to eat we, too, had—lots of eggs, white rice, noodles, chicken, dried fish (or unrefrigerated week-old, water buffalo meat), and an occasional pineapple and papaya. Because everything was prepared on the same wooden block as the rotting water buffalo meat, it was flavored with that same *delightful* flavor! When there are no choices, *one eats to live rather than lives to eat!* But, I must say, I struggled a bit—had diarrhea and was losing weight. One day, as we were walking through the village, we saw large, round chunks of fresh meat lying on a table out in the sun—it looked tasty and even tempting. We were told it was boa constrictor. On another occasion—upon arriving back at our camp at suppertime—we noticed that our cook was preparing fresh hamburgers. Though I am vegetarian, by choice, and not tempted by meat, I must say that I was tempted that afternoon—only to learn that it was fresh pork—a product God had declared as unfit for food. Does that mean even when one is starving? Or does one trust God to take care of those who put their trust in Him? Those are questions that are hard to answer.

"A couple of days after a storm, two little orphan girls became ill and came to us for treatment. It turned out they had been swimming in the rain-swollen stream filled with the washoff from the surrounding hillsides—the same streams that served as *latrines* and from which our drinking water came. (Fortunately, it was boiled before we drank!) I worked hard, as had others before me, to get the people to make and use latrines, but they, obviously, had other more pressing needs—or so they believed.

"I arrived here on Sunday. Aware of the military conflict in the area and hearing the big guns in the distance each day, created a bit of discomfort for me at first; but, as time went on and the gunfire remained in the distance, I found it easy to adjust and become comfortable.

"It is now six days later, April 19, Sabbath—a quiet day—morning rounds—no classes—still afflicted with upset stomach, so not too rambunctious today. It's one of those days when one might wish to be back at home in the comfort of an easy chair, with a glass of cool water—without dirt on the bottom! I guess the hardest thing for me here is the food and water—nothing tastes good except the fruit, and I'm afraid to eat it because of the way it is prepared! Sanitation is something else. I would like to be able to write, but no thoughts worthy of writing come. Miss the family—though not my work. I would like a few days at our cabin along the Little Wolf River. The way it appears now, this will be a long *vacation!* The weather is warm and humid—but beautiful; I can't complain about it. The wildlife is lovely—from the singing birds, to the many butterflies, and to the frogs in the stream. (One day the soldiers brought us a little *mouse deer* that had lost one of its front legs. It was still alive—but very weak. We tied off the artery to the leg to stop the bleeding but, unfortunately, it died in our hands. Standing upright, the little thing was less than six inches tall, but had all the features of a full-sized deer.)

"April 20—A beautiful day—weather is nice—have felt well—able to eat a little again. Hospital rounds, classes, and sector rounds were fulfilling, and we are making some headway, I think, with training the Cambodian health workers. Just at dusk, we heard three shots—found out that a disappointed lover had shot and killed his would-be friend and then himself. Sometimes—after going through so much—life must seem very cheap. One wishes there were a better way to give them hope within—for a happy life here and in the world to come.

"April 21—The shelling started early, off to the north a couple of kilometers—has been going on all morning and still continues into the afternoon—nothing real close. While conducting class at the hospital, we saw everyone filing out of the village with all of their possessions on their backs. That stopped the class! Some of the people are gone; who knows where! Others are sitting on the trail, just waiting—waiting! That's all we have done is to sit around and wait; to stay or to move on is the question everyone asks. So far the officials haven't asked us to go, nor provided escort. It's going to be a long tense day.

"I was thinking, during the early morning hours, how good it was of God to create us with the ability to forget the past, to be able to believe that one can start over again, and to remain optimistic under the worst, most hopeless circumstances. As I sit here, I wonder what the future of this place can possibly be and what hope these people can be holding onto. They can be no match for the enemy should the enemy decide to come, as most certainly they will at the given time. I guess it is this same characteristic to forget that—unless consciously worked at—causes us to forget how God has led us in the past and allows fear to play such a prominent place in our lives.

"As we sit and watch while everyone waits, one can't help but draw a parallel between *this* waiting and the waiting we experience while awaiting the end of the world and the return of our Lord. It is easy to understand why people have difficulty putting their whole heart into the things of this life—which, today, may be here; but tomorrow, may be gone.

"Another thought comes while waiting. Is my contribution to my fellow man here commensurate to the cost? I guess the question wouldn't even deserve an answer, but for the fact that it seems like the contribution is so miniscule. One might not feel bad even giving his life for a great cause but, when the cause is less well defined, the risk sometimes seems hard to justify.

"April 22—It's a beautiful day; there have been a few explosions off to the north throughout the morning, but nothing to frighten the villagers. Things appear pretty much back to normal. Last evening was good for me. It forced me to evaluate my motives and my faith. Though I still wish I were busier, I now know I belong here and will enjoy it in spite of the difficulties. During the next two weeks, I hope to be able to teach the medics how to recognize and treat the most prevalent ills with which they will have to deal and, hopefully, teach them to have some idea of when to make referrals. It seemed God had been so far away since my arrival here—until last night! We had a good confrontation under the light of the full moon and the starry host, with the rumbling guns in the distance and imaginary enemy soldiers lurking in the shadows at the forest edge!

"Kim Song is studying hard and is getting very good at evaluating and treating medical problems. He was just telling me he would be going off to the front lines for the week. I hope we can convince the colonel to leave him here for a couple more weeks, at least. A few others are fairly good, but language is such a problem.

"Another beautiful day! A few big shells again this morning—one casualty brought in with a head injury. We stabilized him and are watching him. He will need special nursing care if he is to survive—he was too close to an exploding shell. Kim Song will stay here to translate and learn for a couple more weeks. Sokoun went off to the front lines instead. It was hard to tell him good-bye, knowing the risk to those stationed there. He was pretty sober—he has been our second-best medic trainee.

"We'll be getting a turnover of people here during the next day or two. Keith and Steve will be leaving, along with a couple of others. I am not sure who will be taking their place. I enjoy their company and working relationship.

"When one of the soldiers came into camp today, he told how he and his companions were sitting on top of a knoll when a platoon of Vietnamese soldiers began marching up the trail toward them. Since they were over the crest, they could see the soldiers as they began coming over the crest, and picked them off one by one as they came. When I heard the story, I found myself actually exulting over the death of these—our enemies. It was a strange feeling, for I had never experienced such an emotion before. In fact, I didn't think I could ever rejoice over the death of anyone under any circumstances. I even hate to see animals killed; yet, here I was feeling pleased about this report. I must say, it took a long time for me to forget that feeling and the strange mix of guilt and exhilaration that I experienced. It is something I will have to deal with—even knowing that God, Himself, experiences righteous indignation!

"Steve was pretty sick with diarrhea and malaria today. We were visiting with him by his tent when a young man came by dressed in a neat, new, military uniform (the soldiers in our camp had only old and ragged uniforms). He told us he was working as a spy for Colonel Prom, going behind enemy lines at night gathering information from the Vietnamese. He carried a very small tape recorder and other special tools in his many secret pockets. We weren't sure what to make of this friendly guy—who even spoke English—but he was soon gone.

"A new French team arrived today. Sitting around the supper table, we were all talking and telling hair-raising stories—relating to them some of the events here in the village and, of course, embellishing them a bit! It must have been about 2:00 a.m. when we were awakened by the most *blood-curdling* scream coming from somewhere down our row of tents. There is only one thing that goes through the mind at a time like this! As it turned out, it was only a dream! One of the new French doctors had been sleeping on his bed while another slept in a hammock above him. In his dream, he was fighting off an enemy soldier and, in the process, jumped and kicked his partner overhead. One can guess where the scream came from! When we were all convinced that the perpetrator was not part of an invading army, we finally settled down to sleep once again.

"April 24—It was breakfast time. I had just finished peeling a mango that the new people had so graciously brought for us, when we heard the hair-raising whistle of a low, overhead shell. It landed a little beyond our table. We hit the dust at once (my ready-to-eat mango and all!) and, immediately, we received orders to leave. While getting ready, two more shells came in and exploded nearby. After assembling and having a group prayer, we joined the evacuating refugees out of the village and down the mountain. Quite an experience! Naturally everyone was tense, but pleasant, as we, together, tried to escape injury. As we left, the shells continued to explode in the village behind us while birds and monkeys chattered in the trees along the way.

"Some of us brought all of our things down with us, suspecting that we wouldn't be going back—at least not to stay. I continue to marvel at the way these people are able to carry on with such good spirits amid such adversity.

"We are spending the day at Co-ji at the foot of the mountain—at the supply depot. Most of the people have gone further into Thailand or, at least, into disputed territory (according to Thailand we are in Thailand now). We are just waiting to see what transpires. The new people who came last night—and the ones who were due to leave—are now gone, leaving only four of us from the SAWS team. The French team is still here with us. All the people are out in the bush, so we have nothing to do. Did see one little girl being carried down the trail, looking very, very ill. We were able to get a little quinine and aspirin into her before they continued on. Haven't heard any official reports of what has transpired back in the village. No wounded have come in yet. There are reports of a number of shells landing in previously-inhabited areas.

"All day, 123 mm shells rocketed into Sac San, until about 10:00 p.m. We spent the night sleeping on the jungle floor under the stars. Awakened about 5:30 a.m. and went back up the mountain to pick up a few more belongings and medications. Except for a bunch of panic-stricken young soldiers hanging out near their newly-dug foxholes, and one sick old lady, the village was deserted (the lady was brought down by hammock). Because some of the shells were landing close to the warehouse where we had spent the night, we all moved further into

We went out and selected a number of tall, straight saplings and put together a new hospital where our patients would, at least, have a roof over their heads.

Thailand where we strung up hammocks for the sick between the trees and hung our IV bottles from the branches. After a few days—convinced that we were beyond the reach of the Vietnamese rockets—we went out into the jungle, selected a number of tall, straight saplings and put together a new hospital where our patients would, at least, have a roof over their heads when the rains came. From time to time, rumors came down to us that the Vietnamese were advancing against the Cambodians and, though we were assured the rumors were false, we noted that the soldiers were digging bunkers around the warehouse—just in case!

"By this time, it was pretty evident to us that the young man we met that afternoon near Steve's tent was not just the *colonel's spy*!

"Meanwhile, we sit and wait in the jungle—I guess the people are getting used to waiting. That's been the story of many of their lives for the past four to five years. We are doing almost nothing from the medical standpoint—only gathering a few meds together and consulting with the medics. In spite of this, they don't want us to leave. Whether it is moral support they want or because of their respect for our God is not certain, but the colonel remarked, recently, to the effect that he thought our God would help take care of them. It was pretty evident to us, too, that His angels had been watching over all of us. (I thought the colonel's comments interesting—in view of the fact that sharing our faith with the Cambodians is forbidden!)

"A couple of nights after coming into Thailand—and tired of sleeping on the ground—I spent the night on top of the SAWS van. The moon and stars in the sky were beautiful, and there was peace and quiet in the camp. I woke with the sudden fear of a possible cholera epidemic sweeping throughout the camp. Though we had not had any cases of cholera, living conditions in the jungle were a perfect setup for it.

"Apart from a few casualties, the next few days remained pretty relaxed. Rumor has it that China is causing trouble in North Vietnam and that, perhaps, this is the reason for the sudden lull in the activity. It would be nice to be able to move back to Sac San—if one could be assured of any degree of safety from the big guns now that they have located the village.

"April 29—It was rumor alright! It was too quiet and pleasant yesterday. Dr. and Mrs. Smith and Dr. and Mrs. Jensen arrived in the late afternoon and brought plastic covering material for the dental clinic and other *buildings*. We had given them a quick tour of the hospital and a late supper. While getting ready for bed, we heard a blast of thunder off to the east. We were not too alarmed—until some seconds later—when we heard the *woosh* of a big shell that exploded a little to the west of us. During the next four to five minutes the shells came in, one on top of another, as we prepared to get out. We tossed our stuff into the Toyota pickup and took off for safe haven, only to discover that the *road* was packed with refugees running ahead of us and hitting the ground every time a shell came in; it was slow going, indeed. The 20 kilometers to the outer warehouse took nearly an hour—and that with the help of *angels* pushing and pulling and holding us up through mud holes and all! It turned out that 23 people, with all of their luggage and belongings, had piled onto our little truck—including the son of the president of the Khmer Seri Ka himself—who had been with us taking pictures and making a report to take back to headquarters.

"Needless to say, the night held little sleep as we waited for injured refugees. Have had only four serious injuries and, so far, have no word of deaths. The refugees walked most of the night and are trying to get settled about three kilometers from here. Because of Thai political concerns, it is uncertain what will happen to them now. The male population is still up in Sac San at the front lines, fighting and protecting their territorial perimeters. They now have no one to take them food. Will have to wait to see if the families decide to move back or be placed in a refugee camp here in Thailand. If so, what will happen to the male army? A lot of unknowns at this point! We have been requested to wait here for further direction and to await those having medical needs.

"One of the injuries was a severe chest/shoulder injury to one of the girls who had been doing our cooking. She is stable and doing quite well. Another had a severe, left-forearm injury; another, a hand injury.

"On the way out, we picked up an old lady and three little kids. Another child was carried most of the way by one of the French doctors who missed getting on the truck; the last few kilometers, he was carried in on a motorcycle that had been sent after him.

"I'm not tired yet today, in spite of the lack of sleep. Sure have appreciated having my pillow along on this trip—bamboo, rattan, and plywood make a pretty hard bed! Today we wait!

"April 30—We had a quiet night's rest—my first experience of sleeping in a hammock. Not bad! In fact, it might even become habit-forming. We're camping on a compound near the warehouse, with no facilities except a table and bench of rattan and a bug-infested thatch roof over the top. The orphans stayed in the warehouse overnight. Most of the rest of us were under the stars. The moon has been so beautiful!

"I am waiting to get back with the refugees; I'm not sure where they are now but would like to go back and do what I can. There are a few here in a makeshift hospital, but there must be a number of ill refugees out there needing attention, also.

"I walked down the road about a mile this morning looking for enough water to bathe in. There are a few mud holes in the stream-bed where we finally washed up. I suspect the mud hole across the road will have to suffice in the future. (There is a deep, open well on the compound, but it is dry at the bottom!) The natives are able to drink from the pond, so I reckon I can bathe in it at least! What I wouldn't give for a glass of clear, cool, fresh water!

"May 1—I finished rounds—only five patients—all doing well. The *hospital* consists of a lean-to shack of bamboo, thatch and plastic sheeting. It is filthy—dogs, pigs and chickens running all around. Maintaining aseptic techniques in such an environment is, of course, impossible and one wonders why there are not more problems. We have everyone on high doses of antibiotics and treat most wounds by open technique.

"They won't allow us to go to the people. The medics are seeing all of the emergencies and will refer whatever they feel they cannot handle. I only wish we could have had a couple more weeks with them before turning them loose. In the meantime, we remain more or less prisoners here at the gate—not allowed to wonder out into Thailand, without permission, and unable to go toward Cambodia. Plenty of time to relax, eat mangos—and write!

"May 2—I can't help but hurt inside as I see the orphans come to the warehouse to sleep each night, after dark, and leave at the break of dawn to spend the daylight hours about a mile away beside a water hole.

"It would sure be nice if some sort of peace could be established in this land. We noted by the paper, yesterday, that there are moves underway to unite the non-communist blocks so that—if and when—the UN or someone moves in to help out, they will be adequately represented. I guess Colonel Prom was at one of those meetings when we evacuated Sac San.

"Later—We went out to visit the people. They are camped all along a little riverbed four kilometers from the warehouse at Co-ji. It's beautiful! The people, again, have shelters up and seem comfortable. I never cease to be amazed at how quickly they are able to settle down after a major attack. We visited the jungle hospital. No dire needs there. We observed while Pastor Hall consulted with the Thai authority and Dr. Gabriel, who was representing the French team. Consensus is that we will stay where we are, but go into the jungle for clinics and maintain an *Intensive Care Unit* out here for the most critical patients.

"May 3—Got up at dawn along with everyone else—walked down the road a little ways and found a nice hilltop with a log to sit on to have my private devotions. The sun rising over the mountains of Cambodia, through the hazy silhouette of lacy trees of the nearby jungle, was absolutely beautiful—and the birds were singing with great enthusiasm—seemingly just for me!

"Visited for a few minutes, over lunch, with a man from CAMA (Compassion and Mercy Associates)—brought him up-to-date regarding the situation here and suggested what some of our needs are. His present responsibility is to oversee the delivery of 300 tons of rice into Cambodia every day.

"Things remained *boringly* quiet for the next several days. One afternoon it rained for a couple of hours. In the evening the sky was beautiful. The magnanimity of God is very evident in the star-studded sky. As I have reflected on my own life in His plan, I am grateful for the way He has led. This has been a good experience for me but am convinced that I am not cut out for this kind of life and work for a lifetime. I find that my talents and abilities are more consistent with my present location back in Chicago.

"May 7—Norman Clark arrived today to take my place. We made some quick rounds in the hospital before my departure. I am now in Bangkok after a comfortable bus trip through a rather scenic part of Thailand. What seemed like an eternity, while there, now seems as but a day! Time perspective is strange. I suppose that—when Jesus comes—we will see this life as but a very short time also; though, now, it seems that sin has gone on forever!

"The next day, I went shopping with the Ehlers. It was a difficult task for me. I was not feeling well at all—so weak I could hardly stand; headache, etc. While they shopped, I watched a little boy sitting by a grinding wheel making brass items for the market. I was happy that he had a means of supporting his family, but sad that he would have no education. On the plane coming home, shaking chills convinced me that—though we had been taking three different medications to prevent malaria—they had no effect on those tiny, almost invisible, mosquitoes that frequented my sleeping quarters (my hammock) each day at dawn and dusk.

"Thus ends my Cambodian adventure!"

Postscript!

"May 9—We left Bangkok at 8:00 a.m. on Friday, May 9, east-bound on Pan Am Flight 002, around the world. I flew in the first-class section as far as Hong Kong. I then got bumped to clipper-class. By mistake, we were placed in the smoking section. At Tokyo, two of our party of five were able to get first-class seats again. It was about 5:00 p.m. Bangkok time, and the Sabbath had just begun when Pan Am, flight 002, started its engines for the last leg of the flight to Los Angeles. It had been a short day. An hour or so out of Tokyo, I could take the smoke no longer so proceeded to search for a place in the non-smoking section with the hope of getting a few winks of sleep. I found a row of four empty seats in the economy-class section of the plane. I thought, 'This is great! I am in luck!' I sat down. After a few minutes, I tried to discover the secret of raising the dividing armrests to make a nice bed. I couldn't figure it out, so I signaled a stewardess and asked her. 'They don't come up in this section,' was her reply. I stayed there for a long time anyway, amidst a large group of Vietnamese refugees with cross and tired kids. When one behind me started, relentlessly, to kick the back of my seat, I decided it was time to search for another place. It was now dark in the cabins. Many people had stretched out to occupy—previously-unoccupied—seats. I found two seats together further forward in economy class. I chose the aisle seat and made myself as comfortable as I could and tried to sleep; I couldn't! I couldn't read! I couldn't think straight—my mind remaining much as it had been for the past 30 days—blank! I tried to dream; I couldn't! I tried to pray; I couldn't! Pan Am's feature movie was now coming on. Maybe I'd watch it. *The Black Stallion* sounded innocent enough; it wasn't to my liking. I switched to the audio channel and listened to orchestral music for awhile—then, tired of it all, I positioned my head on my pillow and tried to sleep. Still, sleep would not come. Little by little, I began to daydream! I dreamed of painting Scriptures on my car pointing out God's love and His soon return. Suddenly, as if out of the blue, the fog lifted from my mind, and I knew the most important reason for my call to Cambodia, and a number of other reasons I had struggled so hard to find for 30 days—but could not. All of a sudden, I understood a little of how Jesus must have felt in Gethsemane and upon the cross. Thirty-three years—God among men—and He had little to show for His labors.

The previously blind, lame, dumb, former lepers; even a couple of people whom He had raised from the dead had pronounced sentence against Him. His chosen 12 were gone—no one to strengthen and encourage Him. Thirty-three years wasted and, perhaps, even God wouldn't have Him back now! Though, only in miniature, I had gone through a similar experience. I had gone to Cambodia prepared to give my life, if need be, in service to less fortunate people. For thirty days, it seemed as though my offering were worthless. I didn't feel needed. There were too many doctors, too few patients and nothing else that I could find to do. Here I, a highly-trained and experienced surgeon was risking my life, daily, with hardly enough work to occupy an hour a day much of the time; mostly work that could have been done, as well, by any of the other doctors there. Oh yes, there were a few serious injuries that I could handle better than the rest. Upon these, I encouraged myself from one day to the next—all the time wanting to believe that I was where God had called me. Thirty days in Cambodia and the feeling of failure! Uselessness! At very high cost! It had taken God thirty days to teach me that one lesson—a lesson I shall never forget. Thirty days for *my* good—perhaps while leaving a few small blessings to others along the way.

"As the thought developed and unraveled in my brain, it was as though all the power of Niagara Falls had been let loose inside my head. I began recounting my experience of those *dark* days—now suddenly made light. Thoughts, insights, feelings, emotions, concentration ability; yes, even the ability to meditate, study and pray as had been my custom—dry for thirty days! Thoughts now began to tumble over each other, trying to get out. For several hours I sat there, eyes closed, head back—thinking! thinking! thinking! It felt so good to be able to do so again. I was hardly aware of the rising sun faintly illuminating the pulled cabin shades. For several hours, the time flew. I wanted to write, but it was dark with people sleeping or trying to sleep all around me. So, I let my mind run. I would go back and record it later—now that I knew it was all stored there!

"The lack of activity had brought my self-winding watch to an unrecognized halt. Whereas, I had thought time was going so fast; all of a sudden, I discovered that it seemed not to be moving at all! It was too noisy to hear my watch and too dark to see; so I wound it anyway! Because of this, we arrived in L.A., about three hours before my calculated time. What a good feeling after 20-some hours of sitting!

Chapter IV

Cambodia, Again!

"When we went out among the houses to look around, it was as though a civilization had suddenly vanished—a few kids here and there were rummaging through the remains."

"After an aborted takeoff attempt, we are finally airborne out of Tokyo once again, headed for the next stop at Hong Kong. Except for this incident, it has been an unusually comfortable flight from L.A. where we were placed aboard Pan Am 001 by the careful arrangement of Pastor Hunter.

"Traveling with me are Dr. Crider, a retired physician, who has spent most of his professional life in Thailand in church-related mission programs; and Dr. Billy Hover, a dentist, and his wife, from Alberta, Canada.

"It is now two years, to the day, since I first volunteered to serve among the Cambodian refugee camps in Thailand and the Cambodian border. That experience, lasting for 30 days, was undoubtedly the most difficult 30 days of my life—and the longest! Words will never express many of the emotions and thoughts then experienced. Yet, in spite of it all—in retrospect—I considered my mission valuable, both for myself and for those whom I went to serve. If a single soul is claimed for eternity, the price will be cheap enough.

"It is difficult to understand; let alone describe the desire—indeed the drive—to return! Yet, deep within, it is something I am compelled to do. At a time when the novelty of the mission has worn off, the needs of the refugees continue. Can I hold back my contribution?

"During these two years, my life has been full. My practice has been busy, and my opportunities to preach the everlasting gospel—by both deed and word—have been many. Some of the questions troubling me about God's *apparent lack* of interest among the masses of suffering humanity have found answers, and His dilemmas clarified in my mind.

"While it is not true that I wing my flight without fear—a fear largely based upon memory—I also go with anticipation and peace. While I recognize the very real risks and dangers, I also am confident of the One who is in control.

"Many wonderful people have sent me off with the assurance of their prayers and with words of encouragement—friends of the truest order. Only a few question my sanity—to my face!

"It was hard leaving home. The years have strengthened the bond between myself and Avonne, making it increasingly difficult to leave her behind. Denyse is now just one week old. She doesn't need a grandfather just now but, still, it's hard to leave her and her parents during these critical times in their lives. My son, Greg, will do well in my absence, but I wish he understood, a little better, the forces driving me. My mother is doing well, but is up in years and of limited days. We both realize the possibility that we may have talked for the last time upon this earth.

"From a more selfish point, I love this season of the year in Midwest America, and I will miss it in exchange for the heat and humidity of Thailand. A month or more away from my practice, now, means that it will be difficult to get away much more during the year. Sure, sometimes I could question my own sanity—but not really! God has been so good to me.

"We arrived at the airport in Bangkok just before midnight. Due to an apparent communication mix-up, we weren't expected until the next day—so no one was there to meet us. Fortunately, there are numerous taxis, and we had no trouble getting to the SAWS headquarters at the Bangkok Adventist Hospital. We were awakened quite early by the local commotion and, subsequently, got our papers and things taken care of at the SAWS office. After that, Dr. Billy Hover and I got on a bus to go sightseeing. We took the bus to the end of the line and ended up at a big Buddhist Wat—26 acres of pagodas, golden Buddhas, temples and schools, etc. We watched as the people brought their offerings of food, flowers and money and presented them to the gods. Our guide answered many questions that we had about the Thai version of Buddhism. It was interesting to learn the meaning of the symbols of serpents and birds, etc.—a throwback to the *flying* serpent in Eden, perhaps—and to get a first-hand explanation of reincarnation. We were shown the 193-foot-long, 200-year-old, reclining Buddha. On the bottom of his feet were pictures of all of his previous life experiences, everything from a seashell to an elephant! The reclining position indicated that he had finally arrived at the highest heaven, Nirvana, and could now rest. There were over 300 *sitting* Buddhas lined up along the walls, collected from all over South China during the past couple of hundred years. While Buddha, himself, taught against idol worship; today, the more images the better. Present Buddhism combines worship to the Buddhas, to numerous spirits, to ancestors and to the king who, himself, is believed to have supernatural powers. Just the day before, as was reported, he presented evidence of his power by stopping the rain.

"The grounds of the Wat had numerous animals running loose. We were told that people—who could no longer keep them—brought them here to be cared for; here, they were honored guests. I was also told, from another source, that animals aren't usually treated well by Buddhists because of their belief that they represent reincarnated people who didn't do too well in life, so came back in a lower form; hence, deserved a little ridicule so they would be encouraged to do better the next time around! In one area of the court, a lady had a cage of little birds which, for two Bat, she would transfer to another cage and give them to the worshipers to release. We were told that the people like to let caged birds go free.

"After leaving the Wat, we wandered down to the riverfront and through some of the warehouses and markets. The odors were horrendous, but maybe one adapts to them—eventually! Next we ended up where the royal yachts were tied up on display. They had apparently been used in a ceremony a couple of days earlier. We noted the royal palace just across the street, so decided to visit it as well. Since this is the beginning of the bicentennial celebration of Bangkok as the capitol city of the country, it was open for public view. All of the buildings have been redecorated and restored. An English-speaking Thai whom we met, told us they have spent 60 million Bat on gold-leaf alone—to say nothing about all of the lacquer, colored-glass, mirrors, etc. There were beautiful pagodas and temples within the palace court; again, with people at worship. One place struck us, especially, as we watched the people buy gold-leaf and place it upon golden cows. We were reminded of the experience of Aaron and Moses when the Israelites retaliated against God and worshipped the golden calf at Mount Sinai. Then, too, we were fortunate to be at the palace, at just the right time, to be permitted to view the royal jewels—golden crowns loaded with the most precious gems, and rings and all sorts of great and beautiful things—probably exceeding any other such collection in the world. Realizing that we were witnessing the palace of the king—with the greatest honor and glory that anyone in Buddhism can ever hope to receive—made us compare this glitter with the promise of the redeemed who shall walk on streets of gold and the sea of glass, and witness conditions such as '…eye hath not seen nor ear heard, nor has ever entered into the imagination of man the things God is preparing for his children' (1 Corinthians 2:9). All free! And without earning their way through numerous reincarnate orders of things. Yet, over and over again, we could see the many resemblances to the ancient Hebrew service with its sacrifices, its offerings and its temples, etc.

"We got on the wrong bus and ended up way on the other side of the hospital. We walked back rather than get on the wrong one again!

"April 9,—We left Bangkok at 6:00 a.m. in a thundershower; dropped Dr. Hover and his wife off at a transit camp a couple of hours out of Bangkok, where he will be fixing teeth. The dental operatory didn't look too bad, but I didn't envy their living quarters. We then went to Sac San to see what was happening there. Ten or twelve days earlier, three regiments (it is reported) invaded Sac San and drove the Khmer into Thailand—apparently about 8,000 people. There were only five Khmer casualties compared with numerous Vietnamese, we were told. The week before the invasion, they had been dropping yellow-rain (chemical warfare) on the village. Just before that, the Thais had made the area off-limits to all SAWS workers so none were there at the time of the yellow-rain or invasion. Today, the Vietnamese were shelling into Thailand and the Thais were volleying back; the Cambodians apparently caught in between. SAWS has been told to close the hospital there at the checkpoint and to get out. Right now, they are waiting to see if the Thais really mean business. At any rate, both the Thais and Cambodians have seen Christianity at work and, even while I listened to the big shells explode off in the distance, I was glad I had the opportunity to be a small part of the witness. I did not get to see Kim Song as I had hoped—I suppose he is busy caring for the ill and wounded out in the jungle.

"From Sac San we came up to the village of Topsai where the housing for Camp Kamput is located. Everyone is out at camp, so am sitting here waiting their arrival.

"After a good night of rest—in spite of the songs of the local frog symphony—we (Dr. Diez and I) were just starting on a tour of the hospital when they carried a lady in on a stretcher with a baby lying between her legs; they said there was another inside yet. This was soon confirmed when a protruding hand was noted. It had, apparently, been about two hours since the first was born. We took her to the O.R. Since our anesthetist had not yet returned to camp, I had the dubious honor. In time, she was adequately anesthetized and a version extraction done. The second baby was dead and joined the first, which had been breathing its last when they arrived. Fortunately, at least the mother did OK. After doing the morning rounds, I was sitting and reading when we got a call to see a man with suspected appendicitis. We confirmed the diagnosis and took him to surgery, this time under spinal anesthesia. After lunch, we joined the Khmers in their worship service. There have been a couple of hundred baptisms here recently. Unfortunately, some of their most capable leaders have found exit to a third country; they need a pastor to work with them full-time. I spent a couple of hours talking with some of them after the service and hope to be able to sit down with them, on a regular basis, and study the Bible with the leaders. All in all, it has been a good Sabbath. It looks as though I will be staying out here at the camp at night. The facilities here are very comfortable, and I think nicer than in Topsai.

"During the next few days, I met regularly with the members of the church, teaching them for a couple of hours a day; and, since they are all new to the church and have no pastor, helping them elect leaders and get organized. In my spare time, I read a most interesting book, *The King Smiled.* It is the story of a Khmer family's escape from Cambodia under Pol Pot. (It gave me some history and insights not known before.) Meanwhile, I was quite busy as the surgeon on-call 24-hours-a-day and the only doctor in camp during the night.

"April 12—Was up three times last night—once to do a cut-down to start an IV on a baby; once to check a lady with a threatened abortion; and once when a man died. (I discovered later, when we did the autopsy, that it was due to a brain abscess). Today has been quite busy. I spent an hour, this morning, with the church leaders and Bible workers. Then made rounds—did a hernia repair on a baby from Sac San; an I and D (incision and drainage) of a scalp abscess; and a vaginal hysterectomy for prolapse.

"April 13—It is the beginning of three days of celebration of the Khmer New Year.

"April 14—Poor night! The electric generator running outside my window competed with the frogs for attention. I was awakened early in the morning to look at a stillborn baby. Shortly after returning to bed, I was called to see a pregnant mother whose baby was in fetal distress with the umbilical cord around its neck—delivered OK. Later called to see a newborn that had gone bad—he died while trying to get IVs started. A rather sad night!

"I met with the Khmer leaders this morning and went over the topic of Inspiration and Ellen White. Rim Pham, the head elder, told of dreams he has had—beginning while living in Cambodia under Pol Pot—where he was shown that he was keeping all of the commandments except one, and that he must keep *it* also. So he started keeping the Sabbath long before he ever heard of Adventists! Last night he had a dream about the danger of his fellow church members worshiping Buddha while trying, also, to be Adventists. He is a very thoughtful man and a pleasure to study with.

"We did a C-section after 24 hours of ineffective labor in a multipara lady (lady with many babies); both mother and baby are OK. We also did a D and C for irregular menses on a lady from Sac San. Heavy rain started about 5:00 p.m. and continued throughout the night. All electricity is off in camp and our generator is not working, so it is very dark here tonight. Many of the Khmers are afraid of ghosts and evil spirits.

"April 15—A quiet, dark night. This morning I was called to see a man with pan opthalmitis (infection of the eyeball); had to do an emergency enucleation (remove the eye). Then we drained two other abscesses, one in the groin and thigh area, and a very bad one deep in the muscles of the biceps—lots of pus! In the evening, before retiring, I studied for about 2 ½ hours with a couple of the leaders. One told about his life in Cambodia and of his escape into Thailand; he was first a soldier of Lon Nol—after Nol was over-thrown, he escaped and lived in the forest for about one month to avoid the forces of Pol Pot. During that time, he became skin and bones. Later, he went to live with his in-laws, until—after a fight—his mother-in-law gave his whereabouts away. He then went back into the forest where—beside a lake for several months—he lived on dead fish, etc., *like an animal.* He joined the Vietnamese forces when they drove Pol Pot out—until his identity, again, was found out. Then he came with his wife to Thailand without anything. When he arrived at Camp Kao I Dang, he used the pages of a Bible to roll cigarettes. Later, after transferring here, he began to get interested in the gospel and, eventually, was baptized. He is quite upset, now, because—if he is forced to return to Cambodia—everyone knows he is identified as a Westerner with knowledge of English and Christianity, etc. He will not join the Seri Ka at Sac San because their president, apparently, threatened that any Khmer who wouldn't join in their liberation movement was even worse than the Khmer Rouge—who were worse than the Vietnamese! So far, there has been no sign of transfer to another country. We were studying about practical Christianity and loving one's enemies. It must be hard when people have treated you so badly!

"April 16—A rather busy surgical ward today with a number of sick patients—required a bit of time to make rounds; then sutured a complicated finger injury in a little kid and did an I and D. I then drove to Chantaburi for supplies—about 50 kilometers distance; it was my first experience driving on the left side of the road. Got there and back! It was an interesting place to shop. One can find just about anything if one knows where to look—and looks long enough!

"I went to vespers with the Khmers. They seem to enjoy a short service with group singing and a sermonette. I was just leaving, when I was met by the nurse telling me of a lady on the delivery table not able to deliver. When I arrived, the head was down but the fetal heart was very slow—tried a vacuum extraction but lost suction, so slipped forceps on. The baby was a little slow to respond, but I think will be OK. The mother is fine. It is my first forceps delivery in more than 20 years—it's amazing how well those skills return after such a long time!

"This morning, I had about 16 Khmers in the Bible study as we went over the Biblical references to the state of the dead, the resurrection, etc. They appreciated some new insights. They are very eager to learn.

"April 17 (Sabbath)—We started the day with Bible study on the book of Daniel, chapters 3 and 4. We then did a D and C for an incomplete abortion, made rounds, Sabbath School and church this afternoon, performed an appendectomy and finished reading a fascinating book about *Good King Hezekiah.* It was interesting comparing his day with ours, and noting the way God leads His people when they will be led.

"April 18, Sunday—a quiet day, made early rounds, did an I and D, took a foreign body out of a little boy's nose, and met a couple of hours with the church committee while they debated—at times, rather heatedly— the problem of back-sliding members. The consensus, I think, was that they weren't ready—a thing that strikes home to my own feelings so often. They were reading the parable of the sower in Matthew 13, to try and understand what was happening and to get some reassurance. I think they are learning a valuable lesson. Later, Peter Wong, the dentist; Mrs. Cummings (Mama Gretchen—our anesthetist), and I went for a ride down toward the Cambodian border in her Toyota pickup. It had just rained, so the mud on the newly-graded road made difficult traveling, and we were forced to turn around on a bridge and come back. Unfortunately, we had come down a steep hill and, of course, had to return! But the mud was deep and as slippery as ice, making the return impossible. While Peter and I went searching for alternative ways to get back up, Mama Gretchen got in her truck, shoved the throttle to the floorboard, and headed up the hill. We knew there was no way she was going to get back up—and certainly not that way—but we saw that she was moving, though ever so slowly, so we ran over and pushed. We could almost see the angels pushing, too, for we should never have made it. (This was a long ways from anyone or anything, so we would have been there a long time—or had a very long walk!) On the way back, as if we hadn't already had enough excitement, we stopped to investigate a suspension bridge that crossed high above a very wild river below. I didn't have the nerve to walk out on the bridge very far but, obviously, the people used it every day—as risky as it appeared to me.

"During the next couple of days, things were pretty quiet from the surgical point of view. We did a few cases—reduced and cast a difficult fracture, elevated a nose fracture, removed a growth from an old man's ear and drained some big abscesses. I also spent some time watching Dr. Wong pull teeth, and visited the craft center and watched as they made bamboo baskets, machetes and musical instruments, etc.

"There are rumors that the camp will be closing soon, and reports that the Thais are clamping down on foreign assistance, etc. Obviously it is intended to cut down the flow of traffic this way and, hopefully, to get it going the other way! Some are talking of going back to Cambodia.

"April 21—This morning, beginning at 5:30, we studied the Book of Daniel, chapter 8, discussing the meaning of the Sanctuary. After rounds at the hospital, I repaired a cleft lip. I was quite pleased with the result. Then I spent a couple of hours with Peter learning about teeth. Tonight, we spent a couple of hours on the Sabbath School lesson and then discussed the concerns of the Khmers for a period of time. They are really quite agitated about the uncertainty of the future. I tried to reassure them that—as long as they trusted God and served Him—He would meet their needs and use them to glorify His name. We read Daniel, chapter 3, together, telling how—when the three Jews refused to bow down to worship the king, they were thrown into the furnace—heated seven times hotter than normal but were not burned; though those who threw them in died from the heat. Some, at least, are resigned to die with the assurance that they will be raised again and have a home in heaven. I, for one, will be pleased to meet them there. How I wish they didn't have to go through what they are going through, but how glad I am that I have this opportunity to encourage them a little.

"April 22—How quickly things change in a refugee camp! Yesterday—though uncertain of the future—people had homes and gardens and jobs and schools; today, an announcement was made that 582 families will be kept here for eventual transfer to the U.S.; all others will be transferred to other camps by bus (about 10,000) at the rate of three to four thousand per day, beginning next Monday. To take their place, 23,000 more will come here in transit to another country. For those lucky ones whose names will appear tomorrow morning to go to the U.S., there will be joy. For those going to SaKau or Kau I Dang, there is fear and apprehension. It will be a restless night in camp tonight. This also means that the church group here will be broken up. Hopefully, there are those with solid-enough backgrounds to carry on in the other places. If so, the work of the gospel may be enhanced by the dispersion. I am grateful for the time I have been able to spend studying the real basics with them.

"Before the rumor became news, I visited the Khmer traditional medicine center and had opportunity to watch herbal medicines being made and used—as well as to observe a fortune-teller, a masseur, and a mid-wife (as she *cleaned* out the water of a newborn's throat), etc. Later, we walked around the camp and watched rice noodles and deep fried bananas in rice batter being made. The bananas tasted good, though a little greasy. We saw the sewing and weaving center and watched the skillful use of hand-operated looms. As of tomorrow, all of these things will stop as people prepare to move again. So frequently, observation of these people who have grown dear to me, reminds me of the masses of humanity who have suffered in war almost since the dawn of human history. I wonder how God can be so patient in allowing the course of sin to reach its natural climax—and I realize that He feels the pain so much more than we can even begin to feel. Many prayers will rise from Kamput tonight!

"Many emotions course through one's soul on a day like today. Everyone thinks they want to go to a third country. Yet, only a few of the present encampment will be able to. The list didn't come out until about noon; after that, there was rejoicing for the few who found their names on the list and depression for everyone else—wondering why! Why didn't God hear their prayers? What next? The next step now for them is a return to Kao I Dang—a thing which none look forward to since they see it as an even worse prison than this place.

"In talking with many people today; Khmers, voluntary agency workers (Volag) and U. N. personnel, it is really difficult to know where these people would be best cared for. The third countries are not heaven either—with prejudice, strange western customs, shortage of jobs and language problems, etc. Few of them are able to understand; from here, all they see is freedom from oppression! The authorities say that Cambodia isn't that bad now, but most of the people here don't agree. Because of these concerns, our Bible studies have fallen by the wayside—people's faith is being tested—some of them will also fall by the wayside! Hopefully, there will be some who remain faithful to carry on the work, both in the camps and back in Cambodia.

"In all of the shifting around, we were asked to empty the hospital as completely as possible. Few patients have time to come to the clinic, so not much work today. Early this morning a lady brought her baby with vomiting and diarrhea to be treated, but it was before anyone was around to translate; I lost track of them while waiting. I looked for them later, but was unable to find them.

"Last night I delivered a second baby, vaginally, for a lady who had had a previous C-section. I used the vacuum extractor, and things went well.

"April 24 (Sabbath)—It's been a long day; awakened at the break of dawn, as usual, to the sounds of birds, frogs, lizards, chickens and people arousing for another day. The spirit here is much different from a few days ago. Those who know they are on the way to the States are happy, but they are few compared to those being transferred to Kao I Dang. We have emptied our ward at the hospital, so the patients we saw today have been outpatients; later, had Sabbath School together and, after lunch, attended the Khmer church services. The attendance was small. The people are being tested to the limit. Those present had a good service, though, as they received their baptismal certificates. One of the men who wanted to be a pastor to his own people in Cambodia, pulled a fast one today and changed his name and joined another family (for a price) in order to get to the States; another is still pulling strings, also trying to find a way. It seems that nothing is as important as to escape. I guess they wouldn't be here if they hadn't learned well; am grateful that some have been true to the principles they have been taught.

"This morning, Erma, UNHCR official in charge of this move, spent an hour or so eating breakfast with us telling of her experiences during the past three years here with the Khmers. While she is very loving, she has no time for foolishness and gets very upset at some of the things the people do. There are certainly two sides to every story. Her side is quite different from the one we usually hear.

"This afternoon I talked for quite a while with Kosal, who was in college in Phnom Penh when it fell—or at least nearly until then. Just before it fell, he returned to the rice farms. While in college, he was studying literature and law and, apparently, was a student leader because once a month he met with the president of the General Assembly of the Government of Lon Nol, who is now president of the Khmer Seri. After going to the farms, Pol Pot's people made him marry a girl he had never before seen. They now have two children.

"He told me a little about Prince Norodom Sihanouk, Lon Nol, Pol Pot, and how each came to power. It seems the people feel that the U.S. could have resisted Pol Pot's forces had they seriously helped Nol. In spite of the anti-American sentiment, they want to go to America where they can be free from oppression. Apparently, the Vietnamese were invited by the present Khmer president to help overthrow Pol Pot—himself an officer under Pol Pot, but who became disillusioned with his methods.

"April 25—This has been a long and discouraging day for many of the Khmers and workers. Much of the day has been spent at the embassy trying to get people's names on the list and included with other families. As a result, a number of the workers will stay here for later transfer to the States. For those, however, who could not beg, borrow, bribe or steal their way, it has been a trial.

"Tomorrow morning, more than 4,000 people are due to be loaded onto buses for transfer to other camps.

"Late afternoon, a lady came in who had delivered her baby at home but retained placenta and lost a lot of blood. After several hours she was stable and out of shock; we weren't able to find any donors at that time of day, so Dr. Diaz gave a unit of his own blood which, along with iron supplement, should hold her. Again we got the impression that, in times like these, life isn't worth much for anyone else but oneself.

"I awakened early to see rows and rows of bright, shiny, red and orange buses lined up—ready to load the refugees. At 6:30 a.m. we began the process of reviewing the medical records of the people as they got on the buses—nothing but mass confusion! As the people got on the buses, we reviewed the cards and recorded all of the names of families; when all was said and done, there were quite a few people who didn't get on. They will have to try tomorrow. I suppose this is better than making

Rows and rows of bright, shiny, red and orange buses lined up, ready to load the refugees.

people walk mile after mile, but it is so hard to see how much suffering must occur. Am certain that most of the few possessions people packed will not be found at the other end and, though they will be provided with their basic needs there, all of the extras will be gone.

"Had a meeting with the UNHCR people this afternoon and discussed the problems of loading and checking—hopefully, tomorrow will be better. The other problem is, Thai soldiers taking what they want from the people. There doesn't seem to be any way to prevent this. A couple of fellows came by this evening to study, so perhaps the day has not all been in vain.

"The next day we loaded another 59 buses in the morning. Things went much more smoothly and quickly, and the people seemed much more at ease. The work was hard and hot—but went fast.

"This afternoon I had a short session again with UNHCR; then spent the time reading and talking with Sambo. He is 21, speaks a little English, and has been working as my translator for the past two days. Before that, he was a medic in the Surgical Outpatient Department. He has been in Thailand about 3½ years waiting to go to another country; now has finally been cleared for the U.S.—along with his mother, four siblings and his new wife (married so she could go along after they learned about the transfer). Before coming to Thailand, he had spent more than three years under Pol Pot doing farm labor. Later, they were put in prison for about three months, put in ankle-cuffs and, finally, liberated by the Vietnamese army. They then escaped to the border area and were rescued by the Red Cross and taken to Kao I Dang. Three siblings had been lost while they were away at school. Pol Pot drove all of the villagers out into the countryside and put them to work. Sambo's father was also lost at an earlier time; he had been employed as a school guard during Lon Nol. All of these are presumed dead. While on the farms, many died of starvation, by bayonet and by guns. When people died while in prison, they were left to rot right where they died! This made life very unpleasant for those still alive.

"Sambo thinks Pol Pot had an army of about 100,000 soldiers. Many were killed by the Vietnamese when they took over. He tells how Pol Pot's men hauled gold by the truckload to be buried in the mountains, after which the truck would be burned and the drivers shot. He awakens at night with bad dreams reliving the events and is very afraid of Communism in any form, but he would like to return to Cambodia if there were freedom. All of his life he has been Buddhist until about eight months ago; he now seems to be enjoying the opportunity to learn of Christianity.

"This evening the director came over and told of the early days at Kao I Dang when there were 28,000 starving people lying there in the jungle, with that many more still in the jungle inside the border with Pol Pot—all while under fire by the Vietnamese. She told how bulldozers made mass graves for the many deaths; she also told about the fire that destroyed the hospital about a year ago with 500 patients evacuated in minutes. Fortunately, the patients had their families there to carry them out.

"I got two letters from Avonne and two from my daughter, Cindy, today—was good to receive their love.

"April 28—The remaining buses were loaded rapidly this morning and were on their way by 8:30 or 9:00 a.m.—11½ thousand people with their belongings—now gone! When we went out among the houses to look around, it was as though a civilization had suddenly vanished—a few kids here and there were rummaging through the remains. It was sad to see things left behind that, one knows, could be useful at their new location but could not be taken. For those 2300 people remaining, there is an abundance of tables, beds and garden produce, etc. As a personal keepsake, I picked up a wooden yoke—as if I needed anything to remind me of this experience!

"According to the latest information, reportedly from the U.S. Embassy, they will start moving people out from here about May 5 on their way to the States. Thus—though 1500 per day will be arriving here on May 1—they may not stay long.

"Tonight—it is very quiet. The fellows didn't show up for Bible study. At first I was upset that they had made me wait for them, but then I remembered—and was reminded by the workers—how fearful everyone is of the Thai soldiers. No one is out walking around! No yelling or singing! Just quiet! For a change I can even hear the birds singing.

"The next couple of days were quiet except for checking in new arrivals to the camp—not much surgery. One day we went in to Chantaburi shopping and I saw an elephant walking along the road with his driver, so we stopped and asked the man for a ride. It was an interesting experience—much easier than staying on a horse—and much slower!

"May 1—It has been a rather hectic Sabbath. The process of transfer of refugees from camp to camp goes on seven days a week. We were requested to help with the medical work when the buses arrived bringing the new people. As a consequence, we were busy with our translators at the time church was scheduled; hence, I guess there was no service today. While the SAWS people were having Sabbath School study this morning, we had some of the Khmer with us. We discussed how close the similarity is between the Khmers going to the *Promised Land* of America and the Christian on the way to heaven. It is interesting to observe all of the different ways the Khmer try to get to America. It is also sad to see all of the heartache and sorrow they go through in the process—again, very much like the road to heaven!

"I saw one pregnant mother coming to register. She had a small child at her side, and a severely, malnourished child in her arms who had a cleft palate. On the way, she had to stop and vomit. Such scenes nearly draw tears. I suppose I will never understand, this side of heaven, how God can sit by and observe the suffering of mankind century after century while sin runs its course. I wondered again today—does God cry? Were it not for my understanding of the controversy between good and evil and the thing God is about to accomplish, I would be very angry with God. As it is, I must sit and cry with Him.

"Tonight, I spent a little time with a couple of medics. One has no family—having lost them all in Cambodia. He is now 18 and has been here in Thailand for three years. He said he is a vagabond! We discussed the suggestions in the book of Hebrews, chapter 11, and 1 Peter 2:11, stating that we are all pilgrims and strangers (refugees as some translations put it) in this world, awaiting the day when we can all go home—to our real home!

"One of the SAWS workers failed to pass his interview with the American Embassy. It seems that the information his *brother* in America sent to the embassy didn't conform to what he had told them. They didn't like that. One of the VOLAGS was commenting this morning that it seems it is the dishonest ones who get to the States, and the honest ones get sent back to Kao I Dang! Hopefully, this isn't as true as it seems at times.

"May 3—Today, we saw people running down the road toward the U.N.—didn't know what was happening. This evening we found out that the man who was the interpreter for the American Embassy, was being stoned because he was doing more than just interpreting. He was telling stories about people that were apparently not correct. He will sleep in the U.N. building (for protection) tonight, and they will try to solve the problems tomorrow. Apparently, he is a very straight and honest man, but used indiscretion in saying the things he did.

"That last night in Kamput was not as restful as some. There was a lot of unrest about the threats on the life of the interpreter. It didn't help that there were drunken Thai soldiers wandering around the road by the house and hospital. The fellow who sprays for mosquitoes was pretty upset about the whole affair and accidently locked himself out of his room. When he finished spraying, he came and slept with us in the SAWS house. That house was pretty much the hub of all of the Falangs (foreigners) and VOLAGA (voluntary agencies).

With all of this excitement, I was on my way home. I stopped at Sac San and spent the night with the Thai merchant who supplies the food, etc., for the village. He has made a place for SAWS workers who are passing through, to stay free of charge. The next day I met a French doctor, whose wife had just left him, and he had come here to have time alone. Also, I finally got to see Kim Song (a friend I had met on my previous trip to Cambodia) and spend a few minutes with him before catching a ride back to Bangkok and my flight home.

The following additional information may be interesting to those reading this account.

As I understand it, Cambodia (and all of Southeast Asia) has a long history of political unrest. Prince Norodom Sihanouk was head-of-state, I believe, when the U.S. bombed the road going through Cambodia from North Vietnam to South Vietnam. He was toppled by a Coup d'Etat in Phnom Penh in 1970 and replaced by the pro-USA, Prince Sisowath Sirik Matak and followed by General Lon Nol, etc. A number of other heads of state ruled until 1976 when Pol Pot, a Communist supported by Red China, came to power and set about to make Cambodia a communist state, Khmer Rouge (red), by eliminating the educated and upper classes. In response, a number of opposing Cambodian parties developed, among which was the Khmer Seri Ka (white)—a free democratic party under the direction of Hen Sen, I believe. Disillusioned, one of Pot's generals left him and convinced the Vietnamese army to take Pol Pot down—a feat they finally accomplished in 1979. Meanwhile, the Vietnamese were not only attacking Pol Pot and the Khmer Rouge but all of the other Cambodian parties as well—including the Khmer Seri Ka. The Vietnamese apparently saw an opportunity to take control of the whole nation and were set to do so.

Under the rule of Pol Pot, millions were killed. Some escaped into Thailand and ended up in the refugee camps where we worked. Aran Pra Thet was a small town along the border, adjacent to the Kao I Dang refugee camp. Sac San was nothing more than a community of Khmer Seri people who had found refuge in Cambodia's mountainous area near the Thai border. It will not be on any map because—though they lived together as a community—their physical location was ever-changing, as driven first by Pol Pot and then by the Vietnamese. Meanwhile, Pol Pot and his army was driven north by the Vietnamese. Eventually, a year or two after I was there in 1980, the various non-Communist parties got together with France, the U.S.—and others — established a new coalition government that, as I was told, retained many of the original trouble-makers of the Khmer Rouge, Vietnamese and some of the democratic parties. I believe Hen Sen was in power at one time. Presently, Cambodia is doing fairly well as a democracy.

Pol Pot died before he could be tried for genocide by the world court. Some of his generals were to be tried, but I don't know if they have ever been prosecuted or not.

Colonel Prom was loyal to Hen Sen, a Khmer Seri leader, and was assigned to Sac San, one of their resistant forces against the Khmer Rouge and Vietnamese.

Kim Song subsequently received training to become a prosthetist, making and fitting prostheses for amputees in Cambodia. A few years ago, he came to Chicago for a couple of months of additional training. Later, he went to Sri Lanka to work with the amputees there. He has since moved to Bangladesh with his family. We keep in touch by e-mail. He phones to wish us a Merry Christmas each year.

Chapter V

Poland

"Before he left, he reached into his tattered jacket, fumbled around in a torn pocket a few moments, then pulled out a small crystalline rock and placed it in my hand, saying, 'Here, this is for you!' There were tears in my eyes as he walked away."

"It is autumn in Poland as I arrive at the Warsaw International Airport to join my friend, Pastor Mark Finley, for a first-ever evangelistic series of meetings in the historic city of Gdansk. Soviet leader, Mikhail Gorbachev, has already launched a policy of openness (Glasnost) for the Soviet Union and expressed the need for economic reforms (Perestroika) for the Soviet States. Poland has experienced high levels of tension relative to the formation of an independent trade union (Solidarity) led by Lech Walesa, with the strong backing of the Catholic Church. Though at this time Solidarity has been temporarily forced underground, it remains a formidable force for the Communist government to contend with.

"Sensing the times, a request had been made of the government about a year earlier for permission to hold religious meetings in Gdansk—a request granted under the authority of Communist leader, Wojciech Jaruzelski.

Announcements of the coming meetings were advertised widely on bulletin boards, street corners and on the sides of public transportation throughout the city.

"Arrangements had been made to rent the famous Kino Theater in old Gdansk for the meetings. Announcements of the coming meetings were advertised widely on bulletin boards, street corners and on the sides of public transportation throughout the city. Thousands of Bibles had been published and were ready for distribution.

"This is now the fourth day since leaving Chicago. The emotional roller coaster upon which I have been riding for the past year—since I was invited by Pastor Finley to join him for this venture—has reached great heights and depths, some of the steepest of these immediately before beginning my journey. I have had to struggle with my thoughts over and over again as I have considered my mission and potential opportunities and risks, not really knowing either. I have been sustained through it all by the conviction and belief that God was the One who was opening the doors, and I could not refuse to enter where He offered opportunity.

"The day was windy, cloudy and cool as I disembarked from my plane in Warsaw and walked toward the small, drab airport terminal. I was met and accompanied by church personnel as I passed through Customs, being warmly greeted throughout. Outside again, I was seated in a *Russian Mercedes* with a young conference leader by the name of Richard Jankowski, and we were soon on our way to Gdansk, the city of our destination, seven hours away. As we traveled, my heart resonated with the scenes of the countryside. It was autumn—called by my driver, Richard, *golden autumn* (English translation). I was taken, in thought, back to my childhood when we, too, dug and picked our potatoes by hand; shocked and husked our corn by hand, and horses pulled our machinery and wagons full of harvest produce. I was already in love with the Polish countryside and its people. I had thought—when first asked by Mark to join him—'Why Poland?' All of this suddenly changed as we traveled and talked together, discussing plans and problems for our anticipated work in the days and weeks to come.

"My home away from home was with the most gracious Krahl family; a pastor, his wife and three children, living in a second-floor apartment with three small rooms and a bath in Gdynia (a sister city to Gdansk). My sleeping quarters consisted of an interesting *hide-away* bed in the dining /living room which was available after everyone retired for the night. I am not sure where the three children slept while I occupied their quarters! The lady of the house spoke some English—the others, very little, but they thoroughly enjoyed the task of trying to teach me Polish.

"One of my first assignments was to speak at a senior high school about the dangers of tobacco and drugs. The faculty and students, alike, were kind and grateful, and enhanced my visit by a gift of three pretty Gerbera flowers (I learned later that the Poles love beautiful flowers, raise many of them in greenhouses and give them as gifts of gratitude for many occasions). It was an enjoyable experience.

"A cordial meeting with the city mayor; an invitation to attend a meeting of cardiologists; a press conference with a reporter from a local newspaper; a meeting with six other reporters representing the press throughout the country; and local television reporters, all gave us the impression that Gdansk—and most of Poland—was aware, or about to become aware, of what was to transpire in the famous Kino Theater. Being, at heart, still a bit of a farm boy, I am not accustomed to such celebrity status—it both embarrasses and frightens me but, at the same time, thrills me to have a little part in the plan of God on planet earth.

"On Friday, the day before the scheduled start of the meetings, Mark and I—with our translators and the local team members—met at the church for worship and testimonies, etc. Already—based upon the reports we heard—the Spirit of God was working upon the hearts of the people of that city, leading us to believe that we could find ourselves holding a second session to accommodate the many interests. My talk for worship that morning was based upon Revelation 18:1 which describes the filling of the earth with the glory of God—a bit of which we were beginning to witness!

"After worship, we all sat together for a lunch prepared by the ladies of the church. Food, being scarce in this country, does not leave many options and this day was no exception. Just a bit of horseradish on the tip of a spoon is enough to make me *cry*, but never had I even considered eating a whole meal of creamed horseradish! If there were a few potatoes mixed in, I could not see them through my tear-filled eyes!

"When the doors opened for the evening meeting in the Kino, the people could not be held back. As expected, the theater filled rapidly—leaving many outside crying for admission. Word was soon sent out that we would hold a second session for those unable to get in. Following a few preliminary remarks and musical selections, it was time for me to speak. My allotted time was twenty minutes. Mark was seated on the stage behind me waiting to deliver his message as soon as I sat down.

"I began to speak with my translator, Pastor Kosofski, beside me. I spoke of the cause and effect nature of the laws that govern our universe, including those that promise us health, happiness and long life. Failing to factor in the time it takes for translation, my twenty minutes were gone, and I had hardly begun my lecture—so I continued on. Meanwhile, Mark was getting more and more uncomfortable, knowing that I was cutting into his time, and that we had a second session to follow. All in all, it was not a good beginning for me! Only time will tell who will return tomorrow night. It seems it would be much easier for God to do His thing if He would just bypass us humans—but, of course, He can't; for we are both the cause and a necessary part of the cure. The crowd stayed with us to the end.

"The next night the crowds were even larger, and they continued to increase each night. My talks were going well after that first fiasco. Mark, too, had captured the interest and attention of the people with his powerful Spirit-driven message about the return of Christ.

"Each day we met with the local pastors and other workers, teaching and planning together. One of our plans included programs designed to help people quit smoking and abusing alcohol. Unfortunately, because of the large crowds, the theater was not suitable for this. But having seen how God had provided until then, we had no doubts that He would provide for this also. I considered it a real honor to have the opportunity to share my faith before such a great and hungry crowd. God's Spirit was quite obviously working, and I deemed it an honor to have a little part in it.

"I had frequent opportunities to speak in the schools and to meet with the press, officials of the government and the church. This, in addition to preparations for the evening lecture, kept me busy.

We were often overwhelmed by people asking us to autograph the Bible they had received.

"By the fourth day, we had made sufficient impact on the city and were given a five to six minute interview that was aired on the evening news; we were told they were considering airing the meetings nation-wide. I don't believe that ever happened, but word truly was getting out. This was made clear to us when, one evening, we met a man from the far south of Poland's hill country who had come to take in the meetings. (One of his daughters eventually studied medicine at Loma Linda University in the U.S.)

"Following the lectures, we were often overwhelmed by people asking us to autograph the Bible they had received. Too, we met people with all kinds of personal problems; with these we prayed and encouraged. I also met with professional people who expressed their appreciation for what we were doing. One lady even commented on a statement made by a friend of hers attending the meetings that, 'Mark was even better than the pope'—referring to the power of his material and his ability to remember his message without notes.

"Thursday was an off day—set aside for rest and relaxation. After doing a little catch-up work at the church, we toured the *old City* and other interesting places. Gdansk had been almost totally leveled by the Germans early in World War II. When the war was over and Poland was being revived, the central part of the former city was restored to its original condition using many of the very materials of brick and stone lying on the ground following the bombings. It is a beautiful sight—from the original *Rat House* (City Hall); to the Kino, just a short distance away; to many other interesting buildings lining the cobblestone streets. Even the large brass fountain was impressive, and I thought it interesting that the saints, as I was told, were the same statues that were once the ancient pagan gods! We visited the Solidarity Church, headquarters of Lech Walesa and the Solidarity movement; we went to the shipyards (one of the largest ship-building complexes in the world), and viewed the monument set up as a memorial to that movement.

"Saint Mary's Church was as beautiful and interesting as it was old. I marveled at its architecture. A winding staircase rises from the ground floor up 360 steps to the top of the cathedral, from where one can look out across the entire city in one great panoramic view. When shown the beautiful art work, I was most impressed with a painting in one of the side rooms depicting a representation of hell and the final judgment. There the judge (God), sat on his throne—along with a few saints—while in a scene below, people writhed in anguish. Though I say I was impressed—for I was familiar with this view of God—to see it portrayed so visually nearly overwhelmed me, for this was not the God I read about in my Bible. At the rear of the sanctuary, there was a large, rather ornate, baptismal tank—the tank having been filled in and exchanged for a bowl from which water was sprinkled upon the candidates. I was then informed that there are still at least a few of those old churches where baptism was done by immersion.

"From St. Mary's Church, we were taken to the site where World War II began. It was here that the Germans overwhelmed the Polish forces; first at sea and then on land. One cannot view the monuments and reflect upon that day without experiencing a profound respect for the Poles, and a dreadful sense of the terribleness of the human state and the wars it generates. Then, as I so often find myself doing, I wanted to cry out from the depths of my soul, 'How long, Oh God, before Jesus comes and this whole sin problem can be resolved?'

"Day six—Another beautiful day! Tonight we had a double session at the Kino, again with a full house at the first meeting and about 500 in attendance at the second. There are still a lot of new people coming and a nice group that is coming regularly. My talk was on the topic of love, lust and adultery—building it around sexually-transmitted diseases, destruction of the family unit, and its consequent harm to society. I would never have believed that—from my mouth—would come such a clear statement regarding the truth about the current sexual revolution. During the second session, we also started a five-day program for those wishing to quit smoking. We were able to find a lovely building several blocks away from the Kino that fit our purposes. It is called *The Fisherman's House,* but I never did understand the full significance of the name. At any rate—while I gave my lecture in the Kino—Mark led the smokers through the streets to the Fisherman's House. He carried a huge inflated replica of a cigarette, stopping traffic as they went. One man even had an accordion along and began to play. During my talk at the Kino, Mark began the meeting at the Fisherman's House and, as soon as I completed my talk, we switched places. Getting the timing down was a bit tricky, but it worked out quite well and turned out to be a very successful venture. Later, we began the same kind of thing with the alcoholic and drug addicts.

"Day seven—During the evening meeting, a man from the press brought a message inviting Mark to meet Lech Walesa at the Solidarity Church on the day after his press conference where he would be talking about his visit with vice president G.H. Bush. Wisely, Mark sent word back to Lech that he was welcome to come to see us at the Kino at any time. The press agent noted that the entire city is talking about our meetings, and knows what is going on.

"The next day was a *dark* day for all of us—a *blue Monday* I guess. We sensed that the devil did not like what was going on in the city. Perhaps he anticipated what was to occur the following day. I spent much of the day with Pastor Kosofski helping him translate a movie, *Understanding Stress and Strain,* for the five-day plan. That evening, Mark presented a powerful message describing the second coming of Christ and the Millennium. At the conclusion of his lecture, he asked those who wanted to follow Jesus to the end—wherever truth would lead—to stand. I expected that perhaps a couple of hundred would stand at best, but my heart was full and my eyes overflowing as I realized what was happening. Everyone in the auditorium stood with one accord—twelve hundred people—nearly all of them only about a week along the Christian way. Then, I concluded, that the dark day yesterday must have been so that we could enjoy the sunshine of this evening even more!

"Day eleven—I have begun doing medical consultations at the Fisherman's House in the afternoons, and have had some very interesting contacts that could well change my way of practice in the future. God works when we put Him in the proper light. Two days ago, I saw a lady who had come in on behalf of her brother who was dying from lung cancer, and who was in terrible, uncontrollable pain. There was little we could do for him—other than to lead her in a prayer to God on his behalf. She returned today, telling me he had his first pain-free night in months. On one occasion, Alex, a young man (age 17) came to see me, stating he had no friends and was alone in the world. His parents were divorced and he lived with his father and sister. His sister, apparently, has no time for him and, at school, his friends don't appreciate him. Recently, when away from home, his most valuable possession—his rock collection—had been thrown away and was gone. I tried to encourage him as we talked and I offered a prayer for him. Before he left, he reached into his tattered jacket, fumbled around in a torn pocket a few moments, then pulled out a small crystalline rock and placed it in my hand, saying, 'Here, this is for you!' There were tears in my eyes as he walked away. Though simple calcite and of no commercial value, I treasure that piece of rock to this day.

"Nearly every day I am speaking in the schools. In one of these, the principal expressed his happiness regarding my presentation and my willingness to speak about the moral motives for lifestyle habits."

"Nearly every day I am speaking in the schools. In one of these, the principal expressed his happiness regarding my presentation and my willingness to speak about the moral motives for lifestyle habits. He assured me that Poland was free and that I should have no hesitation to speak what was on my mind regarding the value of Christianity. On another occasion, I spoke at an evening secondary school for working people. It was a bit intimidating because it was a very large room with terrible acoustics, and I did not have good insight regarding a topic that might be useful to them. Obviously, someone had prepared the way as I discussed AIDS, alcohol, tobacco and drugs. Lives were touched among the several hundred students who were quiet and orderly throughout the entire program.

"During meetings with the teachers and with the school supervisors, I struggled—along with them! They wanted me to give an answer to the problem of alcohol and drugs—realizing that the answer does not lie in programs—but recognizing the problem is the result of a psychologically-devastated society. Still, they are not willing or able (at least as a group) to accept the only real answer based upon principles found in the Bible. This was well exemplified by an article that appeared in a paper from another Polish city about Adventists. It was a very good article, but the last sentence spoke to the effect that, 'It is too bad that it is utopia'—implicating that most people cannot experience it. Unfortunately, this is the view of all too many hurting people in our world today. But I was pleased when, later, one of the teachers came to our meeting at the Kino. It was her first time, and it was because of my talk with the teachers the day before. She was bubbling with gratitude for the message she was hearing.

"One day I was honored to speak to the teachers of a school for ambulatory, retarded children about stress management and health. The school radiated a somewhat more optimistic atmosphere than some of the others; perhaps, because these teachers take their work with the crippled kids very seriously! Everywhere we go with our lectures and demonstrations, we are received warmly.

"On another occasion—on our day off—we were taken to visit the Malborg Castle about 60 kilometers away. This is the largest brick castle in the world and one of the most impressive in Europe. The building was begun in 1274 and was under continuous construction for 230 years. It was being restored when World War II broke out, during which about half of it was again destroyed. At the time of our visit, much of the damage had been repaired. It would take an entire book to describe this fantastic edifice—the surrounding mote, the protective gate guarding the entrance, the fantastic heating system, the great dining room, the collection of rare amber jewelry, other artifacts and so many other wonders—everything one reads about in those tantalizing stories of castles, kings and brave knights of times gone by.

"We are near the end of this experience. Each day has its highs and lows. God is gracious in giving sufficient, encouraging experiences to make up for the frustrations. The evening meeting went OK—attendance probably about 800 but with increasing cohesiveness. It appears that most of the curiosity seekers have now attended or heard about the meetings, so that those who continue to attend are truly interested in what we have to share. Mark spoke on the topic of hell and did a very good job. Afterward, a couple of Catholic individuals approached us with challenges and questions. It appears they are under conviction and seeking certainty of what they have been hearing.

"At a meeting with leaders of the Adventist Church in Poland, we were given a report of the impact of our meetings. From all of the evidence, what we are doing here is being well-received and is making a nation-wide impact. They listened carefully to our recommendations for follow-up, and they also described their plans for following up interests and for developing a strong health outreach throughout the country.

"After dinner one day, we were invited to meet with—and speak to—a small group of Catholic priests, during which we talked about managing stress. Though I was a bit limited without means of illustrating my comments, our presentation was accepted very graciously. This was followed by a meeting with a pro-socialist Christian association discussing the subject of disease prevention. They, too, received us well.

"At our final session of the alcohol treatment program, we broke into groups and discussed various options for managing alcohol addiction. I was thrilled to see about a dozen men with alcohol problems request the organization of an alcohol support group. Initiating such a program has been one of my wishes since the beginning. The group will be led by one of the young pastors. Some of the men are well educated, and it is my hope that they will develop and grow into an organization that will reach out to the entire city and nation.

"Not far from our sleeping quarters, I discovered a large nature reserve. Well-traveled paths wound in and out and roundabout, through the forest and over the hills. Whenever I could find a little free time, I enjoyed wandering through those forests taking in their beauty, speaking with my God and seeking guidance and reassurance. At the far end of the reserve—beyond the foot-trodden trails—back where the deer munched on forest grasses and wild hogs rooted in the earth for choice morsels of food, I noticed that the hills were pock-marked with holes and piles of dirt. Only young trees grew there—no virgin timber. Here and there, scattered remnants of spent artillery poked out above the fallen leaves. Not long before, I had visited the monument marking the spot where Polish soldiers had fought to their death in defending their land from the invading German forces—marking the beginning of World War II. Here, in this unmarked spot, I realized that this, too, was sacred ground; spilled blood still crying out to God above begging, 'How long? How long must the reign of evil prevail? How long untill the last battle is won?' From these hills I returned to the Cine' better armed to fight on for the cause of my God.

"The worship service this Sabbath was held in the Kino. There were about 800 in attendance—most of whom had been regular attendees at the meetings. We were pleasantly surprised, since one Saturday each month is a workday like the other workdays; and, this, was that Saturday. I spoke for about 15 minutes on the topic of answered prayer. After the sermon by Mark, 18 people were baptized in a pool that had been built in the front of the theater. Many more expressed an interest in baptism and church membership.

"During the evening session, I spoke on the topic of the body as the temple of God, reviewed with them the assignments for lifestyle change that I have given out during the past ten sessions, and challenged them—as my last assignment—to make their own bodies the most beautiful temples possible, whereby to glorify our God. Many seem to have taken my assignments seriously. The young man who gave me the stone has been doing better and expresses some strong evidences of becoming a worker in the service of God. Many, many young people and educated people have been among those choosing *Nove Zycie* (New Life). Our efforts here have been received with great appreciation. I have signed hundreds of cards, books and Bibles, circulating far and wide the words, "*Nasz Bog yest tak wspanially*" (Our God is so wonderful)! I am happy, in spite of having a tired hand, to encourage these people to a better way of life—but would not do this for popularity and fame—only for the glory of God!

"After the meeting, the entire staff gathered and wished us their blessings. They gave presents to add to others given by loving new friends from among the attendees and church members. It was a time of tears and joy; an experience long to be remembered by both myself and my wife, Avonne (Avonne joined me here about a week ago). Afterwards, we were nourished with a light meal at the Krahls and then put on the train for Warshawa (Warsaw).

"I am told that one of the newspapers of Gdansk published an article stating that, this month, crime and drunk-driving have been the lowest they have been for a long time. If any of that is attributable to our work, I hope that the effect may persist and grow. Certainly, all of the evidence is that this city has been touched and influenced by the gospel from one end to the other and I suspect, like Nineveh of Jonah's day, it will be spared some wrath because of its response to the gospel. Unlike the Bible story of Jonah—who became angry at God for not destroying Nineveh after their repentance—I am thrilled by the results to this point. God is so good!

Chapter VI

Poland, Again!

"... saw where the band welcomed them, and read the announcement saying they were brought here with only one way to leave—through the smokestack."

"Traveling down a new four-lane superhighway from Warsaw to Katowice reveals a much different Poland from the one we experienced 3 1/2 years ago in Gdansk—then still under communist rule. Tractors now work the fields alongside the horses. Buildings are rising everywhere. Even at the airport, one can sense a different mood in the land. Yes, people still complain that they are poor, but they have much more—adequate food and housing and quite adequate medical care. Of the poorer classes, clothing and other things are still scarce and hard to get, but—for those with money—nearly everything is now available. Long lines are hardly ever seen now, and store shelves are well stocked. Pollution remains a problem with the Silesia area (Katowice region)—one of the worst in the world. Yet, much of Poland is beautiful, well kept, and with productive farmland and forest. There are still entire families and children here—a thing almost nonexistent in the west. With the influence of western television and video now available, one wonders how much longer the family will remain here, as well. Education in the professions, arts and trades is very highly regarded and a major blessing to the land. Many youth still have vision and purpose, it seems.

"But not only is the nation changed, even the preparations for our meetings in Katowice are different from what occurred in Gdansk. We have not had the advertising and promotion such as occurred there, nor the ample, enthusiastic staff present at our previous campaign because many are now involved in their own ministry at various sites throughout the country. Personnel and supplies for our health fair have been inadvertently delayed, and we have only a couple of translators available. Yet, the Kultural Center is a beautiful auditorium with a seating capacity of about a thousand and spacious enough for our health education initiatives.

"Mark and I will be working here in Katowice, while Pastor Peter Neri and Dr. Tim Arnott will be carrying on a similar series of meetings in Pszczyna, a smaller, neighboring city in southern Poland.

"My health has always been good and, though public presentations have always been accompanied by high levels of stress, I suppose this was one of my most trying. My surgical practice at home was very busy. It has always been difficult for me to walk off and leave recovering surgical patients under the care of someone else—no matter how skilled they may be—and, I must say, this was no exception. In fact, as I climbed the stairs of the hospital from one floor to the next in my final preparations prior to leaving that evening, I noted my legs were weak and my heart was pounding—my very first episode, as I soon discovered, of atrial fibrillation. It soon spontaneously corrected, and I was good to go! Perhaps I should not have been surprised then—when preparing for our health fair in Katowice—a check of my blood pressure revealed a significant elevation—something else I had not previously encountered!

"Our living quarters were in a hotel about ten to fifteen minutes away. They were clean, comfortable, very simple, cheap—and in the process of being remodeled. Judging by our meals, the hotel had not yet begun to experience the revolution involving the rest of the country. Breakfast consisted of bread and jam, scrambled eggs and barley tea—or something very similar. Dinners, too, reflected continued scarcity of luxuries of any kind. Even so, it was comfortable and adequate, and nearby there was a lovely forested park to which we often resorted for exercise and renewal."

From my notes of our first meeting I quote, "At meeting time there were about 400 present. All of us were disappointed, I suppose, but we all also recognize that God has not brought us here for naught. Time will tell why. Our talks went well and the audience appreciative as we met them at the door at the end of the meeting."

By day four I could write, "Each evening our attendance has increased. We have put up the Health Expo panels (illustrated life-size descriptions of the various principles governing our health) spoken of in other accounts, and each one is accompanied by a young pastor. This teaches the pastors about healthful lifestyles and gives them opportunity to educate the public, to interact with them and to develop relationships with the people attending. The artistic work, done in the Philippines, is beautiful. Tonight, a lady from the TV station came down and recorded the health fair. She interviewed us and had each of us give a little presentation before interviewing some of the participants. It is scheduled to air both tomorrow and the next evening at 6:00 p.m. We learned from her, during the process, that she is fighting some higher powers by doing this. Her station manager asked her if she had an OK from the bishop to do an interview with us last week, and she replied, 'No, they are doing a good thing for the people, and I don't need permission to do so.' We are told that the mayor and all public officials must have the blessing of the bishop in order to serve. She and her work will certainly be in our prayers.

"As in Gdansk, I was invited to speak in a number of schools—as well as to entertain students at the Health Expo. This has always been a highlight of the trip for me.

"Two issues predominate in all discussions about health: bio-energy therapy and environmental pollution. Many of the young people are interested in the healing abilities of bio-energy and other *unorthodox* healing practices. One couple in attendance claims to have healing powers by focusing universal energy *correctly*—ancient practices still widely utilized in the Far East and in New Age teachings. It has been a challenge for me to present a better alternative as found in the teachings of the Bible and the findings of modern science.

"Pollution is, indeed, a problem in the area. This is a major industrial area consisting of about 1000 industrial plants. Smokestacks belching toxic exhaust containing lead, zinc, cadmium (and who knows what other toxins) are evident everywhere. All of this adds to naturally-high levels of heavy metals in the soil. One evening, an attendee at our meetings brought me an article listing the concentration of three heavy metals in the soil in the area—ranging from safe up to 16 times the maximum-safe levels. People are afraid to eat garden produce grown anywhere in the region for fear of toxicity. But, even more interesting to me, was the fact that almost everyone smoked tobacco, apparently totally ignoring the far greater risk to health from it than from any vegetables they might consume (which naturally contain qualities that tend to neutralize toxins). Perhaps, even more interesting was the fact that—even when confronted with this suggestion, few seemed impressed—preferring present habits and addictions.

"We had an interesting visit with the president of Katowice. He is a rather distinguished-appearing man. He was concerned about the placards (signs) announcing Nova Zycie (New Life) posted all over the city, which suggested to him that they had been put up by some who were overly enthusiastic. Later, when we had explained our mission, he said, 'Put the signs everywhere!' He noted that 'nothing has changed' since communism fell—only the appearance has changed. He stated that structure must change before the country can really change; he didn't explain what he meant. He acknowledges problems with alcohol, drugs and tobacco—he doesn't smoke, but his wife is just out of the hospital with a tobacco-related illness, so his wife and daughter are quitting. He then asked what he should do about people with alcohol problems who don't want to quit. We suggested media promotion and expression of public policy against the use of alcohol, and education—by example! His aide noted that one of the two vice presidents—the one who does not smoke—was just hospitalized with heart disease and wanted to know why the more temperate one got sick. My response to his challenge was simply, 'That is why we are emphasizing all of the laws of health.' He acknowledged my response positively. We discussed the use of television as a medium for health education and encouraged his support. He mentioned the upcoming cable television, with one channel designated for Katowice. Mark also mentioned the need for education regarding health in the schools. The president acknowledged the risk of environmental pollution; but did not offer any solution to it, nor did he ask for our opinion regarding it. I did, however, have opportunity to suggest to him that—though environmental pollution should not be ignored—poor lifestyle practices were a much greater threat to society. Since he is blessed by the bishop, I must assume that his long-term goals reflect the goals of the church; i.e., to use the power and authority of the church to make the changes in society that everyone recognizes are needed. Unfortunately, the power of God to change sin-bound human beings and to give them victory over destructive beliefs and practices is seldom detected in the modern, Christian church anywhere in the world.

"Attendance at the meetings continued to increase until we were speaking to about 700 people each night. It always amazes me the way—though not usually planned that way—Mark's Bible lectures complement my health-related talks. Likewise, the Health Expo has been very well received and is proving a great format for one-on-one interchange with the people."

We could not be so close and miss an opportunity to visit the Auschwitz Berkenau Concentration Camp. I quote my notes from that visit: "There we spent most of a day observing 'man's inhumanity to man' in the very, most extreme way. We walked among the barracks where narrow wooden bunks stacked three high—one above the other—stretched down the whole length on both sides of the long, wooden building. Six people were assigned to each bunk—just wide enough to contain their skinny bodies. One small stove sat near the entrance at one end as the only source of heat for the entire building—even on the coldest days

At Auschwitz, "... we spent most of a day observing 'man's inhumanity to man' in the very, most extreme way."

of winter. There was a toilet at the other end. Rows and rows of these long buildings are still standing, even though the Germans set many on fire as they left. I could not even begin to think of existing in such a place for a day or a week, to say nothing about month after long month. We walked in the court where hanging had occurred, and where others were lined up and shot. We visited the building where some were kept in solitary confinement (and saw a cross scratched in the concrete wall), and others forced to stand four in a cubicle—one meter square—during the night, and from which they were taken to do labor the following day. We looked into the huge crematorium into which four million Jews and others were burned after first being herded like cattle, 2,000 at a time, into the death chamber. We witnessed large bins containing the remains of human hair, eyeglasses, brushes, cooking utensils, and other personal effects. We saw burlap, woven from human hair, which had been used by the Nazis for making furniture. We walked down the railroad track that brought the people in by the carload from all over Europe, saw where the band welcomed them, and read the announcement saying they were brought here with only one way to leave—through the smokestack. We watched a motion picture of conditions at the time of liberation by the Russians, after most of the *death factory* had been emptied by evacuation to Germany. We stood beside the gallows upon which Huss, the camp commander, was hanged—unrepentant—on April 17, 1947, and saw his fancy home a very short distance from the crematorium.

"This evening I attended the meetings being held in Pszczyna and listened as Pastor Neri spoke about the millennium (the thousand year period of Revelation 20), the judgment and the final destruction of the wicked (a fitting end to the depressing experience of the day at Auschwitz). His lecture reassured me, once again, that one day soon such atrocities—as happened at Auschwitz—will be judged, and a loving and just God will do what is right to assure that never, throughout eternity, will such evil be seen again.

"There is a lady, a friend of my translator, who lives in another city far from Katowice, who fell from a 4th story window ten or eleven years ago—breaking her back and ending up paralyzed. She is now suffering with severe pain in her back and spasms of her legs and has requested that I come to see her. Accordingly, after our meeting one night, we started out. About half-way there the rain turned to snow, making a long trip even longer. I spent about an hour with her the next morning, examining her and making some recommendations that I thought might give her some relief. I learned that she writes children's poetry and Bible stories and that her nurse is an artist. Together, they are working on children's books for public distribution.

"On the way back to Katowice, we stopped at Czestajowa for a few minutes to visit the shrine of the Black Madonna. I was disappointed when I discovered that she was merely a picture, rather than a three-dimensional representation as I had expected. Furthermore, the icon is only uncovered periodically during the day—and our time was not her time! I did see a wall upon which hung many pairs of crutches, left there by those who *no longer* needed them. A look inside the adjacent sanctuary made up for my disappointment. It was gorgeous to the point of breath-taking! (This is the place where Pope John Paul II visited for a world-wide youth conference. I was told that our church members helped to house the attendees.)

"My lecture that evening in Katowice was about the effects of Godly love upon the neuro-endocrine-immunological model (brain, glands, and immune system), and noting how the attributes of love (patience, kindness, forgiveness and similar traits) give healing to the body, while attributes of self-centeredness wreck havoc with health. This, when combined with other lifestyle practices, account for nearly all of our health problems.

"Krakow is one of the oldest cities of Europe. It is the home of one of the first universities, the home of Copernicus, and the site of the old Vaval Castle with its fire-spewing dragon beside the beautiful, winding, Wistula River (one of the few rivers in the world that runs north). Roman, Mark's translator, served as our guide on the day of our visit. From him, we learned a lot of history about this famous and historic city. I found the story of the dragon that lived in a cave under the castle most fascinating.

According to the story, the dragon had a voracious appetite for children and caught those that wandered too close. As one might imagine, this posed a terrible dilemma for the king—who, in desperation, offered his beautiful daughter in marriage to anyone who could get rid of the dragon. Mighty men from far and near tried, but failed; none could catch and kill the dragon. Finally, one day, a lowly shoemaker came up with a plan. He killed a lamb, stuffed its stomach with sulfur, and placed it outside the dragon's cave and waited. The dragon fell for the trick and ate the lamb. According to the story, this caused his stomach to burn—sending him down to the river where he drank and drank until he burst! Of course, the king's daughter and the shoemaker lived happily ever after!

"We took a tour through the university where Nicolas Copernicus studied, and we examined the technical equipment he used to make his observations—leading him to the conclusion that the earth is not the center of the universe as commonly believed at the time. It was interesting to me to learn that he did not permit the release of the results of his findings until after his death; knowing that, as a member of the clergy, the church would not accept his findings—findings that, when promoted by Galileo a century later, led to Galileo's house arrest by the Roman Inquisition."

I now quote from my notes made at the conclusion of this second experience in Poland. "It has been a good three weeks—fairly relaxed with no heavy schedules and good fellowship with those whom we have worked and ministered to. I have kept my lectures fairly simple and Christ-centered. I have discussed the basic laws of health and related these to health-maintenance, prevention and treatment of illness, and made personal recommendations to many. By focusing upon the function of the neuro (brain), endocrine (glands), and immune systems of our bodies; noting how these are related to our physical, mental, and spiritual beliefs and practices, I have tried to provide the incentive and the tools needed by our listeners whereby they might enjoy better health and a longer, happier life. During my last lecture, I challenged each one in the audience with the assignment of giving their best to the world of their own unique qualities and talents. I have attempted to share with them the joy and peace of making the body temple the most beautiful monument possible to God, for the indwelling of His Spirit—comparing our bodies to the awesome beauty of the churches at Czestajowa and Krakow.

"Attendance remained very good at about 500 with peaks near 700, with the expression of much appreciation for our efforts. They represent individuals from many different faiths, including Catholic priests dressed in secular garb as recognized by their members! One night, a priest engaged Mark in a discussion regarding the Sabbath, and later he spent another hour or so on the steps of the Kultural Center with another pastor. I don't know what the eternal results of our work here will be, but I feel highly privileged to have had this opportunity to share the beauties of the Three Angels Messages of warning and hope to this influential part of the world. Probably our impact upon the pastors of the local churches and administration of the church has been as important and valuable as anything.

"Mark has been an inspiration to me. He, like me, was terribly exhausted when he came, but he has recuperated well with the more relaxed pace here away from the telephone and a million and one other responsibilities. During our many walks together through the forest, we spoke often regarding the offer made to him as speaker/director of the It Is Written television ministry. He is anxiously awaiting the final decision regarding this.

"It has been a good experience. 'Nasz Bog Jest Tak Wspanially.' "

Chapter VII

Brazil

"Everyone tells stories of disasters with piranhas—a man, just across the river, had been severely injured by an attack just the week before."

"The Amazon is beautiful as the full moon rises over the flooded jungle around us; its reflections gleam, like diamonds, on the ripples of water flowing out from among the cocoa and palm trees and around the dark silhouette of a lone home along the river's edge. It is July, the rainy season, and the mighty Amazon is at its highest level since 1953. I find myself gently rocking in my hammock on the deck of the Luzeiro, *Light Bearer to the Amazon,* which is moored to trees growing from the bank of the river. In many ways, it seems as though we have just crossed the Jordan River and entered into heaven and the Promised Land!

Danny Shelton of 3ABN, though not speaking either Spanish or Portuguese, was understood by all as he sang his heart out, night after night, to the glory of God.

I was invited by Danny Shelton to join a team from *Three Angels Broadcasting Network (3ABN)* to tape a nation-wide Youth Congress for television. We were located just outside of Brasilia, the modern capital city of Brazil. Pastor Alejandro Bullon, an internationally-respected evangelist, was our evening speaker for the ten-day event, grabbing the rapt attention of nearly 10,000 young people from all around the nation—leading many to a full commitment to Jesus as Lord of their lives. Even Danny, though not speaking either Spanish or Portuguese, was understood by all as he sang his heart out, night after night, to the glory of God at the evening service. I was there to help out with a large Health Expo and to present seminars on health for the young people.

Upon completion of our duties at the Youth Congress, several of us found ourselves flying high over the Amazonian jungles on our way to Manaus, a modern city in the heart of the Brazilian jungle, where we were to join the staff of the Luzeiro—a mission launch ministering to the needs of the Amazonian peoples.

Manaus is a city of about one million that arose out of the Amazon rain forests by the discovery of natural rubber at the beginning of the twentieth century. More recently, its designation as a *free zone* by the Brazilian government has opened the way for it to become a major manufacturing city of electronic appliances, bicycles and motorcycles, etc. It is, also, the home base of mission organizations serving the needs of those living along the Amazon's banks.

The Seventh-day Adventist Church has maintained a hospital in Manaus, as well as a fleet of mission boats (and a few airplanes), along the Amazon for at least 70 years. As a child in Sabbath School, I would listen with rapt attention to stories of heroism and miracles coming from the Amazonian jungles, and would place my meager offerings in the basket in support of them. Later in life, while attending a lecture by Pastor Halliwell, one of the original missionaries to the region, I was amazed as he unrolled the skin of an anaconda—stretching 48 feet across the front of the auditorium. I had heard stories of human-beings consumed, in minutes, when attacked by Piranhas, of children eaten by crocodiles as they filled their water-buckets at the river's edge and of unnamed *monsters* inhabiting the waters. Now, at last, it was my privilege to serve for a few days in this land in which stories are born.

The Luzeiro—meaning Light Bearer—is a two-story wooden craft, powered by a diesel engine, that provides a medical and dental clinic and a church. It is also the home and office of the captain, his family, and volunteer staff that, sometimes, accompany him to assist in his multi-task role as doctor, nurse, dentist, counselor and head pastor for the many little churches along the river. For purposes of emergency—and for accessing villages beyond reach of the launch—a small canoe is towed along behind.

One of the first requests, upon meeting the captain, was for an outboard motor that he could put on the canoe; one of his most difficult tasks was ministering to those villages located far away from the main river along small streams and tributaries. Upon being told the expected cost and finding it reasonable, I volunteered to put up the cash to purchase such a convenience. However, I was taken aback when we were able to find one available in the city and discovered that his estimate was less than a third of the asking price! But purchase it we did!

It was a bright, sunny morning when we walked past the many warehouses adjacent to the port area—not exactly spick-and-span, nor smelling like a rose! The scene did not improve as we walked out onto the boardwalk leading to the boarding area. It was the rainy season, and the water was higher than it had been in many years—the reason one could not walk to the dock on dry land. The boardwalk was impressive—not for its beauty, stability, or safety but for its utility. Everything that was carried on the many ships and barges supplying this city, and those along the more than 2000-mile run to the ocean, crossed this boardwalk. Missing and broken planks made it rough-going, even for those of us who carried only a few necessities. I marveled as the natives seemed to navigate across easily, carrying 100-pound sacks of rice and all manner of other commodities. The beauty of the blue-violet water hyacinths, too, was nearly completely suppressed by large amounts of garbage distributed among their leaves and gorgeous blossoms. Everywhere, overhead, were the ever-present buzzards scanning the earth for rotting flesh.

The Amazon, the largest and, many claim, the longest river in the world, drains the largest land-basin in the entire world, carrying about one fifth of the fresh water that enters the oceans of the world. Its tributaries extend many hundreds of miles to the west, reaching places nearly to the Pacific Ocean. Two primary rivers, the Rio Negro (named for its deep, black water—stained by organic matter and other chemicals picked up along its course), and the Rio Solimoes (of much lighter color), meet at Manaus to form the Amazon River itself. But it is most interesting and notable that these two rivers run side-by-side as two separate—but distinct—black and brown rivers long before they finally blend into one, many miles downstream. We were told, with some good evidence to support it, that the Rio Solimoes derived its name from ancient times, when ships from Israel (Judah) during the reign of King Solomon, sailed up those waters collecting gold.

Joining me for a week on the Luzeiro was Rony Ries, a Brazilian student attending Wiemar College in California; Joilo Barbosa, a Brazilian student studying medicine in Chicago; the captain, of course, and his family; and a sailor who kept the engine running and kept us safe. It was early afternoon by the time we were loaded and ready to begin our adventure.

We tied up about 10 miles down-river to a tree along the invisible bank (hidden by the flooding waters). Water was lapping at the top of the steps of a home belonging to one of the parishioners. (It also served as a church and a site for clinics when the boat was present.) Three children played in the shallow water surrounding the house, while the lady of the house washed portions of her clay pot, water-filter in the same river water! I wondered later, when offered a drink, if the water could indeed be safe to drink—but it tasted good! Then, I rationalized by calling to memory a truism often quoted in the operating room when dealing with contaminated wounds, "Dilution is the solution to pollution!" I knew there was plenty of water in this river for dilution!

Hardly had we secured the moorings, before people began arriving in their wooden canoes seeking medical and dental care. For several hours, we saw people of all ages with all manner of problems, but the one thing that struck us most was the poor dental condition of the kids. Nearly everyone had irreparable, rotten teeth—beginning in early childhood. One of the things we learned to do, early on, was the art of anesthetiz-

Hardly had we secured the moorings, before people began arriving in their wooden canoes seeking medical and dental care.

ing and pulling teeth. I must confess I discovered I was a better surgeon than dentist! (Note: Rotten teeth were found only among children eating primarily *refined* and *junk* foods readily available all along the river.

Children living inland or along waterways without access to the outside world, have no such dental problems.)

Please permit me to quote from notes I made at the time. "The Amazon is beautiful. We sat and watched as the full moon rose over the flooded jungle—slept in hammocks on the upper deck, and awakened to a beautiful sunrise after weathering a little wind and rain during the night. After breakfast, we paddled our canoe back in—away from the river; checking out the wonders growing there—water lily pads four or five feet in diameter, beautiful hyacinths and an infinite number of other tropical plants—watched the birds in the bushes and trees, and picked a bright-yellow cacao nut hanging low overhead. It is amazingly pretty here!

"Last evening I talked with Rony a long time about the work on the Amazon. Since his father is a pastor, well acquainted with this part of the world, he was well versed on the history and needs of the area. Lots of things could be done if one had money with which to work. Short of that, I suggested that *boy "foot" doctors* (care-givers with only basic training and widely utilized in China) could be trained to serve in the smaller villages along the rivers.

"Several mosquitoes came through my netting during the night and pestered me until I got up and applied repellent. Other than that, it was a perfect night—sky full of stars, an almost-full moon, frogs and all kinds of nightlife singing their hearts out at the mouth of a little river where we had tied up for the night. Some time before we had moved to this site, we had spent the afternoon upriver a bit, seeing many patients and worshipping with the people in their homes. It was interesting going to church in a canoe and walking over a string of canoes to get to the door. (Earlier in the day, I had almost taken a dunking when my canoe skirted sideways as I attempted to step from it!) We had a nice meeting with about 45 people present, mostly kids, many of whom we had treated earlier.

"Yesterday morning, we bathed in the river beside the boat (not far from where we had watched the kids swimming the day before)—a most enjoyable and refreshing experience; today, we all chickened out! Everyone tells stories of disasters with piranhas: a man, just across the river, had been severely injured by an attack just the week before. They told us, too, of alligators six meters long, taking off arms and legs! Maybe we'll get enough courage to try again some other day! My bath today was with a bucket dipped from the Amazon! Many patients are anemic; many headaches and epigastric (stomach) pain. Others suffer from otitis (ear infections), and pneumonia and many with rotten teeth (mostly 8-14 years old). The people are having a very difficult time with the flooding. Most houses are surrounded with water, and many are still flooded. Everything is done from canoes and boats.

"The food is good—rice, beans, potatoes; many, many different kinds of fruit and juice; and, for those who eat it, lots of fish. Everyday there is something new. The sunsets and sunrises are so beautiful.

"This morning we saw 40–50 patients and are now on our way to another site. The sky is looking a little stormy!

"We arrived at a little village yesterday at mid-afternoon and held clinics. I then went for a canoe ride up a jungle river with Joilo, winding our way along a trail that was cut out among the vines and trees. We saw lots of birds—bright-red, green and blue parrots; heard the monkeys playing in the trees, but saw none of them. Haven't seen any alligators, anacondas or jaguars yet! Today, while awaiting engine repairs, we, again, saw patients all morning—headaches, anemia and parasites, etc. Later, we were taken to a place in the jungle where they grow cassava. We saw how they soaked the large roots in the river to *leach* out its poison; then roast it in huge pans over an open fire to produce farina (a staple food for many along the river). A little later, we were introduced to Brazil nuts and given opportunity to taste them fresh from the shell. Many other jungle fruits and foods are also available. Unlike most previous trips abroad where I have had trouble getting enough to eat, here I find myself eating too much—rice, beans, dried milk, fruit shakes, farina, etc.—three times daily!

"Some kids were swimming and climbing up and jumping off from a tree leaning over the river near where our motor was being repaired. We decided to join them in the fun. That evening I gave a talk at the church, but found it a bit difficult drawing the people out and involving them in discussion; yet, it appeared they were grasping the lessons I was trying to convey.

"The waters are receding slowly—have gone down six to eight inches since we started our journey—still many empty and/or flooded homes along the river.

"Today we went up a tributary river to visit with Elias' family (our on-board sailor). They are cattle farmers living on the land and, presently, clearing more land by *slash and burn* for the enlarging herds. When we arrived, we saw a dead snake lying near the house. They told us it was a reticulated python. A little later, we went with them to the place where they were clearing the land; there they had a rope around the tail of an anaconda they were trying to pull out of a hole under a tree. Both snakes were about 12 feet long. Because their pasture-land was flooded, it was necessary to find and haul grass and other feed for the cattle. It was here that we saw some of our first blooming, wild orchids. After dark we, once again, boarded our canoe and paddled through jungle trails feeling like little kids on a treasure hunt; one eye on the nearly-full moon, the other on the land and water—looking for Jac-a-rays (alligators) and anacondas. We didn't find any!

The church was still flooded, but the school—built on stilts—was dry. It was the Sabbath, so we joined them in worship.

"This morning we arose early and went back down the tributary river to the Amazon where we had previously held clinics and spoken with the people. The church was still flooded, but the school—built on stilts—was dry. It was the Sabbath, so we joined them in worship. I taught the Sabbath School class and Joilo preached. Following a baptism (no shortage of water here!) we were invited out to eat and had the usual beans, rice, fish and a vegetable patty of some kind. Everyone we spoke with seems to sense the need for sharing the gospel with others.

"That evening we moved down-river, in the darkness, to the mouth of another tributary where we tied up for the night. For all of us, being kindred spirits, those trips—whether in daylight or dark—were always rewarding; watching the sights along the shore, viewing the glories of the heavens, sharing thoughts about the work of God along the river or at our respective missions at home.

"At almost 9:00 a.m., we left our night-time mooring to go up another river. It has been a veritable paradise—so many birds, flowers and beautiful things, but no animals—apparently, because of the flooded conditions.

A day later!

"I am sitting in the town of Itacoatiara waiting for a bus to take us back to Manaus, where we are scheduled to board our plane tomorrow morning for home. The region that we went to yesterday was lovely, about three hours up-river from the Amazon—where the huts are made of thatch, most of the canoes are made from dugout logs and families live far apart. After several stops to let people know we were around, we stopped at a government school to see patients. Many came from far and near. That evening we had a meeting in the school with about 75 people in attendance. There were stories, singing and preaching. Many of the people expressed the desire for a series of meetings to be held there and for a church to be built.

"As we were ready to leave on our trip back to Manaus, our diesel engine refused to start. We were many miles down-river—a long day's travel, even with a *good running* engine. What do we do! I have patients waiting for me back home, and I need to meet my plane. The remainder of the evening was spent in searching for a way to get back, but to no avail. Our search continued the next morning. Finally, we found a family who was willing to trade canoes for a few days—so that we could place our outboard motor (the one I had paid for before we started out) on their bigger canoe and travel up to Itacoatiara where we could catch a bus for the four-hour ride to our destination! Taking shortcuts through the flooded jungle and watching, carefully, to avoid hitting hidden logs, we finally arrived with a little time to wait. Hungry—we ordered a bit of food from a very restricted menu at a restaurant near the bus stop. Small pieces of locally-made cheese, on white bread, were filled with sand—reminding us of our visit at the farm along the way where the cows were milked at the sandy river's edge.

"We stayed at the mission in Manaus for the night. While there, we were given a tour of the beautiful new Adventist hospital nearing completion—but for lack of funds it has not been finished. It seems that someone, stateside, worked hard to collect used equipment for the hospital and had it shipped. Unfortunately, duty on the equipment cost far more than the equipment was worth and, furthermore, exhausted the financial resources that were to be used to complete the building. Sometimes, the best laid plans of mice and men do, indeed, go astray!

"Unlike most of my overseas missions that have often been very demanding, I have enjoyed my time here very much. It wouldn't be difficult for me to spend my whole life in the beauty of this pristine place were it not that God has given me a different mission, I believe. There is so much that could be done here, but the greater world beckons to me. I am tired of treating symptoms, while the world dies for want of real restoration. And, it seems to me, that as honorable as it is to treat the temporal needs of our hurting society, it is time to free the world from the entanglements of sin and to stop the root-cause of most of the suffering we see around us. This is my real burden at this time. The experience, here, has been a good vacation—and though I cringe as I anticipate the responsibilities awaiting my return, I know that I must go. God will provide the grace to do His purpose, whatever that turns out to be.

"My itinerary took me here to Rio de Janeiro where I spent the night in a hotel with Joilo and took an early-morning walk on the beautiful, white, sandy beach. The flight between Rio and Asuncion, Paraguay, was rough—but so beautiful! Tall, white, fluffy clouds towered high into the sky, with thick layers of cirrus clouds above. But the most beautiful experience occurred during the last 30–45 minutes of flight coming into Paraguay—it was as though we were flying through a rainbow! I could look down at the ground through a bright emerald or, sometimes, amethyst haze; sometimes there were blues; and, occasionally, yellows or faint reds. I have never before experienced such a beautiful phenomenon.

"Nossa Deus é munto maravilhoso! (Our God is so wonderful!)"

Chapter VII

Karachi, Pakastan

"... a truck with about 15 young men pulled up ready to torch the bus. When they saw the meeting, they decided to go inside and toss the gas there instead."

Salaam Gi! (Greetings!)

Some events in one's life are never forgotten. Karachi, Pakistan, provided the perfect setting for some of those events to take place.

My friend, Pastor Mark Finley, was serving as the ministerial director of the Trans-European Division of the Seventh-day Adventist Church—a division that included Pakistan as a part of its territory. Sensing a need to carry the gospel to this predominantly Muslim nation, Mark called to ask if I would assist in a series of meetings in Karachi. We both knew that—if we were to make an impact in this nation—we would only do so by meeting people at the point of their felt-needs. It would be a "first!" None had ever tried such a thing before. I could not turn him down.

This account follows closely the chronology of my notes recorded at the time, with only a few vivid mental pictures added from time to time.

"Immediately upon disembarking, I knew I was in a different world from any I had ever been in before. My nose told me so—for the smells of the city overpowered the smell of the plane's exhaust! This was just the beginning of a month-long challenge. I had in my luggage, a video camera, a tape recorder, and many illustrated materials for health presentations. Only by the grace granted by the airline personnel in O'Hare, had I avoided paying $100 overweight on my luggage; here in Karachi, it was Customs on my camera. They were not about to let me through without paying a heavy toll, even after explaining that I was coming into their country for their benefit, and that I would be bringing the camera back out with me upon leaving. That was not good enough. So I waited, wondering what to do, and hoping that the people picking me up would be able to help. Unfortunately, I saw no one around the crowded reception area who looked as though they might be looking for me; nor did I have contact information to locate anyone! So I found myself with two major problems immediately from the start—someone who wanted my money and no one to meet me and take me where I was supposed to go. When, at last, they recognized my naiveté, stamped my papers and let me on through, I was met by a mass of hungry taxi drivers seeking to take my luggage—hundreds of them—or so it seemed! I stalled, believing someone would still show up to meet me. Someone did!

My home for the next three weeks was an apartment on the campus of the Karachi Adventist Hospital that I would share with Mark. The hospital is located at the crossing of a couple of the busiest streets of the city—a fact that one is continuously reminded of, day and night, by the never-ending racket and thick, black exhaust of the motorcycles, motorized rickshaws, taxis and trucks passing that way. High concrete walls—topped with shards of broken glass—rim the lovely campus where the hospital, a nursing school, an apartment high-rise and numerous other buildings and garden areas are located. Outside the wall, garbage collects in great heaps on the sidewalk, and men face the wall to urinate. There, too, hawkers hawk their wares and the homeless lay out their beds of newspapers or corrugated boxes.

My home for the next three weeks was an apartment on the campus of the Karachi Adventist Hospital.

The hospital was started in the middle part of the last century and had developed a very positive reputation, known throughout the country. Unfortunately, at the time of my arrival, conflicts between the medical staff and the administration had risen to a zenith, threatening its continued existence—and our meetings as well.

"Dr. Dunn and his wife live in an apartment in our same building. They are lovely people—taking it upon themselves to keep us comfortable, feeding us wonderful meals and attending to our other needs. After breakfast with them, I met Dr. Walayat, a young Pakistani doctor who had recently finished his training in the Philippines. Together, we visited the theater where the meetings would begin in a few days. It was a beautiful facility with a large lobby suitable for our planned health fair, and an auditorium seating nearly 1,000. Afterward, I was given a little tour of the city, taken to Cliff Town, the beach and other places of interest.

Since it was a holiday, traffic was light. That evening, we attended a Friday evening worship service with the *Logos*, a Christian group meeting a few blocks away from the hospital. We asked them to pray for our meetings and invited them to come.

"After worship at the hospital church the next morning and a lovely dinner with the Fowlers, we went to one of the suburbs to do a children's program among the poor Christians—only to find they were away on a church picnic. That was my first real experience with Karachi traffic. No one obeys any traffic laws—anarchy on the highway! Not much consideration around, it seems.

"That morning, a Muslim lady was in Sabbath School with her little boy. Her father had recently been a patient at the hospital, and she wanted to become a Christian. 'It will likely be hard,' I wrote!

"Bright and early the next day, I met a group of workers from the hospital going out to Rural Karachi (Moidan Territory) to spend two days conducting clinics in the village of Jan Mohamed Ghoht, about 130 kilometers northeast of Karachi. We arrived in the early afternoon, set up clinic in the school and, together, saw about 130 patients that day. I could have rolled out my blanket on a cot in the school but, wishing to experience a night in the desert wilderness as Abraham and the other patriarchs had done, I chose to sleep out under the stars. In the darkness I walked in the desert and, in what appeared to be a quiet place, I knelt to pray—seeking direction of my Father in heaven during our work there. It was an interesting night to say the least. I slept little—watching the stars, meditating, praying and, yes, becoming chilly and soaking wet by the heavy dew!

"The next day we saw about 200 patients, many very sick and some who came from a long distance away. One patient had a bloody growth in her mouth that was bothering her greatly. Somewhat against my better judgment, I agreed to try and remove it—knowing it would be difficult since it was arising from her bony mandible and was adjacent to worn and broken teeth. Oh yes, her hemoglobin (blood count) was very low! I excised the tumor and tried to place a stitch to close the wound and stop the bleeding—only to have my greatest fears realized. The tissues would not hold the stitches nor control the bleeding; the hospital is four hours away and our work is not yet done here! Fortunately, dry tea-bags and tincture of Benzoin do work! At another time, I was asked to do a consultation on an old man who was very ill. I was taken to his home where I was met by a number of very sober, village patriarchs—all with long, pure-white hair, long, white beards, and long, white mustaches that curled around the cheeks. I examined the old man and made my recommendations—I was honored to have the privilege of serving him. Upon completing our work and packing up our supplies, we were treated to a delicious meal provided by the villagers. I watched as the men patted out the whole-wheat dough into thin, round chapattis and baked them over an open fire. (In many places this fire is fueled by dried cow dung; our hosts used wood!) Then we all sat around a pot of stew in the middle of a blanket and ate our chapattis, breaking off pieces and dipping them with our fingers into the pot of stew.

"I must note that this trip has been arranged by Ayub, a brother of Dr. Walayat, and Naomi, an Australian lady, both of whom work for The Child Survival Projects of Southern Asia. The people love Naomi and she loves them; she lives with them in their villages, sleeps with them in their humble homes and completely immerses her life with theirs. Also in this village, ADRA (Adventist Development and Relief Agency), had dug a well and installed a pump to supply water to the area, providing the means for turning the desert into a garden. Now they are able to raise melons and other produce for city markets, as well as providing drinking water for the people and their sheep and goats.

"It was late in the day when we headed back on the long trek home — cross two hours of desert ruts carved by heavy trucks and cross-country vehicles—and many kilometers of high-speed, two-lane, paved road carrying three or four lanes of traffic! Wrecked vehicles scattered along the roadside told the story. (Traffic deaths are one of the leading causes of death in many developing countries of the world.)

"By the time of our return, Mark had arrived from meetings he had been attending in Peshawar, up along the border with Afghanistan (a place which has been very much in the news in recent years, but now the home of many Afghan refugees). We met with the director and assistant director of the provincial television company and were assured that we would have news and current-event coverage on television, but they would not commit to interviews. Later, Mark spoke at the hospital mid-week prayer meeting about forgiveness and acceptance, and he encouraged prayer-bands for the hospital and for the upcoming meetings.

"The next day—in addition to preparing for the health fair—we went to Hyderabad to meet with Mr. Momen, the Provincial Minister of Health, to speak with him about our meetings and invite him to be a part. He plans to be in Karachi later in the week, but did not commit himself regarding attending the meetings. Most of the conversation with the minister was about the Child Survival Projects. As often happens, that conversation started the wheels turning in my brain—crafting dreams of how we might use television to conduct health education to the masses of poor and needy throughout Pakistan and other needy places around the world. A day or two later, there was an article in the paper about children—projecting 10 years ahead. The article forecast, among other things, a literacy of 26 percent, and an increase in violence in keeping with popular television and cinema programming. (Since programs on sex are not permitted, violence fills the void in Pakistan!) No plan was suggested for altering these projections but, again, my dream for television education awoke within me. (Note: It has taken nearly 20 years, but that dream is now becoming reality with a new 24-hour Children's IPTV/ Internet/TV Channel launched by Three Angels Broadcasting Network (3ABN) in January 2009)

"One of the interesting aspects of life is the uncertainty of it! In advance preparation for our health fair and lectures, I had arranged for a series of beautifully-illustrated canvas panels, depicting healthful lifestyle practices, to be sent to Pakistan. Unfortunately, it came to the time for the health fair to begin—and no panels. The courier who was responsible for them had sent them on their way six weeks earlier via Bangalore, India. Though we eventually located them, customs would not release them. In spite of that—by innovating with the things we had—we created a nice fair that captured the attention of television and the press and gave us good coverage. Many people were helped.

"Things were not going well for the meetings, either. Even though a lot of money had been given to an advertising agency, nothing had been done—nothing in the newspapers, nothing on television, no banners, nothing—and we had a thousand seats to fill for Christian meetings in a Muslim Society! Even an article that I had written for the press was hardly mentioned in the papers.

"In addition to the troubles at the hospital threatening the meetings; the trouble with the illustrations for the health fair; and the lack of advertising, Karachi was restless—as illustrated by the experience of one of the workers returning from Peshawar. As the taxi he was riding in approached his home district, they found the street blocked to traffic. He instructed the driver to go on through—only to take two bullets to the taxi. Fortunately, no one was injured, but it definitely increased the tension! Later, Mark just missed a serious accident as a motorcycle and motorized rickshaw collided right out in front of the hospital—sending bodies flying!

"On Sabbath, I had the privilege of speaking at one of the village churches; I guess it was as close as I have ever come to culture shock."

"On Sabbath, I had the privilege of speaking at one of the village churches; I guess it was as close as I have ever come to *culture shock*. I didn't know what to expect as their response, since almost all attending were illiterate. I discovered that—though illiterate—they can understand good logic and explanation as well as any.

"There is no way to express the feelings of my soul tonight (after the first meeting). Never before, in the history of the earth, has the opportunity for a Christian to talk to a Muslim been experienced as it was for us here in Karachi tonight (probably the largest Muslim city in the world). We do not yet know the number of Muslims who attended—and it doesn't really matter—but we know there were some, and it thrills me that I have been so blessed as to have this chance to share that which is of such value to me, with these who are also seekers for the Kingdom of Heaven. The auditorium was nearly filled. My talk on natural law went over OK. For illustrations, I used luminous chalk on a blackboard lighted with ultraviolet bulbs. Mark was filled with the Spirit and poured his whole being into the sermon. I believe the crowd was satisfied. Before dismissing the crowd, Mark and I, with our translators, went to the exits and shook hands with everyone as they left—a 'No! No!' in that society, especially for a man to shake hands with a woman—but they loved it!

"The next evening the auditorium was full and overflowing. (We had rented buses from many of the outlying suburbs to bring those who could not afford transportation.) People from all faiths and walks of life came. I built my talk on the contention that all of the laws of life are from God, and that understanding them leads to understanding Him. Mark followed with a sermon presenting evidence that the Bible is true.

"On the third night, about 1200 crowded into the theater; we tried to deal with the kids in another location, but that didn't work too well—need another plan for them! We are told that our audience remains very diverse and that new people are coming in off the street daily. Some say they are in danger for doing so. Judging by the show of hands, about half of the people tonight appeared to be here for the first time. It is too early to really know what is happening, but one thing is evident—the power of God is active! Mark is a real leader and it is, indeed, a privilege to work with him. He walks very close with God.

"Each night the crowds continued to fill the auditorium in ever-greater numbers, filling every available seat and inch of floor space; so much so, that we feared the weight in the balcony might cause it to collapse. People seemed very attentive to my lectures—though I soon learned that my *dry humor* was not working! Mark continued to build his case for the God of the Bible and God's plan to rescue the people of this earth from the slavery imposed upon us by the devil. I had contracted with a new friend of the Catholic faith to use my camera to record the programs for possible later use on television. He was a great guy and shared many insights with me about religious culture in Pakistan. He noted that, since Christians are in the minority—about ten percent of the total population—they feel very suppressed and berated by the majority. He told me education is very difficult for Christians to obtain—preference always given to the dominant religious group. As a consequence, most Christians work at menial jobs as sweepers (sweeping streets and sidewalks with brooms of various qualities); working in the brick yards; or, if fortunate, in the clothing or carpet industry. Unlike in most other places, Christians in Pakistan are *Christian*—not Adventist or Catholic or Lutheran or Baptist, etc., but all are essentially one in the faith—bouncing from one denomination to the other with

There was a Pentecostal minister attending the meetings who has asked to have just five minutes at the end of the meeting to pray for the people—claiming they would be healed.

little difficulty—depending upon who is closest or most convenient! Of course, there are some exceptions.

"Each morning we met with the pastors, hospital managers and other leaders of the Church in Pakistan. During that time I had the opportunity to teach them the rudiments of healthful living—a thing they seemed to accept quite well—in spite of the fact that many of the workers at the hospital are critical of the pastors for not being better examples of healthful living to the people in their congregations. I shared with them my thoughts about the two kingdoms, God's and Satan's, and of the work of double-agents—a lesson I learned the hard way in the Cambodian refugee camps.

"It is now about midway through our meeting schedule. Time is going by rapidly, even though the pace has not been fast or the load heavy. The first week is now history with *The Design for Living* meetings. Tonight, the auditorium was packed to overflowing again, with many intelligent-appearing young people and many mature men. Some were turned away for lack of space. The audience remains very attentive and representative of many faiths. Mark's sermon tonight, introducing the concept of the return of Jesus as the ultimate answer to the world's needs, tied in well with my talk of the physiology of love (the beneficial effects to the health of one who truly loves other people). As usual, we had been seeing patients before the meetings, listening to their woes, checking them out, making recommendations to them, referring some for medical care and praying with them. Tonight, a very poor, depressed man brought his three sons to see us. All were apparently retarded and getting weaker in their legs, so they had trouble walking. He maintains they were normal when younger. At times like this, I'd give almost anything to be able to see God work a miracle of healing for them. There is a Pentecostal minister attending the meetings who has asked to have just five minutes at the end of the meeting to pray for the people—claiming they would be healed. Our approach has been that healing usually comes through compliance with the natural laws of life, and the *real* miracle is one which allows Jesus Christ to come and dwell within and fill him/her with His love. (Note: Not that I don't believe in lesser miracles, but experience has taught me that I must always be suspect of those who claim the powers of healing. And—had he truly had access to such power here—he would not have needed to be at our meetings, for the whole nation would be at his doorstep! Mark arranged to spend some time speaking with him.) Still my heart goes out to those who are in such pain, and it would be so wonderful to see that taken away. Sometimes it is tempting to tell God how to run His

Kingdom, but I know that He is in charge and will do that which will be right in the whole sphere of things.

"One Sabbath evening, I had the privilege of speaking at another of the churches. I shared with them the cost that heaven paid to rescue us from this world of sin and evil. I was surprised to discover that this was an entirely new concept to them, and they seemed most appreciative. (This was a Christian group that did not even know the essential truth of the faith!) After the service I saw a few patients. One little six-year-old guy had been born blind. We had a special prayer for him and encouraged him and his family. Afterward we went to the home of one of the members for refreshments. His wife had been having stomach problems, so our conversation, quite naturally, soon switched to health topics. I discovered that their total food supply consists of refined rice, curry with a few vegetables or dhal (lentils), chapattis and occasional eggs. Eggs cost one rupee; the poorest grade of rice (still with hulls in it) 10 rupees per kilogram; apples and fruit about 40-50 rupees per kilo (more than $2 U.S.), so there is no fruit in their budget and only a few vegetables; legumes are readily available, and occasionally an egg or a bit of fish or meat. Not much chance to alter the diet, even if one wanted to do so, and most of their neighbors are poorer than they. The man of the house works as a gardener for wealthy homeowners.

"On another occasion, I was invited to John Peters' home for lunch. John is a pastor in one of the villages on the north side of Karachi. I did an interview with his wife for television. She was a Muslim who went to an Adventist school, having been sent by her wealthy father. Her mother wanted her to marry a wealthy man whom she had arranged for, but Mary did not want to do this, so she went to nursing school instead. When she finished, she accepted baptism and joined the Adventist Church; then married John. Her mother and brother set out to kill her and John. They escaped by hiding in a small room—over an oven in a kitchen where people made chapattis—and could not leave for about three months, hot and confined day and night.

"They now have two little boys and a neat and clean home. She is home-schooling the older one. They are a lovely family. John recently received notice that his father was kidnapped and torched for *irresponsibility* on the job. Apparently, while he was on vacation, someone cheated or stole a large amount of money from his company. Since he was responsible for the financial work, he was held responsible for the loss and, of course, was unable to pay.

"One evening, while seeing patients before the meeting, a patient was brought to me who was oppressed by devils. She wanted freedom; Mark offered a prayer, asking God to cast out the devils. Therewith, she collapsed to the floor—shaking all over—not a seizure-type of activity. Afterward, she had no recollection of what had happened.

"Mothers bring their children and babies in their arms, their blind and lame and deaf to be healed. Our hearts break as they walk away—or are carried away—little different from the way they came! Why? Why is the power of God limited? Why can't those who come with hope have their hopes fulfilled? One lady, tonight, was waiting with her little baby—18 months old—who was not able to sit or even hold up her head; two boys with withered legs and arms, the result of polio, most likely—though the mother alleged immunization; a little girl of seven who was deaf and dumb. What limits the power of God? Certainly, His heart is even heavier than mine! We have reasoned that—if such miracles were to occur in this society—people would flock around us, day and night, with their sick and lame but would not hear the message that, alone, can give them lasting healing. It is a very rational explanation, but is it the real reason? Or am *I* still the limiting factor in what God can do in and through me? I pray that it may not be so! Meanwhile, like Jesus who sorrowed over the beheading of John the Baptist but would not be dissuaded from His mission; we pushed forward, teaching health principles, helping people gain victory over life-destroying habits and preaching the gospel.

"After the meeting on another night, a Parsee man met with Mark to talk with him and to tell him that he knew the message was true (Mark had spoken about the divine nature of Christ); also, a Pentecostal minister has been very friendly and helpful; earlier in the day, a young Muslim man came to our apartment to talk. God is truly moving many and varied lives. All glory goes to Him.

"One night, as Mark was speaking, I was called out of the meeting to see a young man who was sick with a fever and hyperventilating (breathing very heavy and excessively). He was experiencing tetany (spasms of his muscles)—the result, I concluded, of his excessive breathing. He and his family were, of course, very frightened. It was interesting to me to note that when Pastor Robin prayed, the man calmed right down and—as long as he prayed—he stayed calm. Soon afterward, he would again begin hyperventilating. As I had my hand on him, I could feel the tension disappear during the prayer. We later had him taken to the hospital where he was treated and later released to go home. I am not sure of the cause for the fever.

"Again, mothers brought their mentally retarded to be prayed for. This is the hardest thing for me to deal with here. Though they may get some consolation by our prayers, I still really struggle with the reality that they must leave as they came. After all—as the Muslims reason—if the Christian God is the true God, He should be able to do miracles of healing! Only God knows why this is not always so! I must trust Him, but it is not easy. Yet, I know that the Spirit of the Lord is working here with power as we continue to speak to a full house each evening, with people of all faiths and walks of life. A number of non-Christians have already indicated a desire to follow Jesus.

"Today we were called to the American Consulate to be advised regarding precautions, here in the city, as violence has recently been on the increase. A Squibb (Pharmaceutical Company) representative from the U.S. was recently abducted by men with automatic weapons. He only lost his watch—by talking them down and advising them that taking an American hostage would not help their cause! Every day there are many murders in the city, and whole areas are under curfew at times. It has, apparently, not affected attendance at our meetings; every night we speak to an overflow audience. Many of the attendees are now identifying themselves and indicating their desire to follow Jesus. For many, the cost is great. Tonight was no exception. People appreciate what we are doing. We had hoped to meet with the Muslim intellectuals for an exchange of ideas; there is a Muslim man at the meetings trying to arrange it, but they told him they wouldn't meet with us.

"Our presence and our work here have apparently served to help 'cool' things down at the hospital: The hospital has been such an important instrument for touching the whole country, and beyond, I am sure. Adventists are well known in this country for what they stand for, teach and do. It makes one proud to be a part.

"This afternoon I was talking with a Goan man for an hour or so. He told me Adventists are much closer to Muslims in teachings and beliefs than are most other Christians, since both Adventists and Muslims accept both the Old and New Testaments of the Bible. He indicated to me, as fact, what I had suspected before; i.e., that the Muslim religion arose as a peaceful movement in response to the irregularities of the Christian Church. (Unfortunately, some soon accepted violence as a means of survival.) He also confirmed other things that I had heard about the St. Thomas Christians of India. (Tradition teaches that the Apostle Thomas took the gospel to India in the early days of the Church.) The Portuguese

Inquisition, under the direction of St. Francis Xavier, began in Goa India in the early 16th century. Terrible atrocities were carried out, and people of all faiths were forced to become Catholic or be killed. He tells me that we can learn more about those times from archives in Lisbon, Portugal; nothing remains here. He was not able to confirm or deny my understanding that— before the inquisition—the Christians were Sabbath observers.

"We visited a carpet factory one day and watched the finishing of the making of fine hand-woven carpets. I found it most interesting. All of the carpets are woven in the villages by women and children on looms provided by the cottage industry. At the factory they are washed, trimmed and washed—again and again—until they are perfect and beautiful.

As noted earlier: "This is apparently the first such evangelistic series ever to occur in Pakistan, and it is getting the attention of Christians everywhere in the land—and likely beyond. Adventism is a conversation-piece far and wide. And people are coming! Tonight, Mark spoke on the beauty and truth of the Sabbath. The audience appears to be with us. My lecture on cholesterol control was also valuable to the more well-to-do Muslims who are developing heart disease at a younger and younger age.

"One Sabbath evening, I was invited to speak at John Peters' church at Bald Mountain on the north side of the city. It was a joyous occasion—joining in with hundreds of people singing and worshipping together out under the starry heavens. I used the Bible verse in Revelation 18:1 that describes the last days of earth's history, as the gospel is taken to the whole world in one final triumph. Among those in attendance was a Muslim man who had had a dream the night before, in which he was told that what we were teaching was right and that he must follow. After the meeting, we were thronged again by people who wanted consultations—just as it must have been in Jesus' day; it was very easy to identify with the experience of the lady with the bleeding problem for those 12 years, and who pressed through the crowd to touch Him. The only major difference here is that—for reasons that only God can know for sure—power does not flow through us with the same intensity that it did through Him. And—though I can rationalize all kinds of reasons why—it is still so hard to see the lame and halt and blind leave, still carrying their problems. This is one of my most difficult things to deal with here. God is, however, working all kinds of miracles—many of which would, likely, not be possible if healing of the kind we desired was occurring—so I must rejoice that He knows how best to work.

"Raza, a young Muslim man, came to visit me searching for answers to the *hypocrisy* he perceived in Islam—the high ideals promoted by the Qur'an, but with problems occurring in all the Islamic States. We talked a lot and read a few Bible passages. He asked what would happen in a Christian society if a Christian married a Muslim; I told him that we would love the Muslim into our family. Here in Pakistan, both parties to the marriage would often be killed. I went on to explain the difference between true and false religion—from the perspective of love that restores and saves, versus religion that kills to gain converts. I encouraged him to make a choice for Christianity without fear, for God can take care of all. He fears that if he were to convert, he would have to run away for his uncle would have him killed. I did not urge him, but advised him to consider, carefully, what he must do with his life.

"Then I heard this story: 'Once upon a time, there lived a wealthy king who had seven sons. When it came time for him to consider who should inherit his wealth, he decided to test them to see who loved him the most. He called them before him, one by one—beginning with the eldest, to the youngest. He took from his ring his most precious jewel, laid it before each son and commanded him to break it. Each, in turn, told the old man that they could not break such a precious jewel of his. Then he called his trusted servant and asked him to break the jewel; whereupon, the servant took an instrument and crushed the precious jewel. Sometime prior to this, the king had commanded his servant to take the life of his own son as a test of loyalty. The servant obeyed the king and went to kill his son. As he lowered the sword, he was interrupted by the king's men—having previously been instructed by the king. So—on the occasion of the jewel—the king knew he could depend upon the servant.' I wasn't told who inherited the king's wealth, but Raza told me—during our study of the Bible and the Muslim faith—'The story demonstrates that honoring the Sabbath is a test of our loyalty to God. Can God depend upon us the way this king depended upon the faithfulness of His servant?' He also told me many interesting things about Muhammad, his birth, childhood and marriage to his earlier widow benefactor who taught him religion.

"A lady that I had seen in the clinic in the desert arrived in Karachi, one day, ready to have her thyroid removed. I had told her, then, that if she could make the arrangements and find a way to the city, I would do the much-needed surgery for her. I did! It was my first and only opportunity to use the operating room at the hospital. It was an interesting experience! I struggled, just a little, with bleeding, because the microwave cautery that I am accustomed to using for this type of surgery was inoperable. In spite of that, the procedure went well and without complications—I thought! Walking into the recovery room after completing the paperwork on her chart, I noticed that she was not breathing. As it turned out, the medication used to paralyze her muscles during surgery had not yet been completely reversed! In no time, we had the problem corrected and she did well, but I feared what the scenario might have been had I not gone by to see her!

"The meetings are coming to an end. Tonight and tomorrow night will be the last here at the theater before the weekend meetings, under a Shami Ama, on the hospital grounds. And, it appeared to us, the powers of darkness did not like what was happening. As usual, the place was packed with the largest crowds yet—some seats with two or three people sitting on top of one another. It took a long time to get the audience quieted down. Then microphone problems developed. It was necessary to give my presentation in parcels—between singing songs—while technicians worked on the microphones, a very trying experience. Fortunately, by the time Mark came on to speak, they had most of the *bugs* worked out. Throughout the evening, the audience was restless and began to talk and leave from the balcony—even before his call was made. But as much as it seemed the Netherworld was against us, I was encouraged by a young man who stopped to talk on the way out. He worked in an administrative office at the Aqu Kahn Hospital, a new modern hospital in the city that has become a major competitor of our hospital. It was his first time at our meetings, and he told me how much he appreciated what I had to say. My topic was about the relationship between love and brain function and body health.

"After the meeting, Mark and I were walking and talking to get our exercise. As we passed the hospital gate, we saw a distraught family there looking for their 12-year-old daughter. She was supposed to have been on the bus that returned from the meeting, but was not. After an hour or so, she arrived home. The story is that, when the bus to her village left, she had failed to get on. As she stood waiting outside of the theater wondering what to do, she noticed a man standing there on the street that she recognized. He lived on her street (alley). He, too, had been left behind. Together, they hired a ride home, but what if he hadn't been left there? What might have happened to her? A 12-year-old in the midst of this city could be bad news. As I reflected upon the incident, I remembered that—in my comments at the meeting that night—I had challenged the audience to look for God's providence working in their lives. It was very evident to us in the experience with this young lady!

"Our last meeting in the auditorium went much better than the night before. Afterward I had a nice visit with a Parsee man, a recent convert to Christ. I had been aware of a bit of unrest during the meeting but made nothing of it. Only later did I learn that, *a whole army of angels had been watching tonight.* Because the buses were packed each night, a decision was made to limit riders to women and children, expecting the males to find other transportation. As one of the buses was leaving the village on the way to the meetings, several young men were causing trouble and insisting on getting on the bus with the women and children. They were not allowed on so they threatened the driver, telling him they were going to torch the bus. When the bus arrived at the auditorium, the women told us what had happened. Hearing this, Pastor Ditter told the guards to keep watch over the bus. A little later, a Suzuki truck with about 25 young men pulled up—ready to burn the bus. When they saw the meeting, they decided to go inside and toss the gasoline there, instead. Fortunately, the guards and police who were waiting were ready for them; ten got away, fifteen were taken to the jail where they were beaten by the police. I was told it was a bad scene! After the meeting, our head pastor went to the jail to meet with the authorities there. After some discussion, he requested the beatings to cease and asked that the young men be released. He said he would assume the responsibility for their future behavior. Touched by this act, their hearts were melted and decisions were made to follow the Master.

Several young men were causing trouble, threatening the bus driver and telling him they were going to torch the bus. Only later did I learn that *a whole army of angels had been watching that night.* Their hearts were melted and decisions were made to follow the Master.

"The Shami Ama is a large, flat-roofed tent made of brightly colored, heavy cloth. Electric lights are strung along the aisles of folding chairs. It was set up in the garden of the hospital grounds, where they had also built a large baptismal tank. To one side, there were fireplaces and very large kettles ready to prepare food to feed the throng expected to arrive on Sabbath for worship and baptism. That night as I spoke, I used the text in 1 Corinthians 6:19, 20 in which the Apostle Paul noted that our bodies are the temple of the Holy Spirit. I had kids come up from the audience and draw pictures, on paper fastened to an easel, of their concept of a temple for God. Mark spoke about the *unpardonable sin* to more than 2000 people gathered there.

"The next day, following morning worship, about 275 people were buried in baptism into a new life with Jesus. It was a grand occasion. Many more were preparing to follow these initial ones in baptism. After dinner we signed autographs, initialed the children's hands, saw patients, laid hands on the heads and shoulders of the sick, and prayed and mingled with the people. It was a nice occasion and, I believe, a happy day for all.

"After supper with the Dunn's, one of our Muslim friends came by for a visit. We exchanged addresses with him and had a prayer for God's protection over him. His future was uncertain, as he had made plans for travel to another land where he would be safe as a Christian.

"Mark leaves tonight—I will leave early in the morning. We have had a great time during the past month as we have planned together, prayed together, shared deep spiritual things and, together, devoted our lives to touching this land with the precious gospel of Jesus Christ.

"It is May 27, 1990. Below is the Bay of Oman and the Arabian Peninsula—the water is pretty; the desert, too. A tanker here and there—otherwise, not much evidence of life down there.

"There is no other place on earth quite like Pakistan. My exposure hasn't been very broad, so I am sure that fact affects my limited perspective. I only got as far from Karachi as Hyderabad. Christian women are not bound by the Islamic laws, perhaps; but since Christians are the minority and discriminated against, this affects the women as well as the men. Most of the women are, therefore, sweepers and laborers. I am told that Muslim men cannot be cared for by women nurses, and the nursing profession is held in lowest esteem. Apparently only about ten percent of the nursing students are there because of their own desire, but it is one of the few opportunities women have to obtain an education. So families who can afford it, send their girls; it doesn't make for the best motivation for study.

"Christians account for about ten percent of the population of Pakistan, but because of discrimination practices—legal and otherwise—they have very little opportunity to get a good education and jobs. There are some exceptions; at any rate, Christians feel very imprisoned by their society. They do not like their situation but are powerless to escape; this doesn't make for a lot of happiness (Khooshi).

"Did we do any good in Pakistan? It is a difficult question to answer—perhaps more difficult if one doesn't believe in the Biblical Hope. We spoke to hundreds of people—people of all classes, creeds and economic levels. We taught poverty-stricken *sweepers* the ideal way to live—but wonder, is there any hope that they can change? We taught Muslims and Parsis how to find physical health, and we shared with them the beauties of the Christian walk—but, will their society allow any of them to change? We preached Biblical truths to Christians of many faiths—aware of the accusation of those who say the Christians in Pakistan are just *Rice Christians* and will go where they think there is something to be gained. We placed our hands on the heads of the lame, the deaf, and the blind; blessed the mentally deficient and cast out devils in the name of Jesus Christ. We instructed and encouraged the church leaders and local pastors, and we ministered to the hospital workers. We ushered many—through the pool of baptism—into a new walk with Christ; and we watched as people publicly declared a new direction to their lives. We drank boiled water and soda in the homes of the poor, shared food with the workers and families, provided medical care to a few each day, cried with some, laughed with others, counseled a few, listened to many—and learned. We prayed a lot and watched as, time after time, unseen agencies brought beauty out of potential curses. We watched as hardened guards softened before our eyes and treated us like friends and princes. We encouraged the villagers to take a stand for Sabbath observance and helped many get rid of tobacco and drugs. We opened the Scriptures one on one with Goans, Parsis and Muslims, and we watched the marvel in their eyes as the gospel unfolded. We visited the villagers in the vast desert lands and slept on folding cots under the stars—while sheep dogs barked at the crescent moon. We breathed the exhaust of a million, motorized rickshaws and coughed the black smoke of buses. Our ears fought to shut out the sounds of the traffic noise in one of the noisiest cities of the world. And we marveled at the faithfulness of donkeys, the strength of camels and the fortitude of skinny men behind their carts or on their bicycles. How does one make an impact in a world so destitute? How can anyone be such a fool as to think he can change a troubled city where babies get killed by stray bullets, automatic weapons aid the thief, curfews often confine large areas and responsible people are wont to take bribes? Is it possible—or just idle dreaming—that a people dominated by colonialism could rise, again, to self-rule—independent of the influx of the almighty dollar and the power and control of expatriate leadership?

"What if—like the seeds of the elm tree that provide nurture for one another—whereby, one here and there may grow to maturity, some lights have been lit in the hearts of a few in Pakistan that will grow as the trees in the forest or shine like the sun at noonday; and, thereby, build on the little that we may have sparked? Has it been worth it?

"Over and over again, in my mind, there rings the tune of a beautiful song: 'I walked today where Jesus walked, and felt His presence near.' Only in heaven will we know the answers to our questions. Only there, will we see the real fruit of our labors and enjoy the full reward of our service. Until then, we have had a fantastic experience. We have been granted a valuable education; we have enjoyed many friends, and gained new perspectives about life and its value. Truly God is good!

"This is a huge desert under us. We stopped for an hour in Bahrain where I bought a flask of expensive Arabian perfume for Avonne. Any man would have to be a fool to lead a million people out into a piece of real estate such as exists down there (as Moses did)! But then, maybe that's what real men are anyway—fools for God!

"I have been home for three weeks. Only now am I beginning to rise above the emotional disruption accompanying my return. I suppose my experience can best be compared—though on a much different scale—to that of Elijah after his experience on Mount Carmel when he was confronted with the 400 prophets of Baal. Values, purposes, motives, attitudes, hopes—everything seems to have changed; whether transient or permanent, I don't know. In my conversations with Mark, it sounds like he has also struggled with similar feelings—something hard to pinpoint or describe; yet so very real—like a dream from which one never really awakens. And over and above it all remains the plaguing question: How long, Oh Lord; How long until you return to put an end to sin? What can I do to hasten that day when this world is finally released from slavery to the fascinations—and heartaches—brought on by the devil?"

Chapter IX

Russia

"As we prepared, word came to us that the communists and Nazis were demonstrating against us outside, blockading the entrance, and trying to prevent the people from entering!"

Communism had only recently fallen. The Soviet Union had finally come to its end. Nothing short of a miracle could have made the Kremlin Congress Hall available for the preaching of the gospel to this godless, atheistic nation. Yet, here I was an invited participant in a three-week series of health and gospel lectures to the Russian people. I would be working with my friend, Pastor Mark Finley, with whom I had worked a number of times, before, in other challenging places around the world. The following account describes this experience as abstracted or copied from notes made at the time—plus a little memory etched deeply in my mind.

Notes from O'Hare International—March 11, 1992.

"As a child, I dreamed of speaking for my God before kings and governors, never expecting to realize the fulfillment of those dreams! Now—in the prime of life—it is my privilege to share my faith in the very citadel of atheism. I feel greatly honored, humbled and, I suppose—in a sense—fearful.

"It is not my style to lecture without a drawing board of some kind. I am told that I will not be able to use this where we will be speaking. I will have a slide projector available, but the slides I have been trying to get for the opening lecture did not come through—though I thought I had started my preparations in plenty of time. I will have to be content with what I have.

"It has been a couple of very busy weeks. Today—just before leaving for the airport—I did two operations, and three yesterday. Last week was a rather trying week spent at Thousand Oaks, California, working with *Lifestyle Magazine* to produce the next set of 13 television shows. Dan Matthews, host of the program, and Jeff Wood, technical producer, have been most pleasant and understanding to meet my agenda, but all of us struggle over the challenge of producing programs that will attract the public and still say something valuable to those viewers.

"Financially, I am strapped with all of the commitments I have accepted with the television ministries of *Lifestyle Magazine*, Three *Angels Broadcasting Network (3ABN)*, and everything else. Just yesterday I learned there will be ten students coming to Chicago for the summer to help raise money and prepare for the Chicago drug program that we have been dreaming about and moving into by faith. As I was going over my books yesterday, I noted—with interest—that there is adequate means to support the immediate needs, but with little to spare! It will be tight-going for the foreseeable future; but, I am assured, that what God honors us to undertake, He also provides the means to make it happen.

"I am working much too hard. I enjoy it to the fullest, but am tired—am hoping the change of pace at the Kremlin will allow some much-needed recuperation, but I know this is unlikely. The time at Thousand Oaks last week was nice—except for the stress of program development. Still—knowing the time in history in which we live and with the opportunities presented to me—I cannot control the fire that burns within. If it is to go out, God will have to be the one to quench it. I just heard an interesting statement the other day that seems relevant to my life and work: 'People always come to watch a fire burn!'

"It was about 5:00 p.m. when Victor, the beekeeper from the Seminary, met me at the airport in Moscow as I arrived. He wasted no time taking me to my hotel and getting me settled before returning to the seminary two hours away. The Russian Hotel, the largest in Russia with more than 3,000 rooms, was adequate but not fancy. The building was laid out in a big square with an open court in the center. Each floor was divided up into sections separated by security doors. Near the center of each section was a security station staffed 24 hours, daily, where the room key was kept for occupants while out of the room. The window of my room looked out over the court. When—on occasion—I happened to be in my room during daytime hours, I found it amusing to watch the large, playful, gray and white crows performing their antics (one of which, I was told, was to slide down the golden domes of the Orthodox Churches—a problem for those responsible for keeping the gold on the roof)!

"In marked contrast to the hotel was the Kremlin Congress Hall. Located within the walls of the Kremlin complex, the marble and glass building is truly a work of excellence. Its gorgeous auditorium seats about 6,000 people. Natural woods accent the plush, red carpet and seats. A full-time professional stage director designs and directs the appearance and functions of the stage. Acoustics in the hall are perfect, as I discovered during my first visit there. Then, as the choir rehearsed on stage, I, from the center of the auditorium heard the sound as though the voice of angels were singing all around me—it was beautiful!

"We spent most of my first day in Moscow in the hall working to get the stage set up to prepare for the meetings to begin the next day. As it turned out, the stage director was a real artist. He had spent a great amount of time and energy preparing a beautiful stage for the programs. He had created the illusion of fluffy, white clouds moving across the blue sky—or a starry sky—as the situation called for; it was lovely. Unfortunately, his plans did not include the ability to project slides on a screen, as we were planning to do for our lectures. Eventually, after some pretty tense moments, everything was worked out to the satisfaction of all. That evening, we had a *practice-run* with about a thousand believers attending. It was a new experience for me to speak without my blackboard prompts, and blinded by the spotlight I could not see the audience and read their reaction. I was glad this was just a test, but I resolved to be prepared for the real thing the next day.

"Following morning worship and a powerful sermon by Mark entitled, *The Five Faces of Jesus*—encouraging the members to be faithful—we returned to the Kremlin Hall to prepare for the first public meeting to begin at 3:00 p.m. As we prepared, word came to us that the communists and Nazis were demonstrating against us outside, blockading the entrance and trying to prevent the people from entering. Then, too, news reporters came to interview Mark—asking why he was here and what he thought about communists, etc. Many news reporters came to the three o' clock session. Their report appeared on the evening news,

We returned to the Kremlin Hall to prepare for the first public meeting. Despite word of trouble, there were nearly 6,000 people attending that first afternoon session.

expressing the hunger of the people for the Word of God. As it turned out, there were nearly 6,000 people attending that first afternoon session. Following the meeting; Pastor Wilson, President of the General Conference; and Pastor Kulakov, President of the Russian Adventist Church, brought two men backstage to our dressing rooms to meet and talk with us. One of the men, Professor Sotz, an educator, had served as an aide to Mr. Gorbachev. He was the one responsible for orchestrating the move providing for the freedom to worship according to one's conscience. One of his comments went something like this: 'I have sat in meetings in this hall since it first opened its doors, and I have listened to all of the great ideologists of this country describe their plans for success. Tonight, I have witnessed that victory which they only talked about.' He had heard a message of hope unheard of for more than 70 years—since the suppression of Christianity by the atheist leaders—and was exuberant about it. With him was one of the Russian officers who had led the Soviet invasion into Afghanistan some years before. He was a huge man who no longer works with the system. He is working to assist widows, children and veterans of that war. Both agreed that any good change that would come into this country would have to come from inside the people themselves. They then gently reminded me that the Russian people were well educated! I took the hint.

"About 5,000 attended the second session that evening. My somewhat more scientific lecture on natural law—as relates to health—went over well. Between sessions, a lady brought her granddaughter to see me. The little girl—now eleven years old—has been paralyzed since the age of nine months and three days, when she received an immunization injection. She is very crippled—her back twisted with scoliosis. She is able to feed herself, but little else. Unfortunately, there was not much hope that I could offer for her as a cure. Her grandmother understood this, but requested help in getting a motorized wheelchair so that she could, at least, get around a little. She said she would return with pictures to take home with me the next day, and that perhaps a chair could be donated? I had a prayer with them before they left, but the thought that kept ringing in my crying heart was, 'How long, my Father, before this sort of thing can all end?'

"On Tuesday the 17th, the communists requested to use the hall. Since it has already been rented to us, the authorities turned them down. That didn't change their plans. But, praise God, He is bigger than any of us; we'll have to wait to see what happens!

"Both sessions on the following day were filled to overflowing. The choir, composed of volunteers from all over the former Soviet Union, is absolutely impeccable. My topic, heart disease, went well. Mark spoke on the return of Jesus. When he made mention of the new freedom present in this country so that the gospel can go to the whole world; the audience broke out in clapping.

"We have received a great deal of news coverage by the media—most everything positive so far. The audience is responsive—fun to work with for a few minutes—before all goes dark for the slides. Some are worried about Tuesday. There have been some acts of minor violence, but nothing of note until now. For worship this morning, Mark used passages in James, chapter 5 and Ezekiel, chapter 43:1, to suggest that they have special meaning for the Russian people just now; as the long-promised Holy Spirit is, even now, being poured out upon the earth.

"Monday morning was spent at the church folding Bible study guides. We then met together on the 21st floor of the hotel with a view overlooking the Kremlin for lunch. We learned, then, that Professor Sotz had called Pastor Wilson with concern about demonstrations scheduled tomorrow by the communists. We were told that, during their demonstrations on Saturday, they had carried a picture of Mark with a black frame around it—a sign of death. One sign said, 'Bush, leave our souls alone!' We considered asking for protection but elected to leave the matter in the hands of God. There is no number of soldiers that can protect us—unless He does; and with Him—no others are needed. Mark met with the assistant director of the Kremlin after lunch, enquiring as to whether we should hold our meeting as planned tomorrow. He assured Mark we should, indeed, go ahead with our plans. He also told Mark they wanted us to hold the meetings and that we—and all attendees—will be protected. These meetings are the subject of extensive discussion at the highest levels, even President Yeltsin himself. We have been much in prayer—and keeping a very low profile (especially Mark). Mark keeps saying, 'This is modern Acts in the making.' At the end of the meeting tonight, a man stood up in the audience and said, 'You will not be here tomorrow. They will be!'

"It's Wednesday now! I didn't write last night. Tired! Exhausted! We had all been so spirited up for a major demonstration in the evening—an event that turned out to be almost a non-event! (We learned later that—though the communists planned to take the Kremlin by force with thousands of demonstrators, the whole thing fizzled at the last moment!) Having pled and begged God to put His hand over the opposition, my proper reaction ought to have been an even greater exclamation of joy and thanksgiving! God is good, and today has been a fantastic day. More than 13,000 in attendance, I suppose, at the two meetings. We gave out 12,000 Bibles—to the common people, to many educated former party members, to atheists, etc.; most of the people have never even touched one before! They kissed them, pressed them to their hearts and held on to them as if never to let them go. And, yes, they are actually reading them!

"A physician met me today and expressed his gratitude for my lectures, stating he did not yet know how to deal with the Christian part, but he was open. After a lifetime as an atheist, change doesn't always occur in a day. Later, I did some short interviews with him for TV.

"We have met many people, since, who joined the church after Mark's meetings here in Moscow; they are so happy they can hardly contain themselves! What a marked contrast to the sadness and hopelessness seen on the faces on the streets, in the Metros (trains) and everywhere else in Russia! Sometimes, we are tempted to wonder if it is all worth the cost—is it really worth it to bring the gospel to the people? Here, there is no reason to wonder. And, too, our audience is warm, grateful, receptive and hungry for the message. Yes, I wish the whole city would repent and experience the goodness of knowing God as did Nineveh of old, but God's heart must be warm, too, for what is happening here. We have given out about 16,000 Bibles. The demand for them is great; people, sometimes standing in long lines waiting their turn to get their hands on one. Because of the reception we have had here, Mark has arranged for 100 sets of his slides and lectures to be made available for the Russian pastors in their language. They should make a real impact across the country. For my part, I have been laying the groundwork for programs dealing with the problems of alcohol and tobacco. Tomorrow, I will begin a session to help those who wish to quit smoking. Later, a program for managing alcohol will begin at the church. For that, I have been working with the pastor of the church and one of his physician members to carry on after my absence. Avonne and Mark's wife, Ernestine, arrived today to join us. It is nice to see them and for them to share in the excitement of this mission.

"While the auditorium is a perfect place for the meetings; there is, unfortunately, no good place for smaller groups. We ended up doing the first two sessions of the Stop Smoking Program in the entryway and on the stairs; not the ideal location. Fortunately, the people are so hungry

We ended up doing the first two sessions of the Stop Smoking Program in the entry-way and on the stairs; not the ideal location.

for help they will go through most anything to get it. And, yes, some have already realized the victory over the cigarette. Today, a man from a Christian broadcasting network was present at the stop-smoking session and made a video recording of it. He later asked me if he could broadcast the sessions to the public. Of course, I was happy for the free distribution of the material. Articles in the newspapers continue to make mention of the meetings. One advertisement for a new western movie said that Mark would be there—ahead of time to talk—using his name to draw a crowd! I was also told today that our pictures are being sold in the subways. As if that were not enough, some are claiming that my picture has magical powers! I am now wondering if those are the pictures I have been autographing the past couple of days!

"I find it almost overwhelming as I walk down through the audience, to sense the fact that thousands of people are studying the Bible and considering the values it promotes. It is impossible to describe the feeling! It's not really as though we had persuaded them of the validity of our claims, nor is it that we had provided free food to a starving multitude (sometimes referred to as 'Rice Christians'); it is, rather, as if divinity were doing something special and something I have never before experienced. Yes, it is certain that, even here, Jesus' parable about the seed and the various soils will find application. Not all of the seed is falling upon fertile, well-tilled ground, but what is obvious is that something *out of this world* is happening in this auditorium—and I am sure there will be an abundance of fruit.

"My wife, Avonne, lost the cap from one of her teeth during the night—not a pleasant thing! Fortunately, Roman, a new Russian friend, came to the rescue. He took her to a dentist who was able to make a very good replacement—for a mere 75 cents!

"We have been working in Kremlin Hall for about two weeks now, and today will be our last session here. It has been such a powerful experience to speak to more than 6,000 people at one sitting, and to share the values of the gospel that have become the very warp and woof of my being. There are always those who get missed or lost in such a large audience, but we have had many good contacts. Tonight, we will graduate those who have successfully quit smoking—and challenge all to make of their bodies a beautiful temple for the indwelling of the Spirit of God—just as described by the Apostle Paul in his letter to the believers at Corinth. Each night, I have challenged the audience with assignments—things to practice and to do to reduce the stresses of life and to make their days more enjoyable and productive. They have followed my recommendations enthusiastically—more than any previous audience I have had the privilege of sharing with. Little gifts—some certainly given with significant sacrifice—flowers, clapping their hands, words of gratitude, etc., all suggest that our gift to them is appreciated. After tonight we will be meeting in other halls around Moscow. I will miss this place. It is such a beautiful facility. The staff has been most pleasant and warm. They really appreciate the Bible we gave to each one—all 5,000 of them!

"It would be difficult to imagine a more satisfying and exciting experience than the one we have had here in Moscow. We have been busy—but not too busy to prevent us from visiting Kremlin Square with its famous cathedral, Lenin's tomb, the underground chamber housing the royal jewels, the Industrial Park, the Moscow Circus, and some of the other famous Russian landmarks. For my part, I had the opportunity to visit a new medical clinic in the process of being built. I also visited the Moscow Polyclinic where I met a microvascular surgeon who does a number of interesting procedures—not yet popular in the West; including repair of the valves in the veins of the legs as treatment of varicose veins; and the repair of lymphatic vessels injured by trauma, surgery or X-ray therapy.

"On our last Friday evening, Alexander, a former Rock Concert lead guitarist, and his wife, Helen, invited us over for dinner. We had a lovely time with them and a good meal of Russian food, cooked healthily. He is now working with Pat Mutch from Andrews University in Michigan to develop a youth program. He wants to develop music for the church; and his wife, a children's choir. Accompanying us to their home was Roman, the man who helped us find a dentist for Avonne. He is a graduate physics student, now waiting to switch majors and to get into the seminary. His wife is a former professional skater. They live in a small room in a dormitory with their 14-month-old baby girl on an income equivalent to $4.00 U.S. (400 Rupees) monthly—hardly enough! When asked to tell us about his diet, he admitted that they basically live on dark rye bread three times, daily; with, perhaps, a few potatoes, beets, or a little cabbage and a bit of milk for their daughter. I don't know how representative this is of the public here, but many are struggling for survival. It is better now, than a few months ago—with a little more food available—but at rapidly escalating prices. Fortunately, dark rye bread is still cheap and fairly nourishing.

"Moscow is a huge, gray city at this time of the year, but I have met a people here that I have learned to love and appreciate. It is difficult to leave them. May God bless this city and this land is my prayer as we take our leave."

Chapter X

Return to Russia

"Later, we learned from him that Parliament had passed a law restricting missionaries—from other countrie—from working in Russia"

Again, this account is taken from my notes—this time recorded at the end of the mission, rather than daily as was my usual custom. Due to numerous complexities, some of which will become evident during the course of the story, I was unable to maintain a daily record.

Because of the hunger of the Russian people for Bible knowledge and the fantastic response to our meetings at the Kremlin, the Olympic Stadium, with a seating capacity of 40,000, was rented for this series of meetings. I cowered as I considered the size of the task. Having begun the previous series at near-exhaustion, and after experiencing the untimely death of our daughter; I didn't personally feel ready for another, even bigger, commitment. In sharing my concerns with Mark, he arranged for a colleague, Dr. DeWayne Butcher, to play the lead role in developing the medical program, but not wanting to decline, completely, what I believed was a call from God, I consented to help wherever I could.

The Olympic Stadium, with a seating capacity of 40,000, was rented for this series of meetings. I cowered as I considered the size of the task.

Our plans, in addition to a health lecture at the main daily session, included a large Health Expo under the capable direction of Dr. Dorothy Nelson who has had experience doing Health Expos throughout much of the world—including China and much of Eastern Europe and the Middle East. Health Expo consists of eight stations, or booth—each displaying beautifully illustrated, life-size panels describing one of the eight primary, lifestyle principles governing health and long life—nutrition, exercise, rest, water, fresh air, sunshine, temperance and a meaningful trust in God. Attendees at the Expo have opportunity at each station to view the illustrations, read the accompanying script (in their own language), hear a brief discussion and ask questions. We had plans for three such expos to be set up in the stadium area. Dr. Royce Brown and a team from Hinsdale, Illinois, would man stations for checking blood pressure, serum cholesterol levels, etc. Ten medical students from Loma Linda would help man the booths at the Expo. In addition to the above, we arranged for Dr. Art Weaver, who has helped more people stop smoking through the years than anyone else on the planet to provide programs for those wishing to quit. Jamie Gavin would work with me on Stress Management and Alcohol Control. Dr. Harvey Elder, an infectious disease professor from Loma Linda University, would spend a week sharing with Russian physicians.

An upgrade to Business Class seats on our flight to Moscow made the, otherwise stressful, flight a bit more relaxing. We had big plans and, of course, we wondered if all our supplies and personnel would show up in time, and if we would have adequate numbers and translators capable of useful communication. During the flight, Mark shared with me the story of a lady he had met, previously, who had lived through the difficult communist years when people were sent to Siberia—or worse—for possessing a Bible or worshiping God. Hidden in a small closet in her home, she kept a typewriter. During every *safe* moment, she typed out Bibles with carbon copies and distributed them among the believers so as to maintain the faith. It was people such as she who kept Christianity alive throughout the communist era.

Moscow looked much different in July than it had in the spring 15 months earlier. The parks and countryside were green—much of the dirt and rubble now hidden by fresh, green leaves and grass. Too, the spirit of the people and the economy had improved. Shops and markets were now fairly well stocked with fruit and produce available—for a *price!* While still reserved, one now notes a bit more expression on the faces and hears the laughing of children. Unfortunately, concerns still exist—wondering if the apparent improvements could last. Furthermore, crime is escalating rapidly, and the older generation is smarting over loss of social benefits they had learned to depend upon. Pastor Kulakov illustrated the situation with the example of a lady who sold her goat (essentially her whole estate) for 6,000 rubles, enough to buy a few bottles of Coca-Cola. Whereas, before, she could do fairly well by selling the milk from her goat that could pasture on government land, that source of extra income was now gone. Everyone complains of the high cost of food, especially vegetables and fruit; yet, almost no one appears starved or underweight. Alcohol continues to dominate the beverage scene (It was recently reported that 50 percent of the income of Moscow was spent on alcohol!), but many other juices and soft drinks are also available and consumed. Kavass, a fermented drink made of old, rye bread and sugar is very popular but hard to find because of regulations preferring the sale of beer with which it apparently competes. American cigarettes join local products in sustaining the addiction of many Russian citizens. One of the striking things about Moscow is the degenerating appearance of its infrastructure, buildings, etc. One example is the Olympic Stadium—itself a building only 13 or 14 years old—which is in a terrible state of disrepair with broken doors, windows, floor-tiles, etc. Much of the city appears the same, including many of the *showcase* places. There are two exceptions—they are the Metro, the underground transportation system, and the Kremlin (described in the previous account). The Metro is beautiful. Each station is decorated differently with beautiful stone and artwork—and always on-time trains!

Our hotel was much smaller than on our previous visit—clean, located close to parks and exhibitions—with a river running nearby. We saw no lawn mowers; all grass being cut by hand, resulting in many wild flowers and other plants. Lots of crows, sparrows and pigeons were seen, but few other birds. Monuments are everywhere, memorializing some achievement or successful venture, etc. Many are very beautiful. My favorite is the *Space Memorial*, a neat, shiny-brass replica of a rocket launching into space. Russian Orthodox Churches are everywhere, too. They are being rehabilitated and are also very ornate and beautiful with their golden domes, etc.

For two weeks we worked the Health Expo. For lack of experienced personnel, we could only utilize two of the sets. These were manned by Russians that Doctor Nelson had trained in previous projects. It was interesting to observe the reaction of some of the 10,000 people whose cholesterol levels were high, and how rapidly they came down after changing their diet and lifestyle practices. The satisfaction they expressed convinced us that we had been wise in encouraging a plant-based diet—even under the difficult conditions that exist in Russia. We received a lot of press and had a number of good interviews. One that interested me the most was a Russian Orthodox journalist who was striving to become a priest. As we explained our positions of faith and the rationale of the health message that we shared, he was most receptive and, over and over, he noted how this was "orthodoxy at its original best." Only a few days before, he had published an article in a Russian newspaper shaming the Orthodox Church for trying to interfere with others who were trying to put out the *fires* of crime and evil that are destroying the society. Later, we learned from him that Parliament had passed a law restricting missionaries—from other countries—from working in Russia. It had yet to pass a second time before going to President Yeltsin for his signature. He then told us it would not pose any problem for us because, "There are always ways to get around the law!" A week or so later, we heard that Parliament had passed the law the second time which, if signed by the president, would effectively create a Church-State structure governed by Orthodox Christians and Muslims. Already, the news of the action was appearing on the international press.

For two weeks we worked the Health Expo. These were manned by Russians that Doctor Nelson had trained in previous projects.

Mark Finley and Pastor Kulakov spent a lot of time translating the bill and speaking with the press—including USA Today, NBC and others. It was interesting how NBC became involved. Sometime earlier, NBC's Russian correspondent had picked up an outdated flyer announcing our meetings in the Metro. She was intrigued and came to see what it was all about. While there, she came to the Health Expo and became so excited that she called her video crew to do a program for the North American viewers. The American staff, however, failed to see merit in her program and let it drop. A week later—when news of the parliamentary ruling hit the world press—she was suddenly bombarded with phone calls to get all of the footage she could get from Mark and our meetings. Subsequently, Pastors Finley and Kulakov were interviewed, at length, regarding the meaning and implications of the law and the way it was rammed secretly through Parliament. The program was scheduled to air on NBC and CNBC that evening in America. Meanwhile, Julia, the head of 3ABN's television ministry in Nizhny Novgorod called me to get more information. Julia's brother is the governor of the district of Nizhny Novgorod but had not been informed about the law and knew nothing about its content—though he had close connections to President Yeltsin and was one of the foremost prospects for his successor. Following through with her request, I obtained a copy of the law and faxed it to her for him to read and to be informed. (Avonne and I had just been at Nizhny in response to a request to consult on a patient there who had a glioblastoma of the brain (brain cancer). He was a brother to Tanya, the attorney general for the administration of the law for the province, and who was also secretary to the governor. She had been very instrumental in opening the door for 3ABN to be licensed in Russia so that we could establish our base for creating and broadcasting television there. As it all turned out, through a series of *providential* actions, the Russian Orthodox Church failed to attain the authority it sought. Russia retains a degree of religious freedom to this day. Who knows if the little part we played had anything to do with it, but it makes no difference. What is evident, is that God may be seen working behind the scenes to make his blessings available to the Russian people.

Meanwhile, the meetings at the Olympic Stadium were making an impact on the nation with good attendance and with many responding to the messages given—this in spite of a large sign near the entrance to the stadium reading, "Russia is Orthodox, has always been Orthodox, and will be Orthodox forever," that appeared after Parliament passed its law. (Interestingly, a Jewish journalist then published an article in the paper asking, "Who is afraid of Jesus Christ?"—implying, thereby, that the Orthodox shouldn't have to worry about protecting its turf if it were really fulfilling its role as God's chosen instrument.)

By the time the campaign was over, eight new congregations of worshippers had been established across the city as thousands found a way of life, previously only dreamed of, in this recovering Soviet Republic. The thought I am trying to convey is best illustrated by an incident that occurred to me one evening after the main meeting. I saw a couple rushing toward me—faces joyous and excited. I did not recognize them at first, but they soon clued me in. Fifteen months earlier, this couple, who had come from the former Soviet State of Georgia to Moscow to attend the meetings, had also attended our sessions for control of tobacco and alcohol. Now he expressed his deep appreciation for the help I gave him in getting rid of alcohol. When sharing their testimony before the whole audience the next day, it was thrilling to hear them say they are happier now than they have ever been. It turned out she has been sharing her new-found values with her family and friends in Georgia and has raised up several groups of believers there.

What has happened here in Russia—first at the Kremlin and now at the Olympic Stadium—is nothing short of miraculous. Certainly, I have never before in my life witnessed such a thirst for the gospel and such an enthusiastic acceptance of it. How does one explain it, I asked myself—even as I felt *chills* of excitement continue to tickle my spine. The same effort in the States would have fallen flat. This, I thought, must be nothing less than a repeat of Pentecost. But then, being of the nature that I am, I must question everything. Is this the work of the Holy Spirit, indeed, or merely a social reaction of the Russian people so long suppressed by the power of the KGB? And then I remembered the accusations I had heard—that the rise of the Advent Movement was nothing more than a social reaction to the great disappointment that occurred when William Miller's prediction of the Return of Christ in 1844 failed; I wondered if this might be the same. In pondering the question, I arrived at the conclusion that it really makes no difference! Who can question God if he should choose to use such opportunity to accomplish His goals in His battles with the dragon? Certainly not I!

As I have sat in on the discussions and planning regarding caring for perhaps seven or eight thousand new converts, I am brought to realize, a little better, the challenge that must have confronted the Apostles in Jerusalem after Pentecost—and to understand the dynamics of the new church and its many problems. No wonder Paul was so direct in his appeals to the converts.

Following the Health Expo, it was our plan to begin the other programs for stopping smoking, dealing with alcohol and stress, etc. Unfortunately—due to many unforeseen circumstances—a rock band was scheduled for nearly the same time and place as my meetings. So, Avonne and I decided to go to Nizhny Novgorod to visit the work of *Three Angels Broadcasting Network (3ABN)* there and to see the patient (mentioned previously) that I had been requested to consult on. Accordingly, arrangements were made for a driver and a car to take us there that evening, with the hope of arriving in time to get a few hours of sleep before the new day. We had not considered the dangers of traveling by car—during the night—in Russia. Roads were poor. Our driver was overtired having, that same day, made the trip the opposite way to pick us up. During the early part of the trip we enjoyed the beautiful scenery; the quaint *gingerbread* decorated houses in little villages along the way; the dachas (garden plots allotted to the city folk where they often spent weekends and vacations in makeshift temporary dwellings), and beautiful forests of birch, linden and evergreens. But—as it began to get dark—the scene changed. The roads were narrow and often bumpy, and traffic; though not heavy, was fast. Our exhausted driver kept nodding at the wheel—the car, sometimes, seemingly uncontrolled. Yet, he would not permit me to drive. Eventually, he decided to stop and get some rest. While we knew he needed it, we had also been forewarned that it was not safe to stop along the highway at night. Bad things often happened. Eventually, he awakened and continued on our journey, taking us into the city of Nizhny at 4:00 a.m. just as the eastern sky was turning orange.

After a couple of hours of sleep, our hosts were ready to show us the city. One of our first stops was the hospital where lay the dying patient I was asked to see. I was given opportunity to see and examine him, to check his medical records, to meet with his neurosurgeon and to discuss his case. Though the facility left a lot to be desired, it was obvious to me that the man was getting excellent care. This fact I shared with the family, assuring them he was in good hands and that an all-loving God was looking on. We then visited the 3ABN building site, looked over the facility and the work in progress, and met many of the workers. The architect, a very talented artist, showed us some of his watercolors and gave us a couple as gifts. Since stained-glass was one of my hobbies, he had some questions about the windows he was planning for the building.

Nizhny Novgorod (formerly Gorky), the third largest city in Russia, is located on the great Volga and Oka Rivers, making it ideal for the role it played during the Cold War—the manufacturing center of the nation for tanks, planes, and all of the other implements of war. For this reason, it was a closed city to outsiders. Pastor John Carter, an evangelist originally from Australia, was one of the first from the West to schedule meetings in the city after the fall of communism. He invited Danny Shelton, Founder of 3ABN, to join him for the meetings. People came by the hundreds and thousands, necessitating multiple sessions, and still the crowds pushed and shoved to get in. Julia was a young English teacher who attended, "just to improve her English," since she had never had opportunity to actually interact with English-speaking people; but she was fascinated by what she heard.

Meanwhile, the meetings caught the attention of the bishop of the Orthodox Church who complained to the governor. The governor, in response, called Pastor Carter into his office to meet with him and the bishop. Mincing no words, he went right to the point and told Carter he was causing trouble and would have to stop the meetings. Instead of timidly agreeing to the order, Pastor Carter boldly advised this governor—who claimed to be one of Russia's staunchest supporters of democracy—that there was no room for such discrimination in a democracy, noting that in America and Australia, Russian Orthodox believers are free to worship as they please. If Russia is really earnest in being a democracy, it must do the same. He then proceeded to tell the governor the benefits his people were receiving from the meetings. Finally, he pulled a letter out of his pocket that he had received from a person attending the meetings. It told how much the meetings meant to the writer, praising him for his messages to the Russian people. Then he read, "Signed, Julia Outkina." Immediately, the governor demanded, "Show me that letter!" Julia was the governor's sister! From that moment on, the tone of the session turned 180 degrees. Soon, the governor had Carter and the bishop shaking hands and posing for photographers. Julia, eventually, went on to become the director of 3ABN television in Russia, a position she still holds today as the gospel is proclaimed in the Russian language around the world from our headquarters there. This explains why it was important for me to visit Nizhny, and why it was such a privilege to meet the governor's staff and share with them—though the governor himself was not in town. After completing our tours of the Nizhny Kremlin (palace and government complex) and the other highlights of the city, our hosts learned of our desire to visit St. Petersburg. We thought, perchance, there might be a train going that way so we could spend a day or two there. At once, they were on the telephones and, in no time at all, Tanya, the attorney general, had seat reservations for us to leave by plane that very afternoon—with promises of train tickets back to Moscow from St. Petersburg at the conclusion of our visit. In addition, they sent Max, a young Russian student, along to translate for us.

We arrived in St. Petersburg about 11:00 p.m. and hailed the first taxi we could find to take us to a hotel. "Sorry, we have no rooms available," was the response we heard over and over again as we discovered we had arrived at the peak of the tourist season and that St. Petersburg was one of Russia's favored vacation spots. Finally, when I was told we could not even sleep in the hotel lobby, I approached a couple of young ladies as they closed one of the hotel shops for the night. "Do you speak English?" I asked one of them. To her positive response, I asked, "Do you know of any place where we can stay for the night?" The young English-speaking lady—we'll call her Natasha—offered to take us to the train that would take us to another part of the city where there might be hotel beds available; and then added that, if we liked, we could stay with her. Thanking her for her graciousness, we chose to try another hotel and followed her to the Metro. No! There were no beds there either. It was now past midnight! We decided to take Natasha up on her offer and phoned her home. She gave us the address and invited us to come on over! We caught another taxi and asked the driver to take us to the address we had been given. It was in an area of the city composed of high-rise apartment buildings—all exactly alike, and with very limited street markings and building numbers. He was sure we would never find the place, but God is good. The driver did find it!

It turned out that Natasha's mother and little sister had gone to their dacha (Russian country home), leaving Natasha with her father and brother. We had a good night's rest and awakened to a hot breakfast, prepared just for us. Then the young lady informed us she was a tour guide, that she was free for the day, and would be pleased to show us the city if we liked. How much better could it get! God continued to pour out His blessings!

St. Petersburg, sometimes known as the Venice of the North, is a beautiful city. Our guide knew just where everything was located, and the best time to see it. It was a great day with only one major problem. Bathrooms! I am not sure what the Russians do! At the end of the tour, she invited us to stay at her place for another night, took us home with her and introduced us to her brother. She then informed us she had some things to do and was leaving. We tried to pay her for our lodging and for her services. She refused anything, saying, "All people are good!" Then—she was gone! We did not see her again—nor have we been able to contact her by mail.

In the morning, we went to the train station to get our tickets and our ride back to Moscow, but there were no tickets for us—and no berths available for our intended overnight trip. Finally, after getting shuttled from one office to another, we ended up in the office of the chief of the Russian rail system. After a very gruff first appearance, he broke out with a big smile, and invited us into his office while he made the necessary calls to get us on board. That night we slept "first class" on the express train from St. Petersburg to Moscow, arriving at the dawn of day.

For my last presentation just before the main meeting, I based my remarks upon the passage in 1 Corinthians in which the Apostle Paul likens our bodies to the temple of God. While children from the audience drew pictures of Russian churches on the blackboard, I challenged the people to give God their very best, and to make their *temple* the most beautiful dwelling place for Him that they could give. By their response, I knew they had accepted the challenge.

I had plenty of time to mull over the experiences of the past three weeks as our *British Air* plane soared over the arctic, on down over Canada, and back toward O'Hare in Chicago. Questions that, quite naturally, come to my mind had to be dealt with. Was our trip a success or a failure? Was it a good or poor investment in time, money, and energy? I couldn't know the impact our work at the Olympic Stadium would make for the cause of Christ. I don't know if our calls and faxes to the governor's palace in Nizhny will have any impact on the law for religious freedom. I don't know if my visit with the people of *Your Story Hour, Three Angels Broadcasting Network*—or with Ramon, Neekeeta (Nick) or Amber, my running mates each morning near the hotel, will enhance their lives and ministries—(Nick was an albino, a recent convert from Siberia; Amber, a pastor from Latvia). I don't know which of the patients I consulted with will find renewed life. I only know that God has shown Himself ever present on this excursion with many varied and wonderful miracles and lifelong memories to re-experience, and I know that I can trust him. God is good indeed!

P.S. While Amber, Nick and I were running one morning, Nick made an observation, likening our link with heaven to the umbilical cord that links a fetus with its mother—an illustration I had not thought of before, but most interesting. I will long remember our early morning, barefoot runs at the track near the Bicol Hotel.

Chapter XI

Cuba

"Hey Sis, Dad, Mom—Come on; Your Story Hour's on!"

Your Story Hour (YSH), an international radio broadcast of dramatized Bible and character-building stories for boys and girls, has been on the air since the late 1940s. From humble beginnings in a garage in Berrien Springs, Michigan; Stanley Hill (Uncle Dan), a foreman at the College Wood Products; Aunt Sue, a college student, and a number of other amateur radio enthusiasts began a ministry that rapidly spread around the world. Though I had worked with Stanley at the College Wood Products during my first year in college, I didn't really get acquainted with him until he came to my office in Battle Creek in the mid-60s, during his annual fund-raising drive for YSH. Then, too, I cared for his first wife during her terminal illness. When I returned to the Chicago area from Loma Linda after completing my surgical residency, Uncle Dan, again, contacted me—this time inviting me to serve on the Board of Directors of the *Your Story Hour Ministry.*

It was in the capacity as chairman of the YSH board that David Gonzales, our Spanish language director, requested that my wife Avonne, and I; along with Thony Escota, known as *Tio Daniel*, attend the graduation of thousands of children in Cuba from the *Tu Historia Preferida (YSH—THP)* Bible Club that he had initiated and promoted throughout the Latin-speaking world. Though the radio broadcast was blocked from entering Cuba, the Bible Club became a very effective instrument for distributing audio-cassette tapes and Bible lessons throughout the country.

"Because of U.S. government prohibitions against direct flights from the U.S. to Cuba at the time, our itinerary took us—via Mexicana Airlines—on a 3:00 a.m. flight from Chicago to Mexico City. There we were to pick up tickets and visas to Cuba. Upon arrival in Mexico City, we discovered that we had no ticket agent and no tickets or visas for the remainder of the trip. Those tense moments were only relieved after, finally, making contact with an official of the airline who did, indeed, have our names and confirmation of visas. With this evidence, we were able to purchase our tickets to Havana.

"The flight across the Mexican Peninsula, the Caribbean and the entire length of Cuba was absolutely beautiful with blue sky and scattered, white clouds. Arriving in Havana by mid-afternoon, we were met by Thony and Andrez Rodriquez, head of our work in Cuba. After accompanying us through customs, they took us on a brief tour of the SDA Church headquarters and Seminary in Havana. There we saw an old, old, hand-powered printing press, dating back a hundred years or more, that had been shipped from YSH headquarters in Michigan to Cuba. With it, they were printing Bible lessons for the Bible Clubs—using *used* motor oil in place of ink. Later that afternoon, we went to Pinar del Rio, home of the Rodriquez family. Our trip of three or four hours was interrupted by *only one* flat tire on our rented van! Dinner with the Rodriquez family was delicious. The church was packed, that evening, for the first of a series of exercises for the graduates of the various levels of the Bible Club.

"The next morning, October 22, 1994, was the 150th anniversary of *The Great Disappointment,* the day predicted by William Miller for Jesus to return and for the end of the world. Hundreds of thousands of people in America, and around the world, were ready and waiting for that grand event—only to be devastated when midnight came—and Jesus had not. One can only begin to imagine the embarrassment, frustration and ridicule these disappointed ones faced. Many forsook the Christian faith all together. Some returned to the churches from which they had come prior to joining the movement. A few believed that Miller's calculations of Daniel's time prophecies were correct, but that—instead of the return of Jesus—the prophecy depicting the *cleansing of the sanctuary* pointed to the beginning of God's final judgment of planet earth. From these roots, the Advent Movement (later to become organized into the Seventh-day Adventist Church) had its beginning. While, around the world, Adventists were reflecting on that tragic experience, we began our day by visiting a *house church* in Pinar del Rio. Here we learned firsthand how the Bible Clubs worked.

"Cuba was, and remains, pretty much a classless society. Everyone is poor, though almost no one is destitute. The house-church we visited was a rather typical, small Cuban residence with three or four scantily furnished rooms. Folding chairs filled one room where the adults met for their worship service. Along an outside wall, the young people worshipped under a makeshift shelter. A short distance away, a low fence encircled a pen containing some chickens, and one could see a single, black pig wallowing in the mud of a neighbor's yard! Singing was enthusiastic—the preaching of the Word, inspiring. I saw no one sleeping during the worship experience.

"From there we met Maria Euginia and her husband at their home. As we visited in her simple home, we listened to the story of her involvement with the Bible Clubs in that part of Cuba—her enthusiasm bubbling over as she recited some of her experiences. Then, taking us outside, they showed us the bicycle on which she rode side-saddle while her husband peddled her to Bible groups each week—some of them more than 20 miles away—over dirt trails or bumpy roads.

Thony challenged his listeners to similar faithfulness, even during difficult times, just as the Israelite little maid had unselfishly played an active part in obtaining healing for her Syrian captor.

"This is how the clubs work: Adult leaders organize groups of young people interested in studying the Bible. The groups are self-generating, as the kids share with their friends and invite them to join them. During their regularly scheduled weekly meetings, they study the Bible and review their completed study guides. Bible lessons occur on three levels, beginning at the most elementary level and progressing into more and more sophisticated studies. At each level of attainment, the kids are given certificates of achievement as they advance to the next level. In addition to studying the Bible, the groups are also involved in community service activities which provide opportunity to place into practice the principles of Christian love they are learning in their studies.

"Maria then took us to meet some of her students and their families who shared their testimonies with us. Many of the children have had no previous religious or Christian background (Cuba is communistic and atheistic). From there, we went to the church where Thony was scheduled to speak for the Children's Church that met in a courtyard outside of the church building where the adults were worshipping. The court was packed with kids, enthusiastically singing and joining in the worship experience. Thony used the story of the Israelite slave-girl serving in the home of Naaman, a Syrian general afflicted with leprosy, to illustrate his sermon. He told how that young Jewish slave urged her master to go to Israel to see the prophet Elisha. Thony challenged his listeners to similar faithfulness, even during difficult times, just as the Israelite *little maid* had unselfishly played an active part in obtaining healing for her Syrian captor.

"That afternoon we attended our first graduation ceremony—late, as seems to be fairly normal—the program finally got started about 4:00 p.m. Kids had gathered from Pinar del Rio and from villages and towns far and near, from house-churches, from organized churches and from other unconnected groups many kilometers away. Travel, itself, was a major accomplishment in this country—which has very limited public transportation such as government flat-bed trucks, dump trucks or any other public vehicle that passed by. Rare, privately-owned cars exist in the country, mostly of vintage before 1953. The church was packed, with many more standing outside and looking in. Following opening songs of praise and prayer, the service began with a demonstration of how sound effects are created in the *YSH* studio for radio broadcast, and with puppets used to tell a couple of Bible stories. Graduation then began, as group after group took the stage to share their testimony before receiving their certificates. Some of the stories were fairly typical; others brought tears of ecstasy and joy as one witnessed these kids sing their songs and tell experiences of where they had come from, where they were now in their life experience, and the cost and benefit involved in the process. These were true modern-day miracles of transformation from deepest darkness to real happiness. It was late at night before the program was over, and Avonne and I knew we had just witnessed something spectacular. We had seen the results of the working of the Holy Spirit among these people, akin to the experience of Pentecost two thousand years ago. More than 250 children had received their certificates; most were from non-religious homes.

"I wondered what the future held for these kids. I thought, too, of Jesus' parable of the sower and knew in my heart that some of the seed would fall on rocky places; but rejoiced that some of the seed would fall in deep, rich, *Cuban soil* and reap a rich harvest. Then, too, I was reminded of the elm trees back home in Hinsdale; there many of the streets are still lined with tall, beautiful elm trees. In late February, tiny blossoms—mostly unseen—yield millions and millions of tiny, round, flat seeds that fall to the ground in the month of April. Soon, they are tossed by gentle breezes and rivulets of falling rain into small piles that collect in corners, quiet places, and in sidewalk cracks and crevices. Here—nurtured by one another and urged on by the warm rays of the sun—these tiny seeds germinate and sprout, forming an innumerable mass of tiny trees. As spring is replaced by summer—trampling feet, lawn-mowers, cultivators and hoes destroy most of these little seedlings. Come autumn, numbers decrease further by wind, by rain, by drought or by men. When spring arrives once again, only a few saplings remain to grow and to become stately trees; so it is with the church!

"As I contemplated the future of God's cause, I wondered if there were any way to apply the principles and practices of what we were witnessing here to ministry for kids in other parts of the world.

"Getting up early the next day, we left Pinar del Rio for our return trip to Havana with the team. There we met in the Vipiro Church for a late morning meeting. This was a large church, just recently having undergone renovation by Maranatha Volunteers, a group of builders and workers from the States. The kids presented some first-class musical selections, poems, etc., and gave their witness of what the *THP* Bible Clubs had done for them. Unfortunately—because translation was not always the best—it was sometimes difficult to fully understand the details; I failed to keep notes of their stories—some of which were nothing short of divine miracles.

"That night, as we went to sleep on the floor of an upstairs room at the *THP* Havana headquarters, the moon was full, the stars in the sky, brilliant—in contrast to the dark, unlit streets below.

"Again, we got up early for our trip to Camaguey, further to the east. The meeting was scheduled to begin at 5:00 p.m. We planned on about eight or nine hours to get there, hoping to be there early enough to prepare for the meeting. Our rented van was old; its tires bald. On the way we sustained a very frightening blow-out, so had to stop at a small, rural town to get it fixed. This gave us opportunity to see—close up—a bit more of the country. On our way again, the drive was beautiful—miles and miles of farmland with cattle and goats, rice, sugarcane, oranges and pineapple, etc. There was a lot of land and lots of crops, but very few people working. I wondered how the work gets done! Most all of the roadside is kept cut by pasturing animals—either running loose, or tethered with ropes; apparently, a practice that was planned for efficiency, as few places were missed to be cut by hand-sickles or a rare tractor-mower.

"We arrived at the church in Camaguey much later than desired. While setting up for the meeting, it began to rain—forcing things to a virtual standstill. Finally, after a lot of frustration, many prayers, and a bit of patience; things came together and the program proceeded. Unfortunately, there were some who—because of transportation and distance—were unable to stay for the activities. Many others were not able to come at all. As noted already, transportation is a major problem. Even so, the church was filled to overflowing, which led to an announcement requesting adults to please leave to make room for the kids! The program went well, again, with some stirring testimonies from youth and kids. It was late at night when we finally stopped signing autographs and got things packed up. Because it was late, we obtained rooms in a hotel, hoping to get a good night's rest—which we did!

"The next day, we spent a leisurely morning and enjoyed a late morning brunch at the local church conference office. Before traveling on, we paid a short visit to the home of a very old and devout Cuban lady who had experienced the best and worst of times in Cuba. While we were there, she sat down at the piano and played for us. The song she chose, *Fur-Elise,* stirred deep emotions in our hearts as this was the song played most often by our daughter before her untimely death at age 28.

The kids presented some very nice musical numbers and great testimonies.

"We were then on our way further to the east, to the city of Holguine—our last planned program. We were, now, a long ways from Havana—and only about 24 hours from our scheduled departure-time back to the U.S. We went anyway! It was another beautiful country ride. In one town that we passed through, the main street was lined with very pretty, bright orange, cana lilies. We arrived in Holguine late—after dark. It took time for everyone to get organized, but the program finally got underway. The kids presented some very nice musical numbers and great testimonies. One little guy told his experience of being put in jail for sharing his faith with a friend—a very moving story in a very real land—where communism can remain suppressive if opportunity permits. It was late when the activities concluded but, before our departure, we were fed a delicious, though simple, meal of Cuban black beans and rice.

"It was then time to begin our long and grueling trip back to Havana and our waiting flight. It is hard to sleep sitting up, packed into a less-than-roadworthy van on dark, narrow, bumpy roads. At about 4:00 a.m. we stopped at Camaguey, awakened a family from their sleep and watched as the man of the house pulled out a five-gallon glass jar of gasoline, wrapped a cloth around its mouth as a filter, and poured it into our tank. (Gasoline is strictly rationed. Collecting sufficient amounts of it for travels—such as we were on—is a real challenge that must be done *wisely.*) As the sun began to rise, we stopped along the road to eat breakfast—a fresh baked-in-the-husk, tamale. Not long after, we lost a *tread* from one of the tires (how does one lose a tread from bald tires?) and had to find a place to purchase another tire. By then, our plane was already loading back in Havana. Needless to say, we missed the flight—only to discover that the next one was on Friday, two days hence. Fortunately, we were able to get on a charter flight to Miami for a good price the next day and, later, to purchase *cheap* tickets from Miami to Chicago—a *win-win* trip after all! That evening in Havana was pleasant. Though much of the city was in poor repair; though black smoke billowed from the tall chimney of the power house along the coast; and though hardship showed clearly on the faces of its citizens, the sunset over the bay was beautiful.

"We had a good night's rest and an enjoyable time with our hosts before taking off over the beautiful, blue Caribbean in mid-afternoon.

"At that time, Cuba was still governed by Fidel Castro. Communism was still very much in control, but Andrez had found a warm spot in Fidel's heart—a fact that facilitated his work with *THP*. As a result, most of our work was uninhibited and, perhaps, even encouraged by the governing authorities. However, Cuban citizens were (and remain) poor. Everything is tightly rationed. Each family is allowed a designated amount of food and other necessary commodities. Even produce grown on one's own allotted property is supposed to be turned over to the government. There were few private cars on the roads, mostly American made, dating back from before the revolution. Andrez desperately needed a van for his work with the *THP* Bible Clubs but could not afford one, even if one were available for purchase. Yet, he did not give up. By the side of his house he was assembling an old Volkswagen van from rusty pieces scrounged from here and there. When I saw what he was working with, I was sure he would never get that piece of junk running. But, though it took a couple years, he succeeded! Later, he was able to build a new office building and home for *THP*—with concessions from government authorities.

"What did we accomplish by the trip I wondered? Was it worth the effort? I suppose only in the Kingdom of Heaven will we see the full results of these efforts and contributions. Hopefully, a little bit of what is happening here, with the kids, will begin to catch on in other places as well. At least, we had a taste of what child evangelism might be. Our hearts have been blessed. And another short chapter of our lives has been written to add to the many blessings God has already given."

I had the opportunity to return to Cuba a few years later; this time for an International meeting of *THP* Bible Clubs. Clubs from all across Latin America were in attendance. Fidel was then ill and talk about the future without him was quite prevalent. The country had undergone considerable modernization. Many of the buildings in *Old Havana* had been rehabilitated. Street conditions had improved. There were even a few new cars on the roads—but none American made. Tourists were returning. One could even purchase fresh, hand-rolled cigars at the airport. But, unfortunately, the living conditions of the masses remained pretty much as they had been before.

Chapter XII

Ghana, West Africa

"Seeing the problem, one of the African pastors called us all together to pray. We knelt there, in the dirt, and sought the grace of God to protect us from the storm. As we got up from our knees, the wind and the rain stopped!"

"Thursday 5:40 p.m.—It is almost exactly one day (one *long* day) since departing from Chicago Midway Airport. The TV monitor in front of me that has tracked our flight from London, now reveals reducing ground speed and dropping altitude as we approach Abidjan, Ivory Coast, West Africa, en route to Accra, Ghana. In a few minutes, we will touch down on African soil. Reserved excitement dominates my mood—anticipation, intrigue, fear, uncertainty, joy, sadness; many emotions converge to make this experience real. When Mark first mentioned his dream of *ACTS 2000* with a site in Africa, I secretly hoped I might be invited to have a part. Yet, careful not to mention my secret wish to anyone, I recognized a dream come true when, in fact, he did call and invite me to work with him in Ghana, sharing the gospel via satellite television to thousands of downlinks throughout Africa and the whole world beyond. I suppose, in a way, this fulfills a dream first implanted in my head by the visiting pastor—the missionary to our church when I was but a boy—who put his hand on my knee and said that I would, one day, be a missionary doctor to Africa. Until now, one might properly conclude that the *prophecy* had been falsely uttered. Coming as this does near the end of a busy professional career, I must view it as God's icing on a beautiful life-cake, full of so many benefits from His hand. Yet, while sensing this bonus to my life, there remains a great, big, unknown challenge; i.e., now that I am here, what can I give that might make any kind of impact at all upon the people of Ghana—and Africa at large? I feel totally incompetent and unprepared! Thus it is, that, it will be interesting to see what God will do.

"Undoubtedly, the greatest cost of this trip to me is the difficulty of leaving Avonne (my faithful wife) behind—not that God can't take care of her, but that she won't be sharing in this experience that means so much to me. One day, we will understand the full extent of the battles that go on behind the scenes of human view and between the powers of good and evil that seem to determine the impact of our lives. The Bible is clear that sadness and pain and disappointment are as much a part of the disciplining process leading to sanctification (holiness) as are hope and peace and joy and love; all of which thrills my soul—that I know such a God who cares enough to put us through whatever measures are needful that He might save us for that better world.

"Accra—Capital city of Ghana—gateway to Africa, some say. Arriving late last evening, we stayed overnight in a little hotel until leaving early this morning for Kumasi—four or five hours away by decent, paved, two-lane roads. While traveling, I had opportunity to speak with the youth director from the local Mid-Ghana Conference, and a translator from Tanzania who were traveling with me. From them, I learned a little bit about the health needs and practices of the African people.

This account, much of which is composed of direct quotes copied from my notes, may help the reader reach inside of my mind as I approached this mission of *ACTS 2000.*

"Never before in history had anyone attempted to do what we were embarking upon, to proclaim the judgment-hour message of the everlasting gospel to the entire African continent, simultaneously, via television—not even the apostles at the time of Pentecost! We were going into the heartland of Africa and, from there, up-linking our messages—via satellite television—to the whole continent and beyond, to satellites around the world! Accordingly, thousands of satellite dishes had already been installed in villages and cities throughout Africa where the signal could be received; necessitating, of course that we also broadcast in multiple languages. This would all take place here in the Kamasi Cultural Center, an outdoor park; the only place we could find that was large enough to accommodate the expected attendance. For my part, I would be working with the local health professionals conducting clinics; teaching preventive, lifestyle health measures; and giving lectures on health each evening, just prior to the preached message—this in keeping with Jesus' example of meeting both physical and spiritual needs of his listeners.

"Though the month of March approaches—the end of the dry season in West Africa—we were assured that our out-door venue would not be endangered by rain and storms.

"While Accra is the capital city of the official government of Ghana, Kamasi is the capital of the Ashanti Kingdom. It is the traditional center of the Ashanti tribe, which has played such a dominant role throughout African history in West Africa. It is here that the king resides and where Ashanti kings are encrypted. Lesser chiefs, subject to the king, govern the various districts and towns of the nation. While the kingdom has no official power or authority, the people look to it as their source of inspiration and direction. Nothing of note gets done in government offices without the approval of the king.

"Interestingly, our meetings were scheduled to begin on Independence Day—the day Ghana gained independence from British rule. As it was told to me, Britain's primary interest in Ghana was its gold that was said to lay thick in its riverbeds. They ransacked the southern coastal region searching for it, forcing the Ashanti people north to what is now Kamasi. In many kingdoms, the king sits on a throne; in Ghana, it is a golden stool! Tradition has it that the stool fell from heaven, making it a very sacred object. Learning of it, the British determined to obtain it and take it back to England for the Queen. Finally, to assuage the colonialists, the Ashanti made a fake stool and gave it to them, while carefully hiding the real thing. There was much talk about that original golden stool but, so far as I know, it remains in hiding!

"Ghana is very much a Christian nation. Churches of all denominations abound—meeting both in nice buildings as well as out of doors under the trees; but there are also many Animists (pagans), Muslims and other religions. Traffic is heavy on Ghana's roads and city streets, and almost every vehicle is *decorated* with a message from or about God. It is also a nation of poor people with many youth, but with little employment and limited educational opportunities. Many of those who do manage to get an education, contribute to the *brain-drain,* establishing themselves in England, France, the U.S. or other *developed* lands, leaving the homeland lacking.

"The Cultural center was very nice. When we arrived a large screen had already been erected for projection of illustrations, and the stage had been set and decorations mostly completed for the meetings. Unfortunately, Customs had held up the entry of our television and uplink equipment, demanding huge sums of money to allow it into the country. That issue was finally resolved—but not until the last day before the meetings were to begin! One might only imagine the challenge of setting up all of the necessary electronic equipment to speak to thousands of people on-site and to uplink, via satellite, to the world. Our technical people were taxed to the limit, to be sure. As if that weren't bad enough, they kept *burning up* the electronic equipment—a problem they had hoped to prevent by purchasing our own generator, rather than depending upon the city power supply. Come to find out, the city was connected directly to our electrical circuits, resulting in wide fluctuations in amperage—not a good thing for electronic equipment! That problem was finally resolved, but not before we had ruined vital equipment.

"Fifteen minutes before we were to go *live* to satellite with the first meetings, the technical crew was still working on the equipment trying to get a signal to the satellite. Even so, we proceeded—trusting God to bring it all off on schedule. Just about that time, the sky that had been friendly all day suddenly turned very dark, the wind began to blow—kicking up dirt and leaves and threatening to mess up all of the work of the day. A few drops of rain began to fall. This was not what we had wanted for our first program! Seeing the problem, one of the African pastors called us all together to pray. We knelt there, in the dirt, and sought the grace of God to protect us from the storm. As we got up from our knees, the wind and the rain stopped! The choir came on stage as scheduled and, just as they prepared to sing, we received word that we were live *on air*. After the meeting, a drive around the city revealed that, indeed, a major storm had passed through the city knocking down trees and taking off roofs—all around us! There are those who doubt the power of prayer. No one in Kamasi did that night!

"We estimated the attendance at about 9,000 that first night. Among them was a minister of another faith about whom we heard this story: Preparations for the meetings included door-to-door invitations. When the member of the visitation team knocked on this particular door and began to explain the nature of the program, the man suddenly became very sober. At first dumbfounded, he finally began to speak. About a year before, he had had a dream telling him that a man would come to Kamasi and preach to an international audience. He was instructed—in the dream—to go to the meetings and to take his congregation along with him. When, at that moment, he realized that this invitation was a fulfillment of the dream, he was thrilled and made plans for himself and his entire church to attend.

"A nice, octagon-shaped, brick building—adjacent to the outdoor amphitheater—was chosen as the site for setting up our health exhibits and for holding our clinics. Though quite dark inside, it was clean and dry and spacious—perfect for displaying our life-size illustrated panels, teaching people how to become—and to stay—healthy. I was pleased with the prospects. The morning following our initial meeting, I met with about 30 local health personnel, including doctors, nurses, homeopaths, etc., to plan the events and set up schedules for the next few weeks. Then, too, we put up the instructional panels and prepared the place for clinics and for health lectures.

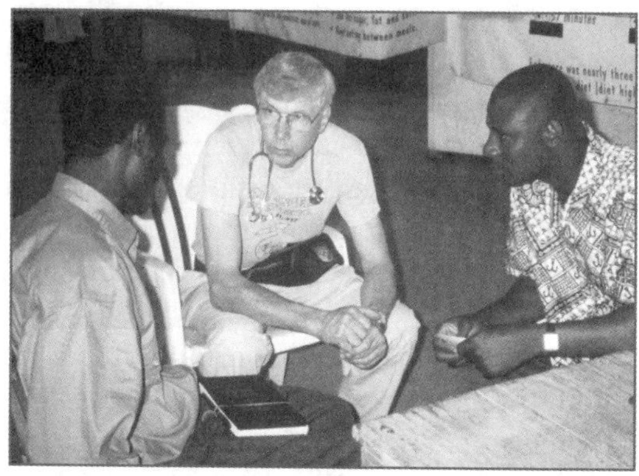

The morning following our initial meeting, I met with about 30 local health personnel to plan the events and set up schedules for the next few weeks.

"My health talks for the main meeting needed to be illustrated for television, but I was a real neophyte on the computer. Fortunately, Mark had brought a computer expert along to help him put together illustrations for his sermons, so he was able to assist me as well. Even so, I spent hours each day working on my illustrations and lectures. Each afternoon—before the meetings—we met with our translators from all over Africa, going over our material with them so they would be better able, when on air, to do simultaneous translation in the various African languages.

"The second night, the program went off without a hitch—sending the signal to groups all across the continent, as well as to English and African-speaking people everywhere. Unfortunately, as we learned later, Ghana and some areas west of us were not able to pick up the signal. Only then, did we discover that the satellite we were broadcasting from did not cover all of West Africa. That problem was resolved by renting transponder space on another satellite.

"The next night was more exciting! We discovered that producing an international television program—in an outdoor theater, in a thunderstorm—can pose real problems. We were reminded, again, that the war between good and evil that goes on behind the realm of human vision is real. God blessed us by diverting the storm the first night, but we failed to take the necessary precautions should another storm arrive. It was necessary for us to learn our lesson. Television cameras and lights, video projectors, the entire audio system, everything except our control room equipment—was threatened. Yes, and we got soaked too! I found it very difficult to look out over the audience and speak to them with rainwater running down my face and into my eyes! To protect the uplink equipment that had to be outside, the technical people had placed a tarp overhead; unfortunately, the tarp filled up with rainwater and settled in the center—threatening to cave in on the equipment. Just at that moment a guard came by and—seeing the impending catastrophe—thrust his bayonet into the canvas, letting the water drain out and saving the day! Fortunately, with the help of a lot of volunteers holding umbrellas over sensitive equipment—and with the blessing of God—we suffered no damage. Subsequently, when the rains came we were prepared—and come, they did!

"Early on I had the opportunity to visit a local medical clinic. The outdoor waiting area was *packed* with the sick. I was shown the pharmacy. Unlike here in America, where most medications come prepared in sealed containers; whether bottles or tubes, these *pharmacists* mixed most of their own prescriptions on site. And, I must say, I was appalled with the conditions under which they worked. It really started me thinking: How in the world can I hope to bridge the culture gap between our healthcare societies? This was my challenge—to touch the world with something of value! Consequently, it was no wonder that I struggled with our work at the Cultural Center, as people insisted that they have the hands of a white man laid upon them. I struggled as I took my clinical histories, mostly through translators, examined their bodies and sought to provide a bit of *real* help. I knew that a few simple treatments and lifestyle changes would work wonders for them—yet they wanted pills. I prayed with a lot of patients, asking God to do for them that which I could not. In addition, I resisted the urge to spend all of my time consulting with patients, so that I could take time to teach them how to prevent sickness and use simple remedies to treat their ills. My efforts were appreciated by patients and staff alike, but one particular experience epitomizes a bit of my frustration. It had been a long and busy day; still, patients were lined up to see me as the time for the evening meeting approached. I was urged to see this one last patient before hurrying off to give my presentation. Her history was complicated; her need great! She literally begged me to help her right then—since she had come from a long distance away and would be unable to return. Yet, it was time for me to go *live* on the air to give a message that would help thousands. My heart was wrenched as I left her to keep my appointment. Even though I assured her I would try and see her after the meeting, I didn't find her again, that night—or ever—and, I still wonder if I made the right choice! Oh, I know that God heard my prayers for her, but—to this day—my heart still aches for this lady.

"One morning before hours, as I walked by the Cultural Center building where we conducted our health ministries, I was taken aback as I witnessed guards beating a couple of young men with long, narrow canes. The men, mostly bare, lay cowering on the ground, flinching with each blow—pleading for mercy. Nor did my appearance seem to work in their favor; the beating continued in spite of my presence. I learned, later, that they were apprehended for stealing from the attendees the night before at the meetings. (We had contracted with the military to provide guards for the meetings, to protect our equipment and to keep order.) But I was troubled. We had come here to bring a message of love and peace, and I saw this activity as bringing a whole different influence. I shared my observations with Mark and the pastors who, in turn, spoke with the guards—sharing our position on brutality. Thankfully, there were no further problems; either of theft or of beatings.

"Ghana was chosen as the nation from which to broadcast this series of meetings because—of all Africa—it has the least incidence of crime and danger. And, indeed, we were impressed with the conduct of the people—on the street and even in traffic. While we were alert to keep our valuables well protected against pickpockets, we sensed little risk when in public. In fact, one could go through the city any time of the day or night and seldom see a police officer or a squad car. I wondered if, perhaps, the strong arm of the military was the reason for this—but was told that politeness and respect for others is present throughout Africa, and it is believed to be due to the strong patriarchal (and matriarchal) hierarchy that exists across the continent, where tribal kings and elders are held in high esteem by the people. (Incidentally, the people of Ghana express great honor and respect for white people as well.)

"On one occasion, in addition to going over my lectures with the translators, I had opportunity to spend quality time with all of the pastoral staff and translators from across Africa, sharing with them some of my values, instructing on the basics of healthy lifestyles and answering their questions. It was a time much appreciated by all.

"Our attendance at the meetings increased nightly. We heard many stories of miraculous healings and of pastors from other churches attending the meetings with their people. On at least one occasion, we were aware of three Ashanti kings (chiefs) in the audience. People were even coming from Nigeria and other countries to witness what was happening in Kamasi. To meet these needs, we had to set up projection screens and speakers throughout the grounds.

"One of the members of our health team is a homeopath. One day I consented to go with him to consult in his clinic, since I was interested in learning more about homeopathy and seeing what he was doing. I saw several patients, together with him, and I believe I was able to give him a few helpful suggestions. But I was intrigued by what I saw. On his desk in the consultation room was a *gadget* which contained a small metal plate, upon which was placed a specimen from the patient. A crystal pendulum hung above the specimen. The nature of the problem was determined by the movement of the pendulum. The doctor next consulted with a large compendium to determine what prescription to provide. With this information, he counted out the appropriate number and type of pills called for and sent his patients on their way. Certainly, I had my reservations about this apparent hocus-pocus, but I didn't say anything. Perhaps reading my mind—or responding to his own better judgment—he told me he was one of only a handful of homeopaths who had been recognized and licensed by the government to practice his profession of homeopathy. Then he volunteered to tell me that he didn't know if there was any physical basis for his practice but, if people were helped by it, he figured it must be OK. I refrained from comment, preferring to teach and share by example.

"As the meetings progressed, I was gradually learning how to use *Power-Point* on my computer and to insert *clip-art* so as to enhance my visuals. Though pretty simple, they were quite attractive and were able to convey my message quite convincingly, or so it appeared by the response. I spoke on many of the health problems common to people of Africa—as well as to much of the world—heart disease, cancer, addictions, parasitic infections and diseases of filth, malaria, etc. I tried to give useful information, both for preventing illness, and for managing it once present. Though I stepped out on a limb a bit in making a presentation on sexually-transmitted diseases, including AIDS (such talk is taboo in public), the information was well accepted, and I was urged to give a follow-up on the same topic.

"We saw many hundreds of patients in our clinic (even requiring the guards to break up a near riot on one occasion)—treating everything from allergies and arthritis to advanced cases of cancer, Parkinson's disease, and all manner of other maladies—some most pitiful. Needless to say, with so little of modern medical care to offer, we prayed a lot!

"Efforts to start a program to help people quit smoking and to deal with alcohol and other addictions fell flat. Smoking is not common, but alcohol is—though talk about it is taboo.

"On Sabbaths I was privileged to speak at various churches in and around Kamasi. I was amazed at how attentive the people were and how well they comprehended the messages I presented—messages of God's final judgment of planet earth and its effect upon those of us living now during its final hours. I had not experienced the same interest in this topic at home. Furthermore, I sensed no need to rush through my *homilies*. In fact, on one occasion, I went on for an hour or more until it was early afternoon, but they wouldn't let me stop and pled for more; so, I spent another hour talking about health as it applies to one's spiritual journey.

On Sabbaths I was privileged to speak at various churches in and around Kamasi. I was amazed at how attentive the people were and how well they comprehended the messages I presented.

"On February 25, a couple of weeks before we arrived, the Ashanti king died; but he was not entombed at that time. Traditionally, before a king can leave this world and enter the afterlife, all cases in court must be judged (which reminds one of earth's final judgment before Jesus can claim his kingdom). The elders of the court had been working diligently for the past month and were, now, apparently done. In view of this, Tuesday and Wednesday were designated as the times for public condolences before his entombment on Thursday. The king seemed to have been well-liked. This was corroborated by the long lines and hours of waiting necessary to pay one's respects. Mark gave a special tribute to him during the meeting that night. Traditionally, the king takes an entourage with him into the next world; an entourage composed of his special people: public officials, deputies, slaves, etc., depending upon his perceived needs. This king had declared he would not be following tradition but, in spite of this reassurance—people were still very much afraid during the next few days—for fear some might still be taken.

"According to tradition, Saturday is God's Day—in the local language, Kwame's Day. Babies born on Saturday receive the name, Kwame. Another word for Sabbath is MIMIEDA, translated as I AM (the Hebrew designation of God). Black African Sabbath keepers are referred to as Kwames. Sunday is White Man's Day. White people (sometimes called, *colored*) are often referred to by the name, Bruni. Therefore, no official activities occur on Saturdays—not even the entombment of the king. This is true, despite the most intensive efforts of Catholic missionaries during colonial days to get the Ashanti people to change the Sabbath day. Historians are uncertain of the origin of Sabbath sacredness among the Ashanti's and many other African tribes. Some attribute it to the days of the Queen of Sheba who came from Ethiopia to visit King Solomon in Jerusalem nearly three thousand years ago. Others wonder if it may not have been the Ethiopian Eunuch (a prominent government official) who came to worship in Jerusalem soon after the crucifixion of Jesus and, while there, converted to Christianity. This occurred in the days before the Sabbath was changed to Sunday. Or does Saturday, Sabbath, go all the way back to creation itself, as many African historians who have carefully examined the evidence believe?

"I was also told that—except for the king who sits upon the golden stool and who wears much golden jewelry—no jewelry is worn by Ashanti women—or men! The reason? The Ashanti people consider themselves to be a royal family. They believe jewelry is only for slaves (royal family as pertains to the Children of God, I presume, though I was not given an answer to that).

"There is another religious curiosity in Ghana. It is the Nyame-Dua tree meaning, *God tree*. Unlike most plants and trees that branch into two trunks as they grow, this tree always branches into three which, I am told, symbolizes the three members of the Godhead: the Father, Jesus the Son, and the Holy Ghost (Holy Spirit). By the pagans, it is known as the *Spirit tree* and is notorious for its magical properties. I saw one such tree that sheltered the home of a local pagan priest.

"One day a colonel invited me to accompany him to his home village of Dome'abra, which means, 'Let them come unto me.' We visited an old,

old lady, whose son had been influential in witnessing to him and winning him to the Lord. The colonel was a new Christian and very much on fire for what he had come to believe. She was one of his *charities* that he supported and—that day—placed a roll of bills in her hand. He showed me the town square. There we saw a big, eight-foot satellite dish and, in the corner of the village square, a huge projection screen. I was told that, each evening, the people of the village come and sit in the street to watch the programs broadcast from our site in Kumasi—a phenomena occurring all across Africa. We then visited a public school and met briefly with the teachers and headmaster. At the time, they were feeding the little kids their school lunch. As we left, the kids chased after us, laughing and joyously waving their hands at us; they were an enthusiastic bunch if ever I saw one!

"Our next stop was at the home of the Paramount Chief for that district of Ghana. He was, also, the head of the Ashanti Kingdom Army. By western standards, his home was very nice; but when compared to the other mud-brick buildings in the town, it was outstanding. A pretty deep-pink bougainvillea plant accented the red-tiled floor of the entry way. He was a middle-aged man and quite pleasant. Since I hadn't been clear regarding the distinction between the government offices and the kingdom, he spent some time explaining the system to me. When asked how the kingdom is supported financially if it cannot levy taxes, he told me it was by selling land in their district. I was also curious to learn about the Ashanti army that he headed. I was told that—in this day and age—it is a title only. There really is no effective Ashanti army; they apparently have no working artillery. Finally, I discovered that his actual home is in New York City in the United States. He was in the business of manufacturing window-blinds, I believe, and only returned to Ghana on special occasions. I never learned if he was an exception, or if this was the typical practice by the chiefs.

"Before leaving, we visited the church and church school under construction. While there we met a lady returning from her garden, carrying the fruit of her labors on her head. I was told that her garden is five miles away. Several times a week she walks to the garden, cares for it, and walks back at the end of the day, carrying her produce. I was amazed, for I doubt I could have lifted the load she was carrying—to say nothing about carrying it on my head! I was also told that those who carry such loads must have help getting it up there and in taking it down. She was walking alone, so obviously it must have been a non-stop journey. But she was not unusual; oftentimes we saw women carrying large baskets filled with pineapples, crates of twelve-dozen eggs, firewood and all kinds of other unimaginable things on their heads. I noticed that their backs are as straight as an arrow!

"On the way back to Kamasi, the colonel shared a bit more of his life experience. He told me it was during a stint in Rwanda—where the Ghanaian army was sent to serve during the genocide—that he became inspired to become a Christian. There he observed Adventist missionaries who refused to leave the country, choosing to risk loss of life rather than to forsake the orphans and students that they were there to help. This was the clincher that led to his decision for Jesus.

"On another day, I accompanied Dan Houghton, our floor director during the broadcasts; and Debbie Finley, Mark's daughter, to the local market. It was quite an experience! Row after long row of little shops selling everything imaginable—except the sort of things one might find in our great department stores in the West! In fact, I saw very little of those things—with one major exception—clothing! Used clothing! Huge bags of used clothing; I presume the product of our donation to charities there. There were also some imports, mostly from China and East Asia, but it appeared to me that most of the common things they use every day were made right there in Ghana. In the produce section, we saw lots and lots of eggplants, chilies, yams and sweet potatoes, tomatoes, herbs, plantain, bananas, pineapples and; of course, many other things. As we were leaving the market, we saw some ladies mashing their plantains for dinner. One of the staples in their diet is plantain mashed into what looks like putty, then picked up with the fingers, dipped into a hot sauce (hot both ways!) and plopped into the mouth. Mashing is accomplished by repeatedly plunging a large-diameter—approximately six foot-long bamboo log—up and down on the plantain in a large wooden container. The setting was perfect for a

Dr. Thompson and a little friend in the marketplace.

picture but, prior to snapping it, we asked the ladies if it would be OK to take their picture. The asking price—five U.S. dollars! Needless to say, we didn't get a picture!

"In time, our work in Ghana came to an end. For my part, I had very mixed feelings—knowing that I had just experienced the fulfillment of a life-long dream; believing that I had made a difference—not only in Ghana, but also throughout Africa—by the health lessons I was able to share (videos of which would be played over and over again in months and years to come). Hopefully, the influence of our lives on the pastors, the translators, and the medical people also made a difference. We had seen a lot of sick people and were able to help many. Yes, but there were so many more that were beyond any help that we could give. For these my heart ached.

"As I sat and listened to the reports of the results of our meetings on our last working day there, I was again impressed with the evidence of the work of the Spirit of God throughout. I have shared, already, our experience with just one storm that passed around us in direct and immediate answer to prayer; and of another that hit us direct and from which we were kept from sustaining significant damage. We witnessed many miracles of that nature—and many more in the hearts of the people. One of these was told to us during that final report. It was of an Ashanti Chief who had been on a tour to the Holy Land sometime before. While there, he noted that most everything stopped on Saturday in Jerusalem. That started him thinking and wondering why he, a Catholic, worshipped on Sunday. He came to the meetings at Kamasi and responded to Mark's appeal to give his life to the Lord and to be baptized. He said to himself, 'Why not! It all makes sense!' So he and his wife were among the thousands of people in Ghana who experienced the death and burial to the ways of the world in baptism, and resurrection to a new way of life in Jesus. One of the early challenges he faced was that of giving an offering oblation to the dead kings. Should he; or should he not, was the dilemma! He was aided in his decision when, at the funeral of the king, he noted another of the chiefs who stepped aside and did not offer an oblation. He followed that man's example!

"Of course, an experience such as we had witnessed here is not the work of one man. This was illustrated by another story told that day. As the story goes, it happened one day that the men of the village decided to go on an elephant hunt. A good animal was found and killed by one of the hunters. Then all of the hunters, together, went to work to pull the huge critter to the village. They sang and chanted together as they pulled and pulled. As they got closer to the village, the man who shot the elephant was heard to be shouting louder than the group. As they sang, 'We killed an elephant, we killed an elephant,' he began to sing, 'I killed an elephant, I killed an elephant.' Little by little the other hunters stopped singing and pulling! Pretty soon, the elephant stopped moving. It wasn't long before the lone hunter changed his song back to, 'We killed an elephant, we killed an elephant!' "

My final notes of that experience read like this! "The trip has been an interesting experience, to say the least. There have been times of elation and times of depression reflecting, somewhat, the situation at the time. While it is thrilling to see God control the storms and to keep the electronic equipment running and to watch as thousands come forward in dedication, it is stressful to face such monumental problems day after day and to have to deal with them. Then, too, the parable of the sower comes to mind again, as one sees commitment of the seeds of new converts—realizing that there will be many among them who will die from the shallow soil, the stony ground, the thistles and the birds—all of which might give reason for pessimism; yet, the parable also describes another type of soil. And, at times like these, I am always grateful for the parable, knowing that some of these seeds will grow and mature and become great workers for the same cause to which I have dedicated my life. Africa is great! I have enjoyed my time here. I would have enjoyed it more if doing surgery, I suppose, for it has been a little hard consulting under the circumstances of the past few weeks. On the other hand, it has been good to pray for many and place them in God's hands. God is good! I love Africa and its people."

Chapter XIII

Rwanda

"He was in the O.R. dressing room when the killers arrived. He had hidden behind a door and watched through a crack as they killed everyone. When he realized he was the last living person, he dove down to the floor under some bodies and pretended to be dead."

"Walt! How would you like to spend a few weeks in Africa? The hospital at Mugonero, Rwanda, needs a surgeon for a few weeks while the doctor is away for continuing education. Can you do it?"

It was Dr. Richard Hart, Chancellor of Loma Linda University, a former missionary to Africa, and who is especially interested in updating the Adventist mission hospitals around the world.

The following account reflects my personal thoughts (recorded at the time), experiences and reactions during a three-week adventure in the beautiful little country of Rwanda.

"What should I say to him? Why should I do this? Why should I venture out on these missions to the far-flung corners of the globe? I don't enjoy traveling that much! I don't like trying to *sleep* sitting up on airplanes! I don't like waiting in airports! Besides, I have enough to do right here at home! Yet, it is a question I have seldom given second thought to. As a child I dedicated my life to serve my fellow man. Even then I dreamed of serving as a mission doctor in Africa. It was the primary motivating force that took me through college, medical school and residency training. And now—an opportunity to go to Africa! How could I turn it down? I have been blessed with an excellent education and skills rarely available in many parts of the world. It seems only natural to share when opportunity avails. Yet, perhaps I am a fool. Perhaps my talents could be better utilized from the more serene position of my home, depending upon my computer and pen to accomplish my objectives of service to God and my fellow man. And another question always arises in times like this! What is my responsibility to my family and their needs? Am I cheating them? These are difficult questions that missionary families often ask! But, on second thought, how can I turn down calls to serve the underprivileged and unwarned of earth's masses so long as I have strength to do so? Some of my travels have come at great cost but, always, I have been blessed far beyond that cost; I am always the one who benefits the most. I suppose—so long as I have life and health—the burden to serve will remain. How will I deal with it over time? Why did the Apostle Paul go to Galatia, Corinth and Rome?

"It was dusk as I flew into the airport in Kilgali—the same place where the plane went down that triggered the genocide here a few years before. I wondered what I had gotten myself into! That night I stayed in Kilgali with the team of workers from *ADRA (Adventist Development and Relief Agency)* who were stationed in Rwanda. After waiting at the *ADRA* warehouse all morning and into the afternoon, Sampson, the local conference church treasurer, finally arrived to take me up to the mission. Thanks to the new asphalt, paved highway the Chinese were building as their contribution to the recovery efforts of the nation, our trip only took about four hours—a trip that would have taken more than twice that long in former times. Here and there along the way, men dressed in pink garb (prisoners of war awaiting trial) were seen working on the highway, doing with pick and shovel many of the things that, in other parts of the world, would have been done with heavy equipment.

"It is winter (near the equator) and it is nearing the end of the dry season. I am told the rains will begin soon. This is mountainous country. Little houses dot the steep mountainsides, their inhabitants cultivating the fields, now mostly barren of trees. Walking trails crisscross the mountains. There are almost no roads apart from the main highway. People walk nearly everywhere.

"Also scattered around the mountaintops, along the way, are little Adventist churches. I was told that many of these are the fruit of our series of meetings in Ghana a year or so before, when Pastor Mark Finley and I were televising our talks all across Africa to thousands of satellite dishes everywhere. Other converts are the result of visits by lay church members to the prisoners of the genocide. I will say more about this later.

"We stopped for a few minutes of R and R at a *resort* in the town of Kibuye, on the eastern edge of beautiful Lake Kivu (which divides Rwanda from the Congo). We then began our ascent by dirt road to the mission further up the mountain. Once arriving at the mission gate, one could look far down the mountain to see Lake Kivu in the distance. It was a beautiful sight.

"Mugonero Mission is comprised of hundreds of acres of mountainous hills and valleys, at a high enough elevation to provide a temperate climate year-round. I am told that, until recent years, not even mosquitoes frequented these parts.

"The mission consists of a large, brick church on one mountaintop (built in 1927); behind the church an orphanage (now in the process of being moved to another location); and across the valley, to the east is the hospital complex—the clinic, the chapel, the nursing school and the dormitories, etc. At the bottom of the hill there is now a fenced cemetery—a monument to those who died at the mission during the genocide. In its pre-war heyday, the hospital at Mugonero was known far and wide for its expert service, and it drew people from the Congo, from all over Rwanda and beyond. Unfortunately, it was raped of all of its valuable equipment and other assets while under government control. The hospital has only been back in Adventist hands a short time, and Dr. Gerson Aroujo, a surgeon from Brazil, has been here for only about nine months.

A monument to those who died at the Mugonero Mission during the genocide.

"My home—for the duration—was the home of Dr. Aurojo whose place I was taking. Gerard, my housekeeper and cook, was also the keeper of the gardens. Besides the avocados, mangos, bananas, tomatoes and peppers from the garden, he liked to make a soybean salad from soaked soybeans, with a bit of chili pepper, etc. It was surprisingly tasty. At night, I was guarded by a crippled young man who lost his entire family during the genocide and was nearly killed himself. On occasion, we would sit outside under the moon and stars and try to communicate. It mostly amounted to a warm exchange of sentiment, for I have no French in my vocabulary, and he—very little English!

"August 31. Weather is beautiful, dry and hazy—surgery is a challenge. I fixed a large hernia yesterday—very difficult! My assistant, the scrub nurse, has only been in the operating room for a month and knows almost nothing about surgery. The instruments are dull. There was no self-retaining retractor to give me exposure. We began the case with local anesthesia but, because of discomfort, switched first to IV Valium and then later to Ketamine. Though the man slept for a long time after surgery, everything turned out OK.

"The electricity was off from 8:30 a.m. to 2:30 p.m. today—the generator is not working (nor has it been working for a long time, I was told). Fortunately, we hadn't yet started surgery when the power went off. No flashlight available. Nursing staff pretty limited—took two days to get an enema for a patient—didn't know how to improvise! Many sick patients—end-stage heart failure, liver failure, AIDS, cancer—others, not as sick but want help. No physical therapy or hydrotherapy available for simple treatments. Hospital charges are 200 francs daily (50 cents, US); poor quality chest X-ray, 1000 francs; other tests equally expensive as compared to the hospital charges. Most patients do not get tests done because of cost. Therefore, most of our treatment must be based upon what we can see and feel—(just like in the old days)! Dr. Edison, a new doctor on staff as of two or three weeks ago, is a Rwandan Tutsi whose family fled to the Congo during the war years. He was born, raised and received his education there, but has now returned here to his homeland to live and work. My impression of him is that he is an astute observer and good at reasoning things out. And he does speak English, so we can communicate!

"Dick Hart and team from Loma Linda were here today. Dick shared with us a bit of the recent history about the ethnic cleansing that took place on this campus. Apparently, the pastor of the Church on the Hill and his physician son organized his members, armed them with machetes, axes and guns, etc., and then marched across the campus to the chapel at the hospital where many of the personnel and people from surrounding communities had gathered en-masse for protection. There was a common belief that the chapel was a safe place. Everyone in the chapel was slaughtered. The frenzied mob then went into the hospital to complete the task. Manasa, my sterile-supply man in the operating room, was one of the very few who survived to tell their story. He was in the O.R. dressing room when the killers arrived and had hidden behind a door and watched through a crack as they killed everyone. When he realized he was the last living person, he dove down to the floor, under some bodies, and pretended to be dead. He remained there until after dark, when he crept outside into the forest. The chapel remains empty to this day—and unused. Several rough, wooden caskets filled with decaying bones rest on the floor. This is impossible for me to comprehend. The pastor had fled to Texas—and is now back in Africa for trial. He claims innocence! Certainly, an example of mass hysteria similar to what must have happened with the crowd that crucified Jesus! (Note: The International

Criminal Tribunal for Rwanda, [ICTR] has since sentenced him to prison for his role in the genocide of Rwanda.)

"One of the patients I saw today was a lady with an injury of childbirth who is leaking urine uncontrollably. She arrived at the hospital a couple of weeks ago from some distance away. She had retained *afterbirth* that was infected and necrotic, which the surgeon has debrided. Her infection is now controlled, but she is completely incontinent. I will try to place a catheter into her some way, hoping to help her. One lady with AIDS was taken home to die today—probably the result of rape during the war. I also did a skin graft today after the power came back on.

"September 1, 2000. This day has been largely taken up by the lady in the hospital who needed surgery. Once we finally had her ready for surgery, the hospital accountant came by to say that she had no money. In fact, she was already indebted to the hospital for 68,000 francs, and the hospital is out of money and has been unable to pay workers for the past three months. What to do? No other place in the country is able to give her free care either. I felt we were obligated to try and help her, even though the likelihood of success seemed poor. How could I send someone home without giving her our best? The surgery was as *impossible* as imagined. I do not know if we helped her; it will be a true miracle of God if we did. Time will tell. But, even if we failed, she and her family will know that no stones were left unturned. Yes, I am a little discouraged with the outcome—but hopeful and, most of all, glad for going ahead. Having given my best in difficult circumstances, we'll see what God can do for His part in His wisdom and love. '… All things work together for good …' (Romans 8:28 NKJV), and I claim that promise.

"Mark, my nurse in the O.R., came over to my place and talked for a couple of hours. Nice young man. He wants to improve himself but doesn't know how. I tried to encourage him and gave him some pointers. I went to worship with him for vespers in the Church on the Hill (noted yesterday). All kinds of thoughts go through one's mind at a time and in a place like this! Tomorrow I'll preach there, God willing.

"September 2, 2000. I was awakened by the crowing of the rooster and the birds in the tree outside my window. The sun was just beginning to show its face through the morning mist as it slipped up over the mountaintop—a beautiful view and a beautiful African morning! Following breakfast consisting of fresh, over-ripe pineapple; bananas; a mango and nuts, I went to make rounds at the hospital. The lady we had worked so hard on yesterday was not doing as well as I had hoped. I am much concerned for her. Other surgical patients are doing OK—so many patients are beyond help.

"I had the privilege of speaking (through a translator) for the worship service at church; I trust God that He was able to use me in a little way. I spoke of the love of God; some of the ways He manifests it to us, our response to it, the benefits of his promises and the power He offers to us to live victorious lives. People seemed to listen and follow my message. Many with whom I could communicate directly expressed gratitude.

"Dinner (prepared yesterday by Gerard, my houseboy) consisted of a bean salad, spaghetti, fake-fish casserole, and (his favorite recipe) carrot cake—with fresh pineapple juice for a drink. Later, I took my camera and went for a walk around the mountaintops to get a few pictures—visited the chapel at the hospital, again (this time alone by myself), also the old well behind the hospital into which hundreds of bodies had been dropped—and where they remain to this day—untouched. Then, meandered over to the orphanage (sponsored by the German government) and visited with the kids who had never seen an old, white-haired, white man up close before! Had a good time with them, but also picked up a nice batch of lice!

Later, I took my camera and went for a walk around the mountaintops to get a few pictures—and visited the chapel at the hospital again.

"Near the entrance to the mission, the road is lined with trees in full bloom with beautiful, orchid-like, purple blossoms and birds singing pretty songs. The view of Lake Kivu is beautiful from there. Later, Samson tried to teach me how to say, Hello—'ma ra ho;' How are you—'amakuru;' and Fine—'meza.' Now I just have to see if people will understand me! Language is really a problem for me here with so few who speak English. Were I to remain here long, French language studies would certainly need to be a priority.

"I am told that the rainy season starts on September 1st—today is the 2nd; a few drops of rain fell earlier today. Now I am hearing thunder!

"Sunday, September 3. I spent the morning at the hospital making rounds and doing minor procedures. Most of the patients are doing OK.

Saw a little guy with a hernia that the mother wanted repaired. She was told she would have to work out a financial plan with the hospital first. She says she is a widow (her husband was killed in the genocide) and has no money and no way to obtain any. Unfortunately, that is the situation with most of the patients. What to do? This afternoon a man came in who had fallen from his roof while repairing the tiles. He broke his right wrist and sustained injuries to his chest, face and head. Fortunately, I don't think his head injury is serious. We set the wrist and placed a cast on it.

"Later, I went with Edison to a local village market—probably a kilometer from the hospital. It was a small village with a small market—only a few things such as potatoes, sweet potatoes, cassava, bananas, mangos, avocados, soy flour, fish and meat—all laying out in little piles on the ground and all very poor quality (except for one very large and beautiful bunch of bananas)! The people are very poor. Life is hard here!

"Last night we had a few sprinkles of rain. Tonight we had a real downpour. The people hope the dry season is over so they can plant their gardens. Things are very dry and the cattle are having difficulty finding forage. I spent some time tonight talking with my house-guard and scrub-nurse. They were full of questions, as was I—as I try to get a handle on understanding what has happened to this country and on this campus.

"Some days have been more interesting than others—and lighter or busier than others. During the busy times, I sometimes wonder what I have gotten myself into. In lighter times, I sometimes feel guilty for not working harder. It was during these times that I began, in earnest, to write a book on health that would help to meet the needs of places such as here in Africa where—if health care is available at all—it is often not affordable.

"During my private devotions this morning, I ran across a concept in the Bible that I believe is often misinterpreted. I have often been told that—since Jesus came to earth—the Law of Moses was eliminated. Since this is believed to be true and, since Jesus gave us a 'new commandment'—to love one another—the Christian world today has great trouble with the death decree, suggesting that our dispensation is different from ancient Israel's. As I was studying this, it became clear to me that Jesus did not do away with justice by his new commandment, and He was not outlining a new way for governments to render justice; He was only describing a better way for loving individuals to respond to people who harm them. Love still demands justice. Love may forgive and forego—which is a heart response. Great, but justice is also an important facet of love and necessary for the sake of a safe society.

"September 5 was a most interesting and challenging day. Several new patients arrived, including a man with probable tetanus (lockjaw); a baby born without an anus—or any way to empty the bowels—and a man with a hernia. We did a spinal tap on the man with the suspected lockjaw, fixed the hernia on the other man and advised a colostomy for the baby. The parents will decide. A baby with an abscess of the neck is not getting better—the drainage actually increasing. We placed a catheter into the abscess for purposes of irrigation. A lady with meningitis is not improving—in spite of doing everything we can for her. We have no other tests to run and no other meds to give. Fortunately, the lady with the leaking urine (vesico-vaginal fistula) is doing surprisingly well since her surgery. Last week's hernia patient is doing well and a skin graft we did is *taking* well.

"The man with the *lockjaw* remains problematic. It is not a typical presentation, but neither does his picture fit anything else. Therefore, we debrided a fistula he had at his anus (a possible source of the tetanus toxin) and are treating him with large doses of penicillin and valium as we would for tetanus.

"One evening, the president of the mission came by my house for a visit. He shared some of the history of the area and also expressed the difficulty the church has with its leadership having such a large area to cover, without any communication system and with few roads (and those in terrible condition). He also told how he had lost his cows, his only form of stable income. He expressed his concerns that salaries of church employees were not adequate and that—for his children to receive a decent education, one had to have another source of income to pay their way. I later learned that cows, not money, signal one's success in this area of the world. Often, as I walked to the hospital, the cattle of the workers would be grazing around the mission grounds. Unlike the cows of my childhood, these cows had long, curving horns that gave them a real aura of stateliness!

"Always seeking to understand the genocide, I arranged to spend a couple hours talking about it and present rehabilitation attempts with Dr. Edison. As already noted, he is Tutsi. He told me that Tutsis have maintained peaceful rule over these parts of Africa for centuries. Even within the church, Tutsis dominate.

"As far back as history goes, Rwanda has been governed by a Tutsi king. Tutsis—though a relative minority—were leader-type people. When the Belgians colonized Rwanda, they were never able to manage the king or work closely with him because of the power he had over the people. This all changed in 1949 when the king died of illness. The Belgians were urging democracy, and the Hutus—finally realizing their majority status—voted in a Hutu president. Conflict and intermittent killings that followed created an exodus of Tutsis—mostly to the Congo— but to other neighboring countries as well. The president had made certain promises when he came into office—promises and pledges he failed to keep. In the 1970s a new Hutu president was elected, largely through the influence of Tutsi refugees in Uganda. He had an agreement with them that—when he was established in power—he would help bring the refugees back home to Rwanda. He attempted to work on the infrastructure of the nation, putting in roads, power lines and phone lines, etc. He welcomed the return of Tutsi refugees—but only on an individual basis—not as a group. Some of these Tutsis were then given high and influential positions in government. Meanwhile, Tutsi refugees remaining in Uganda and surrounding countries organized into a *freedom movement* (RFM) and created an army of refugees in these countries. (Interestingly, the leader and a number of members in this Tutsi movement were Hutus!) Periodically, as the RFM armies invaded Rwanda, remaining family members living in Rwanda became the brunt of attack—killings continuing until hostilities were suspended. This continued until the 1990s when the RFM finally had enough clout to force the government of Rwanda to negotiate a settlement. Unfortunately, radical elements in the tribes of both the Tutsis and Hutus prevented formation of a peaceful return of the Tutsi refugees to Rwanda. Skirmishes continued until May of 1994, when the president was shot out of the sky at the airport in Kilgali upon his return from a peacemaking discussion. To this day, it is not known who shot him down. It seemed unlikely that the Tutsis, who were fighting far from Kilgali, were responsible. Some believe it may have been by Hutu radicals that feared he was making too many concessions in the peace process; or, perhaps, it was some other unrelated group. Whatever the situation, the country was immediately closed to travel and communication, with roadblocks everywhere and communication lines cut. Many people were killed during this time. Also, at this time—with the president dead—the RFM saw an opportunity to take the country back by storm. Within about six months, they had regained control. Meanwhile, about a million people had died.

"Tutsis are typically tall with narrow features. Hutus are shorter with broader faces. Pygmies, the third tribe in Rwanda, were less than

5 percent (and probably suffered the least). After 1996, the presidential regime required everyone to list his/her tribal origin on their personal identity card. Though an outsider cannot tell one tribal member from another (because of intermarriage, etc.), the people *know* one from the other (Hutus comprising about 70 percent and Tutsis about 20 percent of the population). The Hutus were not a totally united group. Some joined in fighting with the Tutsis, and some worked against the government independently. Whereas, prior to 1949, the tribes had lived for many centuries together without conflict of any kind, many now blame the recent problems on the Colonialists that governed them for so many years.

"Edison answered my question about the killings this way: 'Many people were intimidated by the Hutu authorities and leaders, etc. When told by them to get rid of certain undesirable people—or themselves be killed—many complied, taking the lives of entire families rather than die themselves. Some refused to kill as ordered. These were then accused of protecting the Tutsis and siding with the enemy; many of these were, then, also killed. Eventually, everyone lived in fear, not knowing who could be trusted—even of their own family members. To let live was to risk one's own life.

"This was the situation at the mission at Mugonero. People from all around had gathered at the hospital chapel, previously considered a safe place to run and hide from slaughter. Thousands had gathered there on the day that the president of the mission association rallied his supporters in the church and marched to the chapel for the massacre.

"Millions of Hutus fled into the Congo and to refugee camps in other lands where they were safe from revenge by the now-ruling Tutsis. As they fled, they took everything with them—ammunition, guns, vehicles, etc. With these they began formation of an army with the intent to invade Rwanda and take it back. The new ruling president heard of the movements and, by a surprise attack, captured the Hutus and returned them to Rwanda as captives. Here they were imprisoned and held captive awaiting trial. Now—because of the large numbers and the virtual impossibility of the court system to try them—many are being returned to their villages for a traditional trial by the village people.

"Present Rwandan leadership (with much international support and encouragement) is attempting to treat all with justice in an effort to reestablish stability; education, work opportunities, etc., are currently available to all. Calm seems to reign at the present time (four years later) with a fair amount of optimism for the future. Yet, it is not an altogether comfortable situation. Everyone knows that violence could flare at any moment. Only time and the grace of God may solve that. It is encouraging to witness the response of many Adventists in reaching out to others at this time. Many have confessed their part in the genocide and sought pardon. Many go to prisons and reach out to the prisoners, teaching them and baptizing them. The church is growing rapidly, though it does not yet approach the membership numbers present before the war and the flight of many to other lands.

"One wonders how Christians could respond in the way that happened here. There are no answers. Perhaps, however, this is a miniature example of the kind of human response that will emerge in the time of trouble occurring in the world just prior to the return of our Lord as so graphically described in the Holy Scriptures! I wonder how I would respond in a similar situation. Would I accept death to myself and family—rather than to kill a neighbor—if given that choice? Certainly none of us knows for sure—nor can we judge another. In fact, though I must confess that I would like to see justice done to the pastor and son that led the attack on the chapel at Mugonero, I cannot and will not judge his motive. What is more evident to me, is the fact that many of the true *saints* of Rwanda who did stand for right and refuse to hurt or destroy others, paid the ultimate price—and will receive the ultimate reward!

"But I must share just one more account that occurred in Rwanda during this time. As the angry mob entered the chapel, one of them approached a pastor and threatened to kill him unless he followed his orders. The pastor stood firm, and was chopped to death with ax and machete—his wife standing by and watching as his life-blood flowed away. And then it was her turn, but she survived the attack. In time, this lady recovered and began visiting the prisoners, taking them food and other necessities and sharing the Scriptures with them. One day, she recognized the young man who had chopped her husband to pieces and tried to kill her. Rather than retaliate—as she well might have done—this lady began to minister to him, bringing him food, clothing and other necessities. She told him she forgave him for the atrocities that he committed. Eventually, he softened and was released from prison. She took him home to live with her—and made him her son. I wonder—what would our world be like if everyone exhibited this kind of love!

"I cannot find any Biblical precedent akin to what has happened here, wherein fellow believers attacked one another—and yet could forgive and forget.

"I took a walk over to the new orphanage located on a mountaintop, perhaps a half-mile away from the hospital today. The kids haven't been transferred over yet. It is a nice facility. I walked back across the valley following the steep, mountain trails that the indigent people use. Each day I gain new respect for these people and the trials of their lives. Actually, there are probably few places on earth more ideal than here, except for the poverty element. It is beautiful here, and the weather is ideal year round; the food is basic, but nutritious, with all the essentials needed for a balanced diet grown right in their gardens. Beans are a staple; potatoes, sweet potatoes, cassava and bananas are all abundant. Many other fruits and vegetables are also available in season. There are some cattle and goats for milk and meat and a few chickens for eggs but, for the most part, it is a non-refined, plant-based diet. It is not even contaminated with a lot of oil, sugars or sodas as is the case in so many other poverty areas of the world. Of course, exercise is a way of life here; walking is the only means of getting around on the mountain trails, and there are few roads for cars. The air is hazy, but pure and filled with the scent of eucalyptus and pine. The song of birds is everywhere present. Tonight, the nearly-full moon is beautiful in its ascent in the eastern sky.

"As I sat watching the moon and contemplating the evil that exists in this old world—as so graphically experienced here—I wondered—Why? Why does God have to allow evil to exist? Why are pain and sorrow and trouble necessary? I know the answers in my heart; I know that it is consequential to selfishness and sin. I know that if we all lived by the laws of love (as expressed by the lady noted above), it would be a much different world. But why does sin control us? What is there about it that captivates every one of us—even when we can easily see where it leads? I may never understand the answers to these questions, but I must ask. Always, I am pointed back to the power and benefit of true Agape (Godly) love.

"It is planting time. This morning as I awakened, I could hear the sound of ground-breaking in every direction as heavy, steel hoes turned the earth in preparation for planting, now that the rains have begun. Just to get a little better *feel* for it, I went out into my back yard and got Gerard to let me take a *try* with the hoe he was swinging. It is not easy work. The hoe is made of heavy iron, much heavier than the one I use in my garden at home. One swings it high over the head and down into the ground in front with all the force he can muster. Then, lifting the handle, he lifts and turns the soil. It is effective—but hard work—especially on some of these steep mountain slopes which are even hard to stand on!

"I spent the evening sitting out on the hilltop waiting for the full moon to rise in the sky. From every direction I could hear kids laughing and playing and having a good time—something we don't often hear in the States anymore. But here there is no television or radio or things that keep the kids inside.

"The air is filled with the smell of smoke. A wildfire burns, out of control, on a distant mountain slope a few miles away—apparently, the result of unlawful burning. Last night, about this time, the earth was shaking from a mild earthquake. It wasn't long nor hard—and no damage—but scary, nonetheless, as almost all housing is made from sun-dried blocks of clay without reinforcement. A major quake would do serious damage.

"Yes, some days work has been light, but today it was time to work again. Several sick patients had to be admitted. One little girl transferred from elsewhere with malaria and dehydration; she is groggy, but I hope it is just from sedation. Another man was admitted with malaria, with a classical *black-water fever* presentation—dark urine, jaundiced skin, enlarged spleen and liver, and very weak. I also admitted a couple of cases of advanced tuberculosis.

"I met with a team from the International Criminal Tribunal this morning which is here to record pictures of the genocide. They will use these as evidence in the trial of the pastor next November or December when he goes on trial. They were questioning the survivors and photographing everything but, apparently, thought they needed my permission to do it. They expect to open the mass grave behind the hospital in a couple of weeks. No one around here says much, but it must be hard on those living here who have been through the whole terrible affair and lived to tell about it. I was told they have interviewed about 40 personal witnesses, and a few more secondary ones.

"A little girl died last night. No one called me to say she was having trouble. I don't know if it would have made any difference—with no labs, etc, but they should have called anyway. In the absence of medical staff through the years, the nursing staff has become very independent and often takes things into their own hands. Another little girl has a terrible osteomyelitis (bone infection) of the femur. The entire thighbone is involved and will certainly pose a challenge to treatment. We have started her on triple antibiotics. The man with the black-water fever is rallying well. Unfortunately, the lady for whom I had repaired the bladder injury and who had been doing so well, began leaking urine again the day I left. Naturally, both she and I were devastated by the turn of events. I had so hoped she would do well.

"Upon Dr. Aroujo's return, I took him on rounds at the hospital, introducing him to the patients and updating him on their progress. He, in turn, took some time to point out things I hadn't known about the mission and to share his dreams for the hospital. He has had many of the same challenges as I have experienced working with the nursing staff. They tend to do things their way, despite our directives. His wife, too, who is a nursing instructor, has similar problems. He told me that the hospital gets only $8,000 annually from the church. Everything else for capital improvements and operations must come from earnings or donations. As I have already noted, little of this comes from earnings since nearly everyone is penniless. Fortunately, he has friends back in Brazil who have been providing some support. Nevertheless, he has accomplished a lot during his short time here and has big dreams for the future.

"Before leaving, I left a book, *The Ministry of Healing*, with Mark who is my student nurse, translator and friend. With Isichar, the nurse practitioner who worked in the outpatient clinic, I left my copy of the *Merck Manual*. Dr. Edison has just been assigned to work with the district health department in the control of malaria. Gerard, my cook and housekeeper—who has kept my pitcher filled with fresh pineapple and mango juice—can now get back into his regular routine. The Aroujos expressed their gratitude for my help by presenting me with a locally-made woven basket to give to my wife, Avonne. It has been a very good experience, but I am now ready to let the people here take over again. They are very capable, spiritual people.

"Kilgali is now behind me. We will soon land in Nairobi, Kenya, before flying on to Brussels and then to the States. Nearly three weeks in Africa is over. I am grateful for the experience—but glad, too, to be on my way home. I think this trip has taught me that the world can get by without me! I have given my time as best as I know how, but there are others who are very capable. For this—I am grateful. God has been good to me. I have had many interesting experiences in my lifetime and many opportunities to help make a difference in the world. I have no regrets—and have many friends and acquaintances in Africa and in other places. I suspect there will be many greetings in heaven.

"Postscript: Mark sent me an e-mail a few months after my return home. He had seen the lady upon whom we had repaired the injured bladder and told me she had healed and was now dry and symptom-free. The disappointment that I experienced before leaving has turned out to be a miracle after all! Oh yes, and Mark, the same young man who befriended and helped me while serving at Mugonero, has now completed nurses' training and is serving as a nursing instructor in Africa. God is good!

Chapter XIV

Papua New Guinea

"We could imagine all sorts of terrible things happening in the darkness. But it did not! It was as though the angels of heaven had filled the stadium and maintained the peace."

For weeks I had been making plans to join Pastor Mark Finley, Speaker/Director of *It Is Written Television*, for a three-week series of religious meetings in Papua New Guinea (PNG). We had worked together in a number of other interesting places around the world, and I was pleased to be invited to join in this mission. Arrangements had been made to rent the soccer stadium in Port Moresby for about three weeks of daily meetings. Extensive promotion had been done throughout the country and neighboring island areas. We expected a large crowd. The meetings would be televised live, by satellite, around the world with downlink sites in the Pacific Rim nations and Africa. It promised to be a thrilling adventure. Historically, Adventist evangelism has combined the healing ministry, together with the preaching of the everlasting gospel. This was the example Jesus established for touching the world with his love and one we have often accepted as well. My role would be one of presenting a health lecture each evening, being available to see patients in consultation, and whatever else that needed to be done.

Unexpectedly, a few days before our scheduled departure, news hit the world press telling of riots in Port Moresby, our intended destination. This presented a major dilemma. Should we go? Should we stay home and wait for order to be restored? These seemed to be the obvious questions—but not really! We believed that the same God who called us to go could work everything out—in spite of a city-wide curfew! I met Pastor Mark and his wife, Ernestine Finley, at the airport in Los Angeles at the appointed time for the long flight to New Guinea. We had no idea what we would find when we arrived, but we were pretty much prepared for almost anything.

"It was mid-afternoon when we arrived at Port Moresby. Waiting for us on the tarmac were high government and church officials, who took our baggage-claim checks and hand-held bags and whisked us into the official reception area where we had a few minutes to exchange pleasantries and to get acquainted. Our paper-work complete, we were ushered, two by two, down a long corridor and outside, to a large contingent of young warriors, attired in full fighting-regalia—who rushed at us with bows bent and spears poised. Fortunately, it was merely a re-enactment of the reception the *white man* received when they first arrived in that land; then, it hadn't ended so harmlessly. This was followed by other ceremonies, a large marching band and a few speeches. Obviously, the people were glad we were there. About the time that the ceremonies were over, a call came from the Prime Minister to the officials accompanying us, informing us that the curfew would be lifted during the evening hours until 11:00 p.m. so that our meetings could begin, as planned, on Friday evening. Needless to say, we were gratified to know that God had been there ahead of us!

"While at the airport, I met a young PNG man who had just returned from Avondale Adventist College in Australia. His father had been deeply involved in occult practices—casting spells, pronouncing curses and every evil thing imaginable. I don't recall that he described exactly what had happened to him, but at the point when the young man hit rock-bottom and was ready to take his own life, he was rummaging through a dumpster when his eyes fell upon a copy of the little book, *Steps to Christ*—completely unspoiled by the trash and oil in the dumpster. As he read the book, his life was transformed and he gave his life to God. Not long afterward, his whole family joined him in his new life with the Lord. He was excited to be home for the meetings.

"Eventually, we arrived at our hotel. It was very comfortable; the grounds were well kept and the swimming pool most inviting. I was sure there would be time to jump in every once in a while! Once settled, we were clued in regarding the recent riots. They were apparently started at the college by students who were unhappy with the position the government seemed to be taking on globalization. I believe the immediate cause for the crisis had to do with changes in the way the national electric power was to be managed. Though I was never completely clear on the sequence of events, something happened when the students were gathered, in protest, that *spooked* the police—who then fired into the crowd and killed a couple of students. Following this, the students became very wild—overturning cars, setting fires, etc. Fortunately, it had been quiet for the past day or so before our arrival.

"Breakfast the next morning at the hotel was delicious and continued to be so during our entire stay there. Oatmeal was cold and uncooked and contained raisins and nuts. It was my first experience with cold oatmeal, but it was delicious. While there were many other things on the buffet, I could not resist the large slices of fresh papaya and pineapple, some of the best I had ever eaten.

"Following breakfast, Mark and I met with the local pastors at a nearby church. We made a few introductory remarks, after which we heard reports from the pastors describing their assessment of how things were shaping up for the meetings. One pastor told of a church leader (I believe Pentecostal) who was responsible for more than 100 churches, and who planned to come to the meetings along with all of his churches. Another told of a Catholic priest who was encouraging his people to come—telling them to listen and learn, but that he would be there waiting for them if they didn't like what they heard. We were told of numerous other ministers and congregations; Baptists and Lutherans, etc., who planned on coming to the meetings, and were saying, 'We believe the message is right!' People would be coming from all over the country—by chartered planes, buses, boats and on foot—from the highlands, coastal areas, and island provinces. For some, that meant many days of travel. (Note: Papua New Guinea is very mountainous. There are few roads connecting the various cities and provinces.)

"That afternoon, we met with Sir Silas Atapari, the Governor General of the nation. Upon our arrival, we were ushered—on a red beautiful carpet—into his palace. He, along with his wife, greeted each of us. When seated around a table of delicious food prepared for us, he told an amazing story of his appointment to this prestigious position that he has held for the past two+ years. (Though the position of Governor General is recommended by the National Parliament, the Queen of England must ratify the vote and make the appointment.)

"At one time he had been active in politics (I believe in Parliament), but was defeated in his campaign for another term in office. He returned to his home in the highlands, disappointed and troubled. Politics was his whole life. What was he to do now? He fretted and—in his trouble—he decided to pay a visit to an old Adventist pastor friend for prayer and encouragement. While visiting, the old pastor entered into a trance. Upon recovering, he told Mr. Atapari that he had seen an angel—in vision—who told him, 'Mr. Atapari will become the seventh Governor General, just 13 years from now!' (At the time they were being served by the third Governor General since independence—the normal term of office is six years.) Though the numbers did not add up, Mr. Atapari found encouragement by this experience and soon, again, became engaged in politics, preparing for the designated appointment 13 years hence.

"In the meantime, several Governor Generals died or, for other reasons, were only in office for a short time. Thus it was that 13 years later it was the sixth Governor General whose term was due to expire; the next would be the seventh. Just to make it more interesting, the current Governor General decided to run for a second term. A number of others also placed their names *in the hat* to run. On the final day of voting—the day a decision would be made—the presiding Governor General lost by two votes of Parliament, but Atapari's name was not even on the final list of four! It was noon; his colleagues were razzing him about his expectations to become the next Governor General. He said to them, 'Just wait and see! The day isn't over yet!' Subsequently, two more names were disqualified and by 5:00 p.m., he heard over the radio that he had been selected as Governor General. Sir Silas Atapari told us he takes his role very seriously and believes, without question, that he is there by appointment of God. One of the first things he did—upon entering the palace—was to take down the picture of the man behind his desk and replace it with a picture of Jesus.

"The palace is located on a beautiful hill overlooking an azure bay. It was built in 1913 to serve as headquarters of the Australians when they controlled the island nation.

"After spending a little time working on my lecture for the evening, I joined others of the team for a visit to the stadium where the meetings were to be held. It was, then, that I learned of the sad state of affairs at the stadium. It was in need of all new seats, but the government had no budget with which to buy them. Not to be discouraged, the local churches raised K90,000 (kina) ($30,000 U.S.) to repair the seats and clean the offices, etc.—a major commitment to say the least!

"People began to gather early in the evening, and choirs began singing about 5:00 p.m. We were to go—*live*—on worldwide television at 7:30 p.m. but, long before that, the bleachers and most of the infield were filled (estimated to total around 80,000). On subsequent days, the choirs began singing about 3:00 p.m.—one after the other for the rest of the afternoon until meeting time. Choirs came from all over the nation and from many islands. I found their music—mostly a cappella—most delightful to my ear.

"At about 6:45 p.m., the Prime Minister and his wife and entourage arrived. They were entertained by envoys from all of the provinces, dressed in their native provincial dress—very interesting! The choir sang and the program began on time at 7:30 p.m. There were brief introductions, introductory remarks by Pastor Finley and a short speech by the Prime Minister. (He looked harried and tired—obviously still very concerned about the incident and killings of students the week before.) After his speech, he was expected to leave, but he sat down and stayed throughout the meeting to the end. Mark had a private prayer with them before they left. They were obviously very touched.

"According to custom we, again, were all decked out with beautiful leis of orchids and plumeria. During the meeting, the crowd was quiet and attentive; more so than other places I have been with much smaller crowds. There were some problems with the speaker system but, otherwise, things went well for the first night—this in spite of a problem that arose earlier in the evening with the technical staff. It seems that the local church had arranged for camera operators, as had the people from Australia who were in charge of the technical aspects of the broadcast. No one had anticipated the problem, but it did manage to generate a bit of hot debate. Thanks to the wise, cool head of Royce Williams of *It Is Written television*—and the blessing of God—the issue was resolved peaceably. Rainclouds threatened, but no rain. I observed that God's agents had been busy that day. Mark's sermon was about '*hope for the future*'; there was a very good response. My talks would begin the next night.

We were to go—live—on worldwide television at 7:30 p.m. but, long before that, the bleachers and most of the infield were filled (estimated to total around 80,000).

"Each evening the crowds increased, packing the stadium beyond capacity. Things were going well until—following my lecture on the third night (I believe)—we experienced a power failure. The entire city *suddenly* went totally black. Fortunately, we had a small generator that supplied the uplink equipment. We were off the air for about 15 minutes but soon had lights and microphones on stage and were able to continue with the program—though the stadium and city remained dark. Following Pastor Finley's sermon, we still had no power and no idea when we would, but then received word from authorities instructing us to hold the people in the stadium until power was restored. What to do! So, we asked the audience! They asked for another sermon! Choirs sang while Pastor Finley prepared. In no time at all, he had his illustrations in order and began to preach his second sermon. When that was finished, they asked for another. About that time, we received word that power was not going to be restored that night, and we were given permission to let the people go home. They left as quietly and as orderly as they had come. You may be sure there were many prayers ascending heavenward during that time! We were all too aware of the fact that—only about a week earlier—there had been major riots in this city. The people who packed the stadium had come from all over the country; many were only a generation away from headhunting and savagery. We could imagine all sorts of terrible things happening in the darkness. But—it did not! It was as though the angels of heaven had filled the stadium and maintained the peace. No one could deny that a miracle had taken place that night.

"It was interesting to read the comments in the daily paper in the early days of our meetings. Most were very positive. On one occasion, however, a letter from a priest was published in which he faulted Pastor Finley for preaching that the return of Jesus will be a literal event. On another occasion, it was noted that—since the meetings had begun—the incidence of crime in the city was *way down*—apparently in response to the messages Mark was delivering. Though—not in the paper we also heard about this time, of a Lutheran physician working in the highlands. He purchased a downlink dish and had 4,000 people watching the proceedings each evening in their local village far from Port Moresby.

"One day we were invited to visit a village on the coast about 12 miles from Port Moresby. In past times, the whole village had been built on stilts out on the coral reef—quite some distance from land. When we were there, it was still on stilts—but close to land with boardwalks connected to shore. Of course, the sea below them also served as their sewer and primary source of food—as well as their protection from enemies. We were told that these people had never been headhunters or cannibals, though they did enter manhood by killing another man. (Cannibalism apparently ended in the highlands in the 1960s. So, too, did the practice of eating the dead—including dead relatives—a practice causing the disease Kuru, similar to what we know now as *mad cow* disease.) This was the village to which the first Adventist missionary came in 1908 and, from here, missionaries went out to the rest of the country.

"After a brief tour of the village—a rather scary tour on a boardwalk high above the water that had many loose and missing boards—we were entertained with another re-enactment by young people of their battles to keep the white man off their land. After the usual speeches and marches, we were led to a special feast prepared for the occasion. It consisted of yams, sweet potatoes (kau kau), salads, papaya, bananas and sego—a gelatinous glob (cookie) made of the juice of the sago palm tree. For drinks, we were given fresh, sweet, coconut juice—straight from the coconut.

"I couldn't help but notice striking differences between the villagers—too obvious to miss. The entire village had come out to meet us, and all took part in the ceremonies. Those who were entertaining us were well-kept, clean, looked healthy and appeared happy—in contrast to the others who looked depressed, sickly and somewhat less than enthusiastic about life. The scene that day convinced me, as never before, the value of the gospel in transforming people when accompanied with simple changes in lifestyle such as we were teaching and sharing. Never again, would I accept the accusation that the gospel hurts primitive people more than it helps them—as claimed by some sociologists and others.

"Later that day we were taken to the Adventist College of the Pacific. The campus was beautiful. I was attracted to a pond on the campus filled with exotic water lilies and other wildlife. The college also maintains very large, irrigated gardens where fresh produce for marketing is grown. We were told that the gardens had shown a profit of $100,000 U.S. the previous year—which was a source of profitable employment for the students and support for the college. (All of the three to four hundred students are required to work as part of their education.)

"While there, I met a man from the Solomon Islands who was a grandson (I believe) of the man who trained and organized the *fuzzy wuzzies* (so named because of their *Afro* hairdo's, I presume) of World War II fame, both on the islands and in Papua New Guinea. I remembered that—as a child in Sabbath School—I had heard stories of the *fuzzy wuzzies* and, probably, even given offerings to support their work—more about them later.

"My talks were going well each night. I tried to teach the people what they could do to improve their health and lot in life by simple lifestyle changes. We estimated that we were speaking to about a million people each night in Papua New Guinea, alone, in the stadium and via TV—(not to mention other places around the world) most of whom are underprivileged—so I tried to direct my thoughts toward them, as I felt they were being well received and appreciated by them.

"One day, I had opportunity to visit a clinic staffed by a Korean Christian missionary doctor. He was seeing 30 to 40 patients daily. They would arrive about 7:00 a.m., and some would have to wait all day to be cared for. It reminded me of my experience on Guam many years earlier. This man was working in very primitive conditions; he had almost no diagnostic studies available and only a limited supply of medications. The government supplied immunizations and family-planning supplies. Some lab tests were sent out, but it took a week to get the result of a simple blood count and a month to get the results of HIV tests and diabetes checks, etc. Serious illnesses were referred to the government hospital but, even there, things are primitive. I was told there was only one CT scanner in the country, and that was owned by private individuals and available only to the wealthy few. The same was true for mammograms. He had no medications for treating AIDS, but did have some medications to treat those patients and families with tuberculosis. The only medications available for treating malaria were Chloroquin and Quinine, things that are often not effective against the falciparum variant of malaria prevalent there. I admired the dedication of this man; I would have had real difficulty working under the same conditions!

"On another occasion, Dr. George Gand, a surgeon, invited me to go on rounds with him at the government hospital. It was an educational experience that gave me a different picture of the needs of the people. He was well trained and had learned to do good work with little to work with. Many of the patients are from the highlands. Communication becomes a real problem with some, since there are more than 80 dialects spoken in the country. (Of course, that posed a problem for our meetings, too. To try to meet this need, we had translators working in a number of the major dialects.)

"It is always difficult to know how best to make a difference in the lives of one's listeners. Some people are well-educated; others are very primitive. The night that I spoke on addictions and offered suggestions regarding how to deal with them, I asked for people to stand and make a commitment. I was not certain whether they responded or not. It was nearly impossible to see the audience because of the television lights in my face, but I had a sense that not much was happening. I was a bit frustrated by the apparent lack of response but, at least, I had tried. I have discovered by past experience that, sometimes, when one feels like the biggest failure it is the very time that the greatest impact is made. Whether this was true here or not, I do not know but, afterward, a young man approached me expressing his gratitude for the presentation.

"That same evening, a man spoke to me about his success with treating HIV/AIDS. He was an executive working with a local industry. He told me that when he gets off from work at about 2:00 p.m. he spends the remainder of each day caring for people with AIDS, using natural therapies. He prepares a diet composed of natural, unrefined plant foods and administers herbal medications, as well as overseeing their general care and activities. He claimed he was seeing his patients cured of AIDS. He was, obviously, very dedicated to the task and shared many insights about AIDS and the spread of it among the people of Papua New Guinea. What I was uncertain about was whether or not he had actually confirmed the presence of AIDS in his patients. In any event, he was, very obviously, seeing some fantastic results in some very sick people.

"I mentioned that our program was being broadcast, internationally, to downlinks all around the world. One day we received an e-mail from the Philippines, at a site where a volcano was erupting and spewing ash. It had been raining the night before; yet people sat out in the open until the end of the program with wet, volcanic ash falling down upon them—just a small indication of how seriously some people around this world are seeking for truth and meaning in life.

"One night I was awakened by a dream about 3:30 or 4:00 a.m. (I am not one to have—or to remember—meaningful dreams, as a rule.) In my dream I was walking to my duties with someone else who was walking—in the same direction—with his family. It seemed he was questioning the propriety of the message that Pastor Finley had given the night before. My response to him was: 'It is the right message and the right time for it and, by nature, it was bound to bring a mixed response from the listeners.' This seemed to satisfy him, and he and his family went on their way with renewed courage and determination, trusting in the Lord.

"Uncertain of the significance of the dream, I knelt beside my bed to pray for a moment and then returned to bed. But I could not go back to sleep. I tossed and turned until, finally, I knew I must get up, pick up the Bible and read. I didn't know where to start reading, but my eyes landed upon the last verse of Jeremiah, chapter 50. I read, 'When Babylon falls, there will be such a noise that the entire earth will shake, and the cries of alarm will be heard among the nations.' As I went back to read the chapter from the beginning to get the context, I noted that this entire chapter is a prophecy telling, in advance, what was going to happen to Israel as captives in Babylon, and to the ancient Babylonian empire 70 years in the future—before it fell to the Medes and Persians. It also predicted the restoration of Israel to the Promised Land.

"Continuing on into chapter 51, I discovered that the wording here was very much like that found in the Book of Revelation (especially the 18th chapter) describing last-day events just prior to the return of Jesus. In Revelation, the Apostle John describes a vision of an angel lighting the whole world with the glory of God, pleading with the inhabitants of planet earth to 'Come out of Babylon' and avoid her imminent fate. From early childhood, I have believed that these texts (and many similar ones) were symbolically describing God's work of separating His true followers from the evil that exists in the world—all in preparation for His return. Furthermore, I have believed that the angel symbolized is my church that has been specifically raised up—as a movement within Christianity—to call all people to faithfulness to God and the to principles of His government—for it is my conviction that God has His followers in all faith groups, and even among those who have no ties to a religious group. In witnessing the coming of people of all faiths to the meetings each evening, and seeing them drink in the truths from the Bible that Pastor Finley was offering them, sent shivers up and down my spine—realizing that here in Papua New Guinea, something was beginning that I had long believed would happen around the globe. His message the night before had been a call for all men everywhere to join the 'true ecumenical movement,' founded wholly on the truths of the Holy Bible. He noted how the principles of the *Constitution of Love* (the Ten Commandments) that governs God and His kingdom, have been forgotten, ignored, or outright denied by the peoples of the world—even including much of the Christian world.

"It was raining when he gave that message. More than a hundred thousand people had been sitting quietly and peacefully for hours in the rain—while getting soaked to the skin! He called for those of all faiths who were attending to take their stand for the law of God that alone—through the power of the Cross—gives true liberty and frees one from the power and consequences of sin. He noted how the Sabbath—described at the very center of God's law—serves to unite us with God and, through Him, to one another in true, self-renouncing love. He then invited them to come back the next night when he would tell his own conversion story and his search of the Scriptures to find the things he was now sharing.

"I knew that it had been a difficult message for him to give. Later, back in the hotel—as I encouraged him—his response to me was, 'It had to be said—or what are we here for?'

"I had read those chapters in Jeremiah many times before and had, indeed, underlined portions of them, but that morning they stood out like never before. 'Babylon is being taken.' Men are advised to 'flee.' The whole chapter seemed to fit perfectly into our times and mesh with the Revelation message. Over time I had tended to become blasé in regards to the seriousness of our times—knowing that we are living during the end-time judgment, but tending to live as though things will continue on as they always have. That morning I was given a new sense of urgency, convinced that the world will, indeed, be lightened by the glory of God—that the entire world will hear and will know, including all nations, kindreds and peoples—and, yes, that Babylon will, indeed, also meet her fate. And where better to proclaim it from than from Papua, New Guinea. I knew that we were not there by accident; that the vision of the angel to Silas Atapari 15 years earlier had not been an accident, and that the coming together of peoples of all faiths into a unity of faith based upon the Bible and the Bible alone, was the beginning of something great in the plan of God.

"On another day, we had occasion to do some sightseeing along the way to our destination for the day, the Kokoda trail. It was an interesting day. We traveled along the mountainside, with sheer drops to the river below. We stopped to view a waterfall along the way. While admiring the sight, a bus drove up filled with people from the islands. They had come to sing at the meetings. Some of them were descendants of the *fuzzy wuzzies.* While we enjoyed the view, they entertained us by singing songs of faith and hope—as only the islanders of those parts of the world can do. What's more, they followed us along the way that day, and sang for us at nearly every stop! They told us their story. When missionaries first went to their island, they met them with spears and arrows—prepared to kill. The missionaries had only one defense—their faith in God—so they began to sing hymns. Just then a miracle occurred with the islanders, who then invited them to their island home. Those who were singing to us there along the trail, now attribute their musical interests back to those missionaries.

"We were traveling along the Owens Stanley mountain range, a treacherous range that, even today, still isolates most of the villages and cities from one another, making them accessible to one another only by plane, by boat or on foot. We stopped at the grave site of the first Adventist missionary to the country in 1908. He had come from Fiji, worked faithfully and died there six years later—an apparent failure—having never seen a convert to the faith. That did not occur until 20 years later. A Christian school now educates children on that property. Eventually, we arrived at the beginning of the Kokoda trail, a jungle path through the peaks and valleys across the mountain range, to the village of Pompedetta on the northern coast.

"During the month of May, 1942, the Japanese began a march from Pompedetta, along this trail, toward Port Moresby—with plans to use Papua New Guinea as the *jumping off po*int to capture Australia. They were met on the trail by Australians. Many, many casualties occurred on both sides. The *fuzzy wuzzies* rescued the injured and served as transporters for the goods of the Australians. In time, the Japanese were defeated along this trail, and their attempt to reach Australia via Papua New Guinea was blocked—a victory for the allied forces—often credited, largely, to the dedication of the *fuzzy wuzzies*. One month later, the Japanese wreaked havoc with the American military at Midway but—had the capture of Australia succeeded—the war might well have ended much differently.

"While in the area, we met a group of about 20 people from Pompedetta who had been attending the meetings and were on their way back home along the trail. They and others had been walking that trail to and from the meetings. They told us it would take three days and two nights of hard travel, picking up what food they could find in the jungle—ever watchful for dangers along the way. There are no rest-stops, no hotels, stores—nothing! Survival is for the fittest only. Out of curiosity, a few of us started down the trail (a few hundred feet!). There I saw my first rubber plantation—acres of rubber trees—all tapped and collecting latex. Most interesting!

"Before returning to our hotel, we stopped at a national park—hoping to see some wild wallabies. Our trek through the jungle trail was most interesting, but no wallabies. One of the things we did see was a cassowary's nest. The cassowary is a very pretty and colorful bird, a little smaller than an ostrich; it is also unable to fly. Unlike the proverbial ostrich that leaves its eggs in the sand, these birds build a great nest—many feet in diameter and several feet thick—made of organic material from the jungle. There they lay their eggs. And, yes, the local people rob the nests and eat the large eggs.

"On one occasion, Ambassador Tijano, the Philippine Ambassador to Papua New Guinea, invited us to his home for dinner. It was a delightful occasion with nothing but the best Filipino food. He was most helpful in arranging for our meetings in Papua New Guinea and, subsequently, for getting *3ABN Television* on the air there.

"That night, after the meeting, we were stopped on our way back to the hotel by the police, telling us of a bomb threat there. After an hour or so—upon completion of the search by the bomb squad—we were permitted to return. We learned then that—just the day before—a similar threat had been made on the Parliament building and on a bank. Fortunately, nothing turned up at either of these places.

"Pastor Finley spoke about the Sabbath and the change of the Sabbath for the past couple of nights; I thought he handled the topic very sensitively and with compassion. Subsequently, on the radio one morning there was an announcement calling for all Catholic clergy to meet—presumably to determine how to respond to pastor Finley's remarks. I did not hear the outcome of that meeting and heard no repercussions regarding it. In the meantime, entire Sunday-keeping churches were convicted and began worshipping on the Biblical Sabbath. I wondered if I had been right in my assumptions—that a spark had been ignited that would spread around the world! Looking at the signs of the times, it seemed that it must be time.

"Toward the end of the meetings, Pastor Mark Finley spoke on baptism and made a call for those who wanted to experience it. Thousands stood and came to the alter. As noted earlier, this was a sight I had dreamed of seeing—when people of all faiths would accept the Bible truths for this day—without reservation.

"Meanwhile, the crowd at the meetings continued to expand every night. By the grace of God, we were provided with excellent crowd control, and there were no major incidents. Some estimated there were more than 150,000 in attendance. I don't know about the numbers, but I do know there were a lot of people coming regularly. Many took their stand for the Bible truths that were presented.

"Sabbath morning on July 21, 2001, a beautiful day dawned in Papua New Guinea. We arrived at the beach at 7:00 a.m. for the baptism. Crowds were already packing the grounds around the beach, reflecting the great excitement for the coming events. It was an experience I will never forget. We read in the Bible, in the Book of Acts, how thrilled the disciples were when 3,000 were baptized in one day, and—on this Sabbath—we were to see a repeat of that experience as more than 3,000 walked down into the waters to die to their old lives and be buried in the waters of baptism,

We arrived at the beach at 7:00 a.m. for the baptism. Crowds were already packing the grounds around the beach, reflecting the great excitement for the coming events.

and to arise to newness of life in Christ Jesus. As I watched, I thought how interesting it would be to know each of their stories, to hear where they had come from spiritually, and to hear their experience of joy on this occasion. They had come from all over the land and sea, from all types of villages and towns, and from all types of experiences. It was with mixed emotions that I considered what was happening. All my life, I had believed this must happen one day—and now, as it was beginning to happen, my heart went out to those who—for whatever reason—remained in their former churches. In some instances, I knew that whole congregations would be joining the Advent Movement; while in others, many of their members—including some leaders—would no longer be worshipping with them. And I wondered what would happen to them. Are there still honest Christians among those left behind—those who have not seen their way to take this step into a new life? I knew the answer must be 'yes,' but how will they be affected by these events? And how will the new converts be integrated into the present Adventist churches that are already crowded? What impact will this experience have on the rest of the world to awaken and gather the faithful?

"The Bible is clear that all those who are faithful to the Lord will face persecution. Was the bomb threat preparation for that? Will Mark Finley and his staff be safe as they go on from here to Lei and Goroka—and beyond—when leaving the relative safety of the capital city here? For me, this had been an experience I will never forget—but also one reminding me that I am no longer able to meet the expectations and needs of this type of evangelism. Though of good health—and I have tolerated the trip very well—it is time to involve younger, more energetic blood. God has blessed my life immensely, and permitted me to have a part in helping to initiate the world-wide media ministry of the church and laity. I have been most honored. Perhaps it is now time to pass the torch.

"The people of Papua New Guinea are very nice and very friendly; I enjoyed my time and association with them. One wonders how the history of the past could have been so violent with headhunting and cannibalism—or, perhaps, my picture is skewed. They are a timid people. Perhaps much of the past may be linked to this—it being their way of defense when lacking the knowledge of a loving God."

Flight connections required a night in Sydney, Australia, on my way home. That night I recorded the following impressions: "It's been an interesting few weeks. In some ways I feel like Simeon must have felt when he saw the baby Jesus brought to the temple for dedication on his eighth day of life, knowing that now his dreams had been fulfilled and he could rest in peace. I don't know what the Lord has yet in store for me, nor does it matter, for now I know He will soon finish his work in righteousness—with or without me. I have been so privileged, throughout my life, to have had a part in the final events of planet earth. I could ask for nothing more. My life remains in His hands at His command—but I no longer fret about the completion of judgment, for I have seen the Spirit of God working and realize it will soon be complete."

The challenges in Papua New Guinea are many, but God has done a great work there. It is a beautiful land with many beautiful people. Heaven will reveal many, many interesting life stories from that land.

While high above the Pacific—still about three hours out from Los Angeles—I made the following notes: " I have just finished reading a book describing the events of the life and explorations of Michael Leahy as he prospected for gold in the PNG (Papua New Guinea) highlands during the early 1930's—about the time I was born. At that time, the highlands of PNG were mostly unexplored and uncivilized. Tribal war and cannibalism were rampant among many tribes. In fact, I still recall our Sabbath School mission stories, from there, with appeals for offerings.

"According to his writing, Michael Leahy was not much of a believer in the work of missionaries. He wrote that he expected it to take many generations for the country to become civilized, and he questioned whether the changes that were occurring among the people were really better than what they already had. As I finished reading the book I, too, wondered if what we had gone to do was of real benefit. Was it to their benefit to hear three weeks of sermons which included passionate calls for surrender to Jesus and acceptance of the Sabbath, baptism by emersion and membership into the Adventist Movement? And, though I was giving medical talks, it was all part of the overall objective of giving them a whole new way of life; but the temptation was there to suggest that, perhaps, we ought to have left well enough alone!

"As I considered this issue, I knew the temptation was wrong and that what I was a little part of, was not only beneficial—but essential. This world is sick and hurting from the consequences of the evil that exists down here. Yet, all indications in the Holy Bible, in the beauties we see in nature, and in providence, are that God is a God of love. The troubles of this world are inconsistent with such love as exhibited when Jesus gave up his life for us on the Cross. And, as I considered the issue, I became reassured of my conviction—indeed now more than ever—that, yes, even if our work in Papua New Guinea were to cause major disruption of that society by igniting fires of religious conflict, it was necessary for the totality of the purpose of God and the completion of the work Jesus began when he came to earth to save us. On a practical level, this is the way I see it: Though this is primarily a Christian nation, and though it is now relatively calm and tolerant, there are many very dear followers of Jesus scattered throughout the land who have not had the privilege of knowing Him as I have. They do not understand the beauty of Jesus as revealed by the law—including the Sabbath—or of God's patience and unwillingness for any to be lost. I would be amiss should I neglect to share with them these values that have been such a blessing to me, once opportunity was afforded.

"And even more practical, from my perspective, was the benefit that I could give the nation by instructing them regarding those things that are disabling and killing so many of them. I refer to communicable disease, AIDS, diabetes, heart disease and cancer—to name some of the more prevalent ones. Though they have had some instruction regarding these things, the instructions have often come from those perceived as having ulterior motives. I had the advantage because I was seen as being on *their side* and not as some intrusive power imposing restrictions (globalization to them). As such, it seemed that my simple recommendations were able to make an impact across the nation that political powers could not. In addition, maybe I was able to influence some of the present influential leadership, as well as those of the future. So, from all perspectives—though in the opinion of some, perhaps *too religious*—I suspect the nation and the world will now be a little better place. Indeed, as I look at the world around me and realize how sick it really is with violence, anarchy and breakup of the family as the basic structural unit of society, etc., they all suggest to me that Jesus is the only answer to our present world conditions. Biblical principles still make sense when accepted and applied, and they are still able to change hearts and lives.

"When all is said and done, I must conclude that it is not the everlasting gospel nor the information about healthful living that destroys primitive societies, but the distortions of truth that, so often, accompany the preaching of it. Human nature is basically the same among primitive societies as among the more *developed*. We are all born into sin; it is inherent in each of us. All tend to gravitate to the subtle appeals of Satan that satisfy the lusts of the *flesh* (human nature) and that seem to preempt the benefits of the gospel.

"I have given a bit of myself by this experience in Papua New Guinea, but my rewards far exceed anything I have spent by being here. God is so good!"

Chapter XV

India

"... as she left, she said she had come for physical healing, and though disappointed, was thrilled that her heart had been healed!"

In many of my travels abroad, I have been confronted with the question, "Why?" Why leave the comfort and routine of home to travel to the far ends of the earth? Why neglect family, friends, ministries and all of the responsibilities of home to go to a strange place. Why put up with loss of sleep, irregular meals, and unfamiliar and often—less than healthful—foods? Why risk illness, injury and violence?

Long flights between continents provide ample opportunity for reflection and the recording of one's thoughts. The following are some of mine:

"Some do what I am doing to be successful in business or the arts, or for influence to gain a place and a name in the world, or to mingle with the *in* crowd and to enjoy the 'good' life. To my way of thinking, this is a high price to pay for *success.*

"Is my purpose any more worthy? When asked by Danny to join in a joint venture with *Three Angels Broadcasting Network (3ABN)* and Adventist Services and Industries (ASI) to do evangelism in a predominantly Hindu world, I responded positively—without hesitation. I pose the question (to myself) because it is current thinking in our global community that we all worship the same God, though with different names and different practices. I pose the question, too, because it so often seems that—for all of our best efforts to lead people to Christ—so few really make significant and lasting changes in their lives. Have we, therefore, really done any good for our efforts? And, I pose the question because some argue that God is able to communicate with all men directly and that every man is convicted of right and wrong by the Holy Spirit; therefore, why the need to do what God can do as well—or perhaps better—without me. Furthermore, with modern communication technology, we can reach the far corners of earth with electronic media and enter places unreachable by person. Is it merely for my own benefit, therefore, that I accept such missions and travel to such places?

"Yes, there is much personal benefit. For all of the *cost* of travel with its challenges and unknowns and risks, I always return a wiser, more blessed person. A change is always wrought. This is a personal benefit. And, yes, though Jesus' parable of the sower is true and though much of the seed sown fails to land in good soil and to mature to yield grain—some does! And the world is better for it. The Bible tells of a better world after the sin problem is resolved, but I cannot begin to comprehend such an eternal place. Be that as it may—even if heaven didn't exist—the principles of the gospel—when fulfilled in the life—make even this life much better for those who choose to walk this way. I am reminded of a testimony given by a former Hindu lady in my Sabbath School class, as she reflected upon all of the benefits she has experienced since she accepted Christ as her Savior from the slavery of this world. She could hardly contain herself as she recounted her experience. So, yes, even if there were no better world beyond, there may be—for some at least—a better world even now. And as far as the argument that we all worship the same God, I can only argue that we really don't! There are two primary gods and, ultimately, we all worship one or the other—the God who governs by love; or the god who governs by self-centeredness and deceit. Careful observation quickly confirms that one God gives us length of life and meaning and happiness and peace; the other gives us fun that ends in frustration, excitement that ends in disappointment, thrills that kill and anticipation that never quite materializes—enslaved in a mode of ever-striving, ever-searching, but never arriving!

"So, yes, I do have something good to share! And, yes, I am blessed the more for sharing—but not I alone! Others, too, may be freed from the shackles of evil. And, yes, God does speak to all men but requests human input to accomplish many of his objectives. The gospel commission is not a sham. We are honored and privileged to do real things that make a real difference in this world and in the world to come. And, yes, if only one person were to be freed from the slavery of sin by my life—one who may have otherwise remained shackled—it is reward enough. And, furthermore, the signs of the times all foretell imminent global disaster. Our little global community is agitated and about ready to explode and self-destruct if it is not rescued from outer space. And since that rescue from outer space is actually the God who—in love—created, redeemed and involves me in His thing, isn't that a neat honor to share with all who will listen? I paraphrase the Apostle Paul, 'How shall they hear except someone be sent?'

"After an hour in the terminal at Taipei, we were back in the air to Singapore where we had a nine hour layover. Thanks to the generosity of the airlines and the Singapore Tourist Bureau, we were given a free tour of the island nation. It was a good tour and gave us a quick view of that very modern, financial city with the largest seaport in the world (volume-wise). It is also a very pretty island about the size of Guam. Our tour guide made an interesting statement about housing; she indicated that housing is owned by the government and may be bought and owned on a 100-year lease arrangement. This, she noted, was a marked improvement over former times. I wondered how those former times could have been worse than those rows and rows of high-rises all crowded together!

"January 6 After a short night in Chennai, India, we loaded our supplies into taxis and were on our way to Ongole, eight hours away over narrow, poorly-repaired roads shared with bicycles, rickshaws, pedi-cabs, trucks, cows and monkeys all fighting for the same space. Rice fields, sugarcane, fruit trees, and lakes and ponds were interspersed between the many, small villages. Along the way we stopped for directions. A heavy truck, loaded with logs, stopped close by. I noted that—before the truck left—a man placed a little green lemon under each wheel. To my query, I was told this was an offering to the gods for a safe and successful trip!

Time and arrangements were not conducive to keeping a daily log of our activities. What follows is my best attempt to splice together the few notes I was able to keep—with other highlights of our experience as recorded on my way home.

"This mission was a joint effort by ASI (Adventist-laymen's Services and Industries); Three Angels Broadcasting Network (3ABN); Maranatha, (a lay organization composed of volunteers who build churches and schools around the world); the Church of South India, and the North Pacific Union of Seventh-day Adventists. It was all sponsored by Garwin McNeilus, a businessman from Minnesota. Our mission was to the city of Ongole and the surrounding villages within about a 50-kilometer range. Our home for the duration was a two-story house that had recently been redecorated and cleaned. An iron fence surrounded the property. An open sewer ran along the near side of the street in front of the gate, and immediately across the unpaved street, was the local garbage dump!

"I am intrigued by the environment. Everything competes for space on the streets. Cows watch out for no one and sleep in the median at night, with traffic rushing by on both sides. Dogs, cows, pigs and chickens forage side by side at the garbage sites. By the time they are finished, there's not much left except a little plastic and metal. This is the first time I have ever seen cows eat cardboard boxes and seem to relish them!

"Ed and Marcy had been brought from their work at an orphanage in northern India, near the headwaters of the Ganges River, to serve as our cooks and housekeepers. They were well-versed in cooking Indian food—so that we *weak-stomached* Americans would not get sick! The team from Maranatha stayed in a hotel a short distance away. They had been in India for some time and were conditioned to the living conditions.

"A large canopy had been put up on the expansive campus of a Baptist college, a kilometer or two away, and two very large video screens had been erected for use with the lectures and illustrations.

"For three months prior to this, 50 volunteers (Global Pioneers) who had been trained at a center in Vijayawada, had lived and worked and studied with the people in 50 of the surrounding villages that had requested their presence. Our job was to team up with the local pastor assigned to those villages and visit the people, check their readiness for—and to extend to them—the rite of baptism. They were then brought in by trucks and buses to the evening meetings—scheduled to start at 8:00 p.m. Some traveled more than two hours each way, crowded together on heavy, flatbed trucks or buses. They then returned home very late at night, worked the next day and repeated the process all over again the following night. Many of the people are laborers working for the equivalent of about one U.S. dollar, daily, on huge farms owned by large corporations or landowners. One dollar doesn't allow for much more than a little food on the table.

"This part of India has had Christian influence for many years, and forty to fifty percent of the population are professed Christians. Many of the villages are primarily Hindu and, of course, most all (Hindu and Christian alike) are of the lower caste. Most of the connections between the Christians and their mother church—in both the villages and the city—had been lost long ago leaving them to operate pretty much independently—with little direction—and without church or worship centers.

"Our plan was to establish a congregation and to build a church in every village, where the village elders were receptive. Churches were to be constructed by Maranatha volunteers and hired local workers, according to a common plan, and were made of cement and brick. The churches would serve as the worship and community center for each village. Garwin, the sponsor and primary force behind the project, was in charge of the entire campaign.

"Global Pioneers all agreed to stay a minimum of five years to nourish and develop the congregation until the church leadership would be able to place permanent pastors. From these 50 villages, the villagers would go to neighboring villages and extend the outreach; indeed, that was already occurring while we were there.

"Ongole is an interesting, crowded city with, I am told, a population of about four million. Soon after arriving, we were taken to the site of the scheduled meetings—a large field on the campus of a Baptist college which had been hurting, due to lack of attention by its developers and supporters in the west. What we saw was complete desolation. A cyclone had come through about 3:00 a.m. that morning and dumped a *great* amount of rainwater on the recently-completed outdoor facility. Everything was flattened—including the two video screens. It was already about 3:00 p.m. when we arrived, and the meetings were scheduled to begin that evening with buses bringing people from more than 50 villages—some from many miles away. It was too late to cancel. Fortunately, workers had been busy all day on a temporary replacement, and by the time I got up to give my first health talk, everything was in order and functioning—that, itself, is somewhat of a miracle!

"Buses started arriving early and continued coming until the meeting was over about 10:00 p.m.—we estimated four to five thousand in attendance. Because some buses got to the villages late, those people never got to see or hear anything that had transpired. Following the meeting, the people flocked to us begging and pleading for a blessing. We laid our hands on hundreds of heads; said many, many prayers, and blessed them and their children. It was something I had never before witnessed—nor even imagined. While this was taking place, someone came running up, urging me to come at once to see a lady who was convulsing. When I arrived at her side, she was, indeed, on the ground thrashing about—but not in a typical seizure. As I obtained the history, I learned that the lady had gone earlier to Bob Paulson—the speaker giving the message that evening—asking to be freed of the demon possessing her. As he prayed, she began *seizure-like* movements which he first thought must be an epileptic fit (convulsion). In examining her, however, it was very evident to me that this was not a neurological seizure but an intense internal struggle. For the next half an hour or so, we prayed and sang—praying for the demon to be cast out. Eventually—without fanfare—she awakened, got up and walked away with her family in perfect peace. We assured her she would remain the subject of much prayer for her continued freedom. I was extremely grateful to experience and to be a part of that event. Many question the phenomenon of demon possession, often claiming seizure activity, a conversion reaction or some other physical explanation. Though I had seen some in Pakistan who were considered possessed, I was never completely convinced. This night, I had no further reservations! What this lady was experiencing was no explainable medical or psychological problem. We got home late. My talk had been on natural, cause-and-effect law—laying a foundation for subsequent lectures.

"The Scripture text that I opened to in my Bible the next morning was in the book of Joshua, where it is recorded that 'God did as Joshua had said.' God had proven to me that He is, indeed, in charge and—even in our inadequacies and failures—He answers our prayers. He is there, working out His plans behind the scenes of human vision on our behalf.

"Within a couple of days, they had completed replacing the original tent, stage and screens with a much nicer setup and larger seating area. On the following Sabbath, and every subsequent day, we were taken by taxi to our assigned village—sometimes over very rough roads with deep potholes—taking two or more hours each way. After we arrived and the people had completed their preparations, they would come to welcome us with heavy leis of beautiful flowers (mostly marigolds and *nice-smelling* tuberoses) that were placed around our necks (sometimes so many we could hardly see around them)! Then we were led—walking behind a band (mostly drums) or a loudspeaker blaring loud, recorded music; or placed on a highly decorated bullock cart and paraded, with great honor, through the village streets—all the while showered by flower petals. On occasion, firecrackers and bottle-rockets added to the affair. One of the things that really impressed me, in almost every village, was the attention the big, black or gray, long-horned water buffalo gave us.

Following the fanfare, we were ushered to a site—a church, or the site of a proposed church—where they had a short ceremony and where the candidates for baptism were examined en masse and given short talks and encouragement.

Many of the villagers have them tied up near their homes. They are used as a source of milk for the family; as a source of dung to use as fuel; for plastering the yard around the house (to keep insects away!), and to work the fields. They seemed to follow the activities with nearly as much interest as the people, and often followed our every move with their expressive eyes. Following the fanfare, we were ushered to a site—a church, or the site of a proposed church—where they had a short ceremony and where the candidates for baptism were examined en masse and given short talks and encouragement. Following the ceremony, we went to the place of baptism—a nearby river, a canal, the ocean or, if nothing else was available, a 50-gallon drum filled with water. There the name of each candidate was recorded, each person baptized and given a blessing, a prayer and a Bible.

"In one village, where I was waiting to speak, I motioned to some little girls to come over to where I was sitting. One of the girls who came (perhaps three years old) sat on my knee for awhile. The people of the village informed me that she was an orphan who lived with her grandmother, who had to work all day in the fields so that they could eat. In the meantime, this little girl wandered about the village unattended. When I left, I gave the pastor a little money with which to purchase things she might need. Later, I spoke with Garwin who suggested she go to the orphanage that he sponsors (and that we will see on another occasion). This particular village was a *neat* little village with round houses made with mud walls and thatch roofs.

"At another place, I met a young man who couldn't walk because of polio. Because he had some motion in the lower extremities, no contractures and very good torso and arm muscles, it seemed he would be a good candidate for rehabilitation; we initiated arrangements whereby that might happen. There were many other examples of hurting people; some were helped, some apparently not!

"Some village visits were better than others. Sometimes organization was poor. It was our practice to give all baptismal candidates a Bible, but one day we had a riot, of sorts, when we baptized more people than we had Bibles to give! When it got late and it was evident that our presence there was not helping the situation, we left—frustrated, to say the least. A few days later, we were at the same place baptizing people from another village, and everything went like clockwork!

"In those villages where the celebration was the most extravagant, I must confess I had some reservations, but who am I to judge? It was a great celebration—a big event that encouraged entire villages to join in the excitement of the moment. I had to admit—and the evidence clearly indicated—that what was happening here was the result of the working of the Spirit of God. I had very mixed feelings during some of this, until I realized that it was beyond my power to change! I had never before been treated like royalty with such a show of excitement. It was our desire to present the Lord *to* them, not for *us* to get the glory.

"Everywhere we go people want a blessing for themselves and their children. They come to us by the droves; with all who come, I have a prayer. It is a neat experience to intercede for another man, or woman—or child!

"Most of these people are still lacking in understanding regarding the teachings we have come to share. They have not yet had the opportunity to learn of many of the practices regarding healthful living, modesty and extravagant display of gold and jewelry, etc., as generally accepted expressions of the Adventist faith. In some villages, this became a point of contention among various pastors and church leaders—some insisting that—before being baptized—the people must remove their gold and jewelry; others argued that since the gold rings in their nose and ears represent their only wealth—in essence, their savings bank—it should not be an issue.

"In spite of these *minor* challenges, the faith of these people is rich, enabling God to do marvelous things—even miracles for them that He cannot do for others with smaller measures of faith. Still, I wonder—what will happen after we leave? Will the Global Pioneers—who are young and still in a learning mode themselves, be able to keep a growing Christian experience going?

"Attendance increased nightly. Furthermore, we just learned that the messages were being broadcast *live,* by television, to the entire city of Ongole at no cost to us. Many came to us seeking a blessing or a prayer. Some came to me with medical problems, desiring miracles—the blind, the deaf, the dumb, those with withered hands and legs and those possessed with demons. For all, we interceded with our Father in heaven and committed them unto His ways. Some, we were also able to help in tangible ways with advice or treatment. People were freed of pain and illness. Demons were cast out. Many experienced miracles in their lives.

"One night at the evening meeting, I was approached by a little, old lady scooting along the ground on all fours and tugging at my pant leg. I stopped and prayed for her, but that was not enough; she kept tugging! I had no translator with me so could not understand what she was saying nor let her know my limitations. Several times she came up to me, and to others, pleading. After the meeting, she was still there—nearly everyone else was gone. She started slowly scooting toward the exit. Finally, I found a translator—but he was busy working with Garwin. Anxious to speak with her before she disappeared, I interrupted and got them to come and see her with me. It seems she had broken her hip four years earlier and had not walked since. She had come by train, 100 kilometers away, spending all she had on the fare. Once this was understood, Garwin bent over and placed a bill in her hand. She didn't recognize its value and would have thrown it away, until she was convinced to keep it. After we all prayed—both with and for her—Garwin hired a rickshaw to take her back to the train and to her home. The next day we were told by the pastor who translated that, as she left, she said she had come for physical healing, and though disappointed, was thrilled that her heart had been healed. I have had to accept the fact that God does not always choose to reverse the results of sin—but He has proven to me that I can come to Him—in confidence—and intercede and expect Him to accept responsibility for the outcome.

Long-term freedom does require follow-up and commitment to Jesus as Lord and Savior.

"Earlier, I told of the demon-possessed lady we met that first night. As it turned out, I did not see her again, but others did. The next day, she had another brief episode during prayer but recovered rapidly. For several days she did not return to the meetings. We all wondered what had happened, for she seemed so convicted (though we knew that her father and another family member were not happy with what was happening). Then one night, she and her mother and sister returned and continued coming until, one day, they were *all* baptized in the sea—rejoicing in their new-found freedom. Our experiences in India taught me that casting out demons may not always be a one-time event (Jesus cast the demons out of Mary seven times)! Long-term freedom does require follow-up and commitment to Jesus as Lord and Savior.

"Elder Watts, President of the Southern Asia Division of the Seventh-day Adventist Church, is thrilled with what he is seeing and is committed to making it work and spread throughout the land. He shared his convictions that the celebrations were a necessary expression of the people's joy and excitement about the new life they were experiencing. And, I must confess, had I been suppressed for thousands of years, I can but wonder how I would respond to such an escape to freedom that we were providing for these people.

"Each evening I gave an illustrated health talk; on the second night, I had a hoarse voice and could hardly speak. Jay Prakosh then proposed a different format for the talks so, from that point on, we discussed back and forth as physician and patient. It worked very well and was probably the best way to reach the people. Jay was a real blessing to me. He was an Indian who had immigrated to the U.S. and become a businessman. Apparently, he was quite successful in a number of projects in the area of health care. At one point, about five years ago—after climbing the ladder of self-fulfillment and experiencing a couple of divorces—he said he finally *woke up* and decided to give his life completely to the Lord. A number of providential experiences led to the decision. More recently, he has been working as Garwin's *visible presence* in India working with the pastors, etc.

"Bob Paulson is a layman who has been a traveling companion to Garwin for some years. He has an awning business, but for the past couple of years he has begun preaching. He is a very out-going, salesman-type person who loves the people he preaches to. He is also a real comedian an—when not preaching—is always saying or doing something unexpected; in the villages, he would sing and join with the villagers in their fun. (Not at all like me!) His sermon material was good with emphasis on Jesus as a loving Savior, and the Sabbath as a Bible command leading to the formation of a righteous life.

"On the last night, several men came to me challenging our emphasis on the law and ignoring the cross of Jesus. They knew all of the tests usually given which prove the change of the Sabbath, but they were not convinced by my arguments. We were getting nowhere fast! Finally, I told them that if I were wrong, I was willing to learn the truth and change my practices. I asked them to pray for me asking God to make it plain to me. We stood there a long time before, finally, one of them began to pray. As I recall, he didn't pray about my request, but he did pray. I then prayed for them and challenged them to reexamine the Scriptures from a non-biased perspective. As we parted, I suggested that before one year was over, they would find the beauty and value of the Sabbath if they would earnestly study the matter.

"We had begun the meetings with about 5,000 in attendance. This expanded each night—in spite of the fact that some of the trucks were on the road two to three hours each way—carrying their human cargo of people who had been working all day in the fields. They were packed like sardines in trucks and buses (150+ per truck) traveling over very rough and dangerous roads—then getting home after midnight and repeating the cycle all over again the next day. Frequently, we received word from other villages requesting transportation for hundreds of people. By the last night, approximately 40,000 people came to hear the message with more than 150 trucks and buses bringing them. People pushed and shoved to be baptized, and to receive a prayer and to be anointed with coconut oil that they had brought along for that purpose. Some wanted the oil to be blessed so that they could use it on others—something I was reluctant to do for fear of propagating their long-held heathen superstitions.

"The dedication of a church on the last Sabbath had all of the trimmings. Elder Don Schneider from the North American Division came for the occasion. When he and Elder Don Watts arrived at the heliport pad (rice paddy), they were greeted with *the works*. There were bushels of flowers, long volleys of rockets, a bullock ride through the village with nearly everyone joining the festivities, a short ground-breaking ceremony for the new church, a prayer, a drink of coconut juice—then to the baptismal site for that occasion. Truly, it was a big day in that village. Never before had they had a church to worship in and to witness of God's presence among them. Much that I don't understand, but I cannot condemn—and I certainly can't deny the working of the Holy Spirit among them!

"After the meetings were over, we went north to the site of the school and orphanage—one that Garwin had funded and is supporting. He has built most of the buildings and was laying out another while we were there. I flew with him and with Don Schneider via helicopter from the meeting site in Ongole, leaving early morning as soon as the fog had lifted. Unfortunately, it hadn't completely cleared—as we found out when airborne! We were flying along nicely when, all of a sudden, we felt a forceful surge upward—only to learn later that we had almost hit an electrical power-line!

"The school was new and beautiful. I was privileged to have a part in walking with the children from their old run-down quarters into the new

The school was new and beautiful. I was privileged to have a part in walking with the children from their old run-down quarters into the new complex. The excitement and joy on their faces is simply indescribable.

complex and to their new dorm where each child had his/her own bed and change of clothing. The excitement and joy on their faces is simply indescribable. Then I understood what it is that drives Garwin and his family to devote so much time, money and energy working with the orphans and poor children of India! It is the love of those underprivileged kids!

"But this wasn't the end! We were then taken to the School of the Blind where we were entertained by 40 or 50 blind children with songs and poems, etc. Not only was this a school, but every child is seen and evaluated by the best eye surgeons in the country; those who had correctable defects were then scheduled for correction. Each was given any help possible, either in restoring vision or in preparing to meet life without sight—if that be the only option.

We were then taken to the School of the Blind where we were entertained by 40 or 50 blind children with songs and poems.

"These were only two of a large number of schools that Garwin has built, or helped to build, in India, Bangladesh, Myanmar, Indonesia and other lands—a true exemplar of Jesus if ever I saw one.

"Upon completing our visit at the school, we boarded a train for the long seven-hour ride back to Chennai. I found the train ride most interesting—and even a little enjoyable! We had fairly comfortable quarters—compared to some of the other cars in which passengers sat on the filthy floor along with the pigs, chickens and all other manner of creatures! It was—in seeing these—that I finally understood what the poor little lady who had come to see us at the meetings had gone through to get there—she, crawling around through urine and filth on all fours! And we complain with what life, sometimes, gives to us!

"I am so blessed—in spite of my faltering faith! I recall interviews that I did with a few of the baptismal candidates in one village. They told me how they were healed of their ailments in response to the interest and prayers of the Global Pioneers. This, they noted, was the primary reason for taking the stand they were taking. Still, my most difficult area and deepest desire, is to be able to communicate in the tongue of those I have gone to serve. Communication is difficult enough for me, under the best of circumstances, but often terribly frustrating across language barriers.

"I am on the last leg of my flight home, as I bring this account to a close. It has been a long, hard trip. From Ongole to Vijayawata by helicopter; to Chennai by train; to Singapore; to Seoul, Korea, and from Seoul to San Francisco—with ten hours of suffering for Danny as he lay on the floor of the plane with headache and dizziness— well as severe generalized aches and pains—and not feeling too well myself! (We weren't sure if it was food we had eaten in a restaurant in India before leaving, or our first meal on the plane upon leaving.) The only way Danny could find any comfort, at all, was lying flat on the ample and empty floor space in first class—a thing the captain insisted he could not do and that caused no end of contention! By the time we arrived in San Francisco, there was no way he could fly on to St. Louis and home. The only hotel close to the airport had rooms priced at $375. Though this seemed much too expensive—and was certainly beyond our budget—we were desperate and waited for the courtesy shuttle bus. None appeared. Danny was getting more miserable by the minute. We finally hailed a taxi. After getting our luggage loaded, we discovered that the driver didn't know where he was going, but assured us he had been given directions and it would be no problem! We drove farther than we thought necessary and still saw no sign of a hotel; then there appeared a Red Roof Inn where the driver was more than pleased to stop. Rooms were available at $90 per night and were very comfortable. We were happy with the seemingly providential delay of the shuttle.

"The Rockies are beautiful with the morning sun falling upon their snow-packed peaks. It will be good to be home!"

Chapter XVI

Ile Efi, Nigeria

"... the power went out just as we were preparing to drain a large abscess of the flank—so completed the procedure with flashlights. This was Nigeria, one of the world's richest sources of crude oil, but there was no fuel available for the generator..."

In March of 2003, I was invited to serve as interim head-physician of the SDA mission hospital in Ile Efi, Nigeria, for one month, while Doctor Giebel, the president of the hospital, was in the States on furlough; and the other physicians in Kenya, for continuing education in preventive health. The following is a *somewhat* chronological account of my experience and observations while there.

Let me begin by quoting from my recorded thoughts en route to Ile Efi.

"The monitor screen in front of me shows that we are now a little more than one-half of the way across the Sahara; in a few more hours we will touch down in Lagos, Nigeria. When I left Rwanda a couple of years ago, I wasn't sure I wanted to return to Africa. Rwanda was a trying experience, to say the least! Just a week or two ago, the former pastor from the mission where I was working in Rwanda was finally convicted by the UN Criminal Court for his role in the slaughter at the mission at Mugonero where I served. (Though I want to be merciful with him, it is hard to forget the evil that took place there.) When Dr. Hart, from Loma Linda, called and asked if I would go, I stalled a bit, half-hoping to find a good reason not to go. I wasn't anxious to leave Avonne and home. Denyse was about due to deliver her baby, my first great-grandchild, (She delivered Maiya a few days before my departure and is doing well). I write a weekly news summary for *3ABN (Three Angels Broadcasting Network)* radio, and I knew I would not be able to do that from Rwanda; then Joe and Jay, the producers, assured me they could do it in my absence! I didn't want to leave my patients in the clinic in Chicago for that long, but Dr. Jones, the director of the clinic, said, 'Yes, go! We want you to be able to do those things. Foreign mission is one of the things the clinic has been trying to facilitate.' As I review the past few weeks, I realize that God has eliminated all obstacles, so there must be a reason for this mission! Not that I don't like Africa; I love the land and its people, but travel is hard and I don't deal with stress and the unknown as well as I once did—at least in some ways. Even so, I am very comfortable now with my mission and am anticipating what the Lord has in store for the next couple of weeks.

"I arrived in Lagos about 7:00 p.m. expecting someone to be waiting for me at the airport. There was no one in sight. Even after everyone on the flight had picked up their luggage and gone their way, I was still waiting—and wondering what to do next. I had neglected to obtain contact information, assuming I wouldn't need it. Lagos is a big city in a country—at the time, considered one of the most dangerous in the world. I must confess, I was a little anxious. Eventually, someone did show up and took me to the Nigerian Seventh-day Adventist Union Office where I spent the night in the guest house. It was hot and noisy; the bed was hard and I was over-tired, so slept little. In the morning, Dr. Saunders, the doctor from the mission in Ile Efi, picked me up and took me across the city to the American Embassy to register and get a stamp for my medical and dental license. That done, we drove back across the city to the Union Office to prepare for the trip to the mission of Ile Efi. Before leaving, I had opportunity to meet and speak with the president of the union for a few minutes. He expressed his excitement about being able to tune into 3ABN television (based in Southern Illinois and broadcast throughout the world via satellite), and stated that he was trying to make it available throughout the country in homes and churches. He told me the story of a Muslim king in an eastern state who had watched 3ABN, believed the truths he heard there, and—with seven or eight other people—became a Christian. Following the upcoming election, he said he had plans for placing 3ABN on television throughout his Muslim domain.

"The road to Ile Efi was scenic. Every few miles along the way, we were stopped by armed militia for security checks. At the outskirts of the city of Ile Efi four or five hours later, I noticed that all of the buildings were vacant, broken down and overgrown with brush, etc. I was told this was the aftermath of a civil war a couple of years before.

"Arriving on campus and given a room and a bed, I was soon fast asleep. I was tired—and tired of traveling!

"Slinky was to be my house companion for the next month. I was given the house of the Giebel's, since they were on furlough to the States. I am not sure if they thought it would be for my pleasure, or theirs, that they carefully arranged for Slinky to keep me company! Slinky was a pet Genet that belonged to one of the Giebel children. Genets are carnivorous, nocturnal, wild animals about the size of a cat—though longer and slimmer than most cats. Slinky had been found in the jungle as a baby and raised by the Giebels. She was housebroken—meaning I had to leave the toilet seat-cover up so that she could do her business! That she was so well disciplined, I thought, was about her only good quality! We were not on the best of terms. If I got too close to her she'd *spit and snap* at me—though I never got bit! I was told her bite was not serious. I did feel sorry for her; her mistress gone and, she, confined to the house day-after-day without suitable companionship. (I didn't seem to fit her taste!) Slinky was into everything—on the table, in the cupboards, in the flour container—and everywhere! Nor did she make an honest effort at keeping her own food (they fed her cat food) in the dish. Often it was scattered all over, with ants and bugs sharing it with her. Fortunately, my bedroom had a door on it, so I could be free from her at night when she did most of her explorations.

"My accommodations were adequate. Our water came from the sky. It was piped from the eves-trough to a tank on stilts—where it was heated by the sun—and then to an underground cistern for other purposes. It had to be filtered and sterilized for drinking. A student came in every day to prepare the water and some food for me in the evening. Most of the time, it consisted of fresh pineapple—simply delicious! My other meals were taken with the Moons, a retired couple who had returned to the mission to help out for a year to direct the School of Nursing. They were very nice people and took great care of me. I surely didn't lack for good food! The shower was another matter. While the sun may have warmed the water during the daytime, it was pretty cool by the time I was able to use it in the morning. More than that, in the darkness of the morning, I was barely able to see the many little creatures that traversed the drain to frequent the moist shower-stall where I bathed!

"The weather was hot and muggy. Fortunately, there was a window air-conditioning unit in my bedroom; unfortunately, most of the time there was no electricity to run it! Often times I had to do my reading and studying by candlelight.

"I awoke, well rested, the next morning after arriving and met with the medical team for morning worship, reports and rounds. The hospital had quite a few sick patients, many of whom were orthopedic (trauma) patients. The census had been down for the past month because of strained finances. The fact that all of the regular, overseas doctors were gone for two weeks doing continuing education in Kenya didn't help the matter. I was there to oversee and work with the doctors in training. The *fun* was just beginning!

"Upon completing rounds, I was called to one of the hospital wards to see a patient who one of the resident doctors was debriding (cutting away the dead and devitalized tissue). We soon discovered this was no task to be undertaken at the bedside, and we ended up taking him to the operating room to complete the task. His whole left-calf area was dead and filled with pus, as was his whole right-thigh area. After removing the necrotic (dead) tissue and pus, he had large defects in both places. We dressed them with moist gauze, planning to repeat the process the next day, and the next, and the next—until clean and healing. Unfortunately, most of the patients in the hospital were poor—very poor, living from hand to mouth. This man was no exception. Yet, the hospital has no other source of income. That fact was a major handicap that troubled me a lot. For example; intravenous fluids came in pint-bottles, each of which cost the hospital one $1 U.S. With no other source of income, patients had to find the money for their treatment before they could be treated. Nevertheless, with this patient, we cleaned and dressed his wounds regularly and, eventually got them clean and beginning to heal. His care was a daily matter as long as I was there, hoping, eventually, to be able to place skin grafts on the large defects. We were never able to determine the cause for his extensive infections and, to this day, I am still puzzled.

"The lack of resources was a real problem. For nearly all of the patients, money seemed to be the most urgent discussion. Care was often withheld for hours, days, or weeks, while family members attempted to find someone to help them out. Even as I was recording my experience with the above gentleman, there was a multiparous lady (multiple pregnancies) who had had a previous C-section and who was in labor that was not effective. She needed a repeat section, but the family was not able to provide the necessary funds. At the same time, a patient who had come in the day before with a scalding burn covering 40 to 50 percent of his body, needed dressings and medications. When I saw him the next morning, he had not yet had the dressings applied because of lack of money. After *reasoning* with the staff, indicating the foolishness of spending money for IVs and meds if we weren't going to dress his wounds, I finally convinced them to get him treated—but was sure I had not won any friends in the process!

"While caring for the man with the ulcerated leg one Sunday morning, and considering the money problem, it dawned on me that—with a little innovation—most of the things we were using to care for him could just as well be purchased or made locally from things that were cheap and available. For example, cloth could be purchased from the local markets, cleaned and folded by family members staying nearby, and then sterilized and used in place of sterile gauze purchased from the USA, France or some other foreign place. Likewise, we could make our own saline solution with a little salt and water. My problem was to get the staff to *buy into* these concepts. Unfortunately, during my short time there, I was not able to make many, if any, inroads—but was inspired by the circumstances to continue to work on a manuscript on health care that I had begun a couple of years earlier, while in Rwanda, where I had experienced similar problems.

"Following rounds that day, I got a ride to the university where there was a cybercafé—a room filled with computers—where, for a price, one could use a computer to send e-mails, etc. It took me awhile to learn the ropes but, eventually, I got a look at my e-mails and was able to send one. Later that day I worked with Mr. Moon, the director of nursing. He was building a large water-tower for the nursing school and, to do so, he needed to cut down a huge banyan tree. That task ended up a failure—and a concern for me—though he didn't seem to be too worried! The trunk was very large and—even with his large chain saw and cutting on all sides—was not able to get it to fall. It stood as long as I remained at the mission, and I have never heard what happened!

"Ile Efi hospital has been around for a long time and was the favored hospital in the area. The large campus includes the hospital complex that is composed of multiple buildings (separate wards), and connected by a covered sidewalk. There is also a lab building; a building where the generator is housed; a laundry (most everything was hand-washed and dried in the sun); a maintenance (carpentry) building; an outpatient clinic; an emergency department (one large room), and the educational building and office. There is also a large, nursing school and dormitory (about 300 students, with a new dorm under construction) and a large church on campus. In addition, there are apartments for the resident physicians and housing for the foreign physicians and other staff. Besides all of this, there is ample, vacant land for those who wish to grow gardens, etc. At quite some distance from the buildings, there is a spring and pool with a pump for piping water to the hospital facility and nursing school.

Unfortunately, Mr. Moon spent much time trying to keep this working and, much of the time, we had no running water in the hospital. There was a time when this was a beautiful facility.

"The campus is resplendent with mango trees, and with thousands of fruit bats flying around and resting in their branches. I am told they do no damage to the fruit, but I am not so sure. There are also avocado trees, sweet-smelling plumeria, flame trees and many, many others I cannot identify. Out by the spring, some of the locals grow sweet potatoes and cassava and harvest the palm fruit to cook up for palm oil.

"Our *Intensive Care Unit* consisted of a single room, large enough for two hospital beds; three, if one could *squeeze* them in! A single light bulb was suspended from the ceiling. Walls were dark yellow and in need of paint. There was little more—no cardiac monitors; no monitors for checking blood gases; no machines for assisting breathing. Nothing! We did have IV stands and some IV supplies. The remainder of the hospital wards had even less—including the Emergency Department!

"We tried to maintain a semblance of sterility in the dressing rooms and operating rooms, but that was difficult because—though we had some disposable supplies, they were not disposed of—for they were about all we had. Shoe covers were made of cloth, but laundering was not always possible. Gowns were either reused disposables or very tattered and torn cloth. Sterile gloves were disposables that were used over and over again, until falling apart. Suture materials were mostly donated *samples*, necessitating sorting through them, during a case, to find something that might work. Antiseptic solutions often had to take the place of soap and water for prepping before surgery. We did have an autoclave for sterilizing the instruments, but the towels they were wrapped in were often tattered and torn and nearly threadbare. The operating tables were OK, but not fancy. For anesthesia, we depended upon injectable Ketamine for most procedures. Spinal anesthesia was used for C-sections. General anesthesia was possible, but risky, since the electric-powered oxygen generator was not always working and we had no respirator. Even our cautery supplies, grounding plates and cutting instruments were disposables that often shorted-out and malfunctioned when most needed. Blood, if needed, was usually taken from a family member donor, though the bank did maintain some blood. As mentioned earlier, the mission received electricity from city supplies; unfortunately, that summer the government's generators were not working much of the time. We had a generator on campus for the purpose of filling in when the city didn't have power but, unfortunately, we couldn't afford fuel for the generator—if and when it was available. As a result, some operations were postponed waiting for power—or done by flashlight and candles if they could not wait.

"Troops were just moving into place for the invasion of Iraq while I was in Nigeria. Most of our news of the outside world came at the cyber-café when we were able to go there. One day as I was reading the news, I noted how serious the pope was in averting the war. He was expressing hope that Saddam would accept exile. And, yes, I must confess I was a little apprehensive—not knowing what would happen to international travel once the war started.

"One day, after morning rounds, we debrided the necrotic stump of a lady who had had an above-knee amputation—it was obvious that she would need a higher amputation; also took a strange-looking growth off a finger; and placed an external fixator on a bad, compound fracture of the main bone in the lower leg of another patient. I learned, too, that the man admitted with the burn died during the night, apparently from aspiration (choking on his vomit). We had another patient with a closed-head injury that was not doing well, and we knew he would probably not make it; also, a man with a probable ruptured appendix with an abscess, who went home before admission for lack of money. Not a good day! The day was warm, as usual, but except for a few hours in midday, it was pleasant—cooling down well between 5:00 p.m. and 6:00 p.m. Little creatures of the night kept me entertained with their singing, chirping and squawking throughout the night, until the birds began to sing with the dawning of a new day.

"Another day has arrived. I saw a lady in diabetic coma who was not doing well at all. Much of the care of such sick people requires a variety of lab studies. The only thing we could get was a blood sugar and that, only, when lab personnel were available to run it. We did have means to check urine sugars, but they are not much help in such situations. In situations such as this, one is even more dependent upon the blessing of the Lord.

"I must say that the resident doctors (in training) are very knowledgeable; this, in spite of the lack of resources to work with and to learn from. In some ways, this did create problems; I was not always sure how to relate to the residents. Normally, they should involve their supervising surgeon before doing procedures or if they had questions; sometimes they did, but sometimes they just took things into their own hands—apparently thinking they knew the needs of their patients better than I. For a day or two, I thought that might pose a problem; fortunately, it did not. We adjusted well to each other.

"One morning they presented a seven-year-old boy with a compound suprachondylar fracture (a broken bone at the elbow) that had occurred four days earlier and was still unreduced. These are the injuries that are high-risk for crippling the arm and making it useless. (This was the cause of the deformed arm of a lady that we often visited from the New London Church when I was a kid.) We placed him in straight-arm traction, with plans to reduce it the next day. (He eventually did OK without complications.) That same day, a man came in who had crushed his hand in an auto accident several days earlier. It was gangrenous, infected and threatening his life. We treated this with a guillotine amputation—simply cutting it off and tying off the blood vessels—hoping to repair the stump later. Later that day, I saw an elderly lady with a colon obstruction, apparently due to cancer. She was scheduled for surgery the next day. That evening we had a patient with a ruptured appendix and, another, the next morning. Operating on such sick patients without general anesthesia is very difficult and, somewhat, limiting in what can be done.

"Surgery on the lady with the bowel obstruction went well, but she had a tumor in the rectum that was *fixed* in the pelvis. All we could do was make a colostomy to relieve the obstruction. She and the family were not happy about the outcome, but sometimes we must accept the difficult things tossed at us (even modern health care would not have had much to offer her more than what we could do there). The lady with the diabetic coma did not recover, but the man with the head injury gradually woke up and did OK. The guy whose hand we had to amputate was doing well until one of the residents—anxious to go on vacation, took him to the operating room and closed the wounds without first clearing it with me. Then he left. When I discovered what had happened, the wound was, again, badly infected, and I had to open it up and start all over again. Eventually he did OK.

"On another day, the power went out just as we were preparing to drain a large abscess of the flank—so completed the procedure with flashlights. This was Nigeria, one of the world's richest sources of crude oil, but there was no fuel available for the generator—nor was this the first time this had happened, I was told. Later that day, I supervised while the residents did a C-section; I had also helped with one during the night. Finding the right suture to repair the uterus sometimes poses a challenge for these kinds of procedures. Saw another man who had a belly which needed surgery, but he had no money. We placed him on antibiotics and observed him. Major surgery costs about $100 U.S., but almost no one has that kind of money. Another lady died in the night, during delivery of a premature baby. I did not know about it until I heard the people wailing and enquired of the staff; that patient would appear on our list of those that needed to be reviewed and critically discussed.

"Following worship one morning—when I had difficulty understanding the resident who presented the talk—I learned that it was not just I who had problems understanding the language. In fact, I was told that a lot of the workers have difficulty communicating because of so many tribal dialects—a real problem at times.

"Sabbath School and the worship service were enjoyable. Unlike back home in the states, the services are conducted much as I had experienced as a child—except, here, the church was packed and there was a large choir singing beautiful songs of praise to our heavenly Father. It was a pleasant experience—except that I was placed in a special seat—in the front—along with the members of the choir! And, of course, no one was in any rush to meet certain time constraints as so often occurs at home. I thought it interesting how they encouraged people to arrive on time for Sabbath School—by giving awards to those who arrived early and parading them across the front of the church.

"That afternoon, we operated on a man with a gangrenous colon and a belly full of pus. We have a lot of very sick patients in the hospital. I was in the middle of a case in the operating room, when I received an urgent call to the Emergency Department. A young man had tried to get a ride on a moving truck, fell and scraped his side; he was in shock, without any blood pressure, when I arrived. He had no money, but I was able to convince the staff to pump him full of IV fluids (as I mentioned earlier, at $1 U.S. per bottle). With that, his pressure came up and he regained consciousness. He was admitted to the ward with instructions, from me, to continue the IVs at a rapid rate, hoping he would stop bleeding internally and stabilize. When I looked in on him an hour or so later, he was, again, in deep shock, and later died; the staff had not followed my orders for fluids. Of course, I was frustrated but—knowing the situation—what else could they do? Surgery had been out of the question—not only because they had no money, but because the OR was not equipped to deal with such major internal injuries.

"About midway through my time at Ile Efi, I made a note that it seemed I had been there much longer than I actually had! Though, from the above comments, the reader has noted how frustrating rendering quality health care under those circumstances must be, I was, nevertheless, enjoying the experience. I have always enjoyed challenges; especially, if they include trying to help make the world a better place. This place certainly provided that opportunity! But I also began to realize that I wasn't as young as I once was!

"Living without power was becoming a real problem. We had heard rumors about the problems the government was having in reestablishing power, and power was not returning. Occasionally, Ed Moon would be able to find a little fuel to purchase so we could start the generator long enough to do a surgical case; but, for the most part, we lived in the dark. I am sure that fact added to our other patient-care problems. In addition to the man with the gangrenous colon and peritonitis who died, we had a baby who died of neonatal tetanus, and a mother and her newborn baby died from sickle-cell disease and severe anemia. Each of these were reviewed and discussed on our morning rounds; I knew everyone was doing the very best possible with what we had to work with, and I let the young docs know I was proud of them.

"But, there was another problem as well; it was with the nursing staff. Though some of the nurses were very good and conscientious, they were not well organized to meet the changing needs—among which, was not passing information on from one shift to the next.

"From my comments, until now, the reader may be getting the impression that all is dark and dismal and every case a failure. Quite the contrary! In spite of all the challenges, we have had some remarkable successes. The lady with the rectal cancer and colostomy recovered well. Both patients with the ruptured appendixes recovered well and went home healthy. The lady with the large abscess of the flank healed well but, unfortunately, she was also found to have AIDS. The man with the gangrenous legs was doing reasonably well; the wounds were clean and healing ever so slowly. Many other patients have done very well.

"I learned one day while going to the university to visit the cyber café that all of the teachers are on strike, and have been for the past three+ months. This has been a real problem for the students trying to get their degrees. The campus is beautiful—and large; nine miles on a side. Unfortunately, Nigeria, with its abundance of oil, ought to be wealthy and free, but it is not.

"While I have been disappointed with Slinky, *Four Eyes* has become a real friend. She is a young, black, African dog with two white spots, one above each eye that gives her the appearance of having four eyes. I guess that is what makes her valuable! Anyway, in the absence of her regular family, she has adopted me and follows me everywhere. She lies on the steps waiting for me to leave, then accompanies me to the hospital or wherever I go; some different from that *Genet,* though it did lie down on the floor beside me for awhile one day!

"I stopped by the carpentry shop one afternoon, and spoke with the head carpenter about the possibility of making a prosthetic leg for a kid in the hospital who has had an amputation. He asked me to bring him the specs and he would do what he could. We will make a cast of the stump and let him work with that.

"Besides the little creatures of the night that sing me to sleep, the fruit bats seem to have taken a liking to the trees just outside my window. There are so many that they darken the skies while coming to spend the night, chattering and fussing around. Probably more irritating than their noise is the musty odor that accompanies them. Apparently, no one knows how to get rid of them. They look about the size of a pigeon when flying, but I am not sure how big they really are. I remember the ones we had on Guam sat about 10–12 inches tall (or hung *down* 10–12 inches)! On Guam, they were a gourmet delicacy, so they never became an 'over-population' problem.

"Nigeria is composed of three major tribes and about 250 ethnic groups that have their own language; the Hausas live in the north (are primarily Muslim); the Igbo (Ibo) in the east (are primarily Catholic Christian), and the Yoruba are in the west. Ile Efi is the center of the Yoruba tribe (Christian and animist). Every Yoruba town has a crowned chief. Oba, the head (king) of the Yoruba, lives in the town of Oyo, and the chief priest has his office here in Ife. According to Yoruba tradition, Ile Efi was the place from which the creation of the world began, and from which people spread out to inhabit the world. I am not sure I understand the story clearly, but it seems that the Supreme God sent one of the lesser gods to Ife to create the world—which he did. When Esa—an evil god—discovered that he was cut out of the process, he came down to earth to wreck havoc with the work of the creator. In many ways, their story of creation and of the great controversy between good and evil echo the teachings of the Bible.

"Animism, the traditional African religion, has the belief that—living within every animate and inanimate thing—there is a soul. These souls or *divinities*—of which there are many—are not God. They believe in one supreme God who is immortal, creator, controller of the universe, judge and separated from man. The lesser divinities also have the power to create and, of course, do many other things, but God rules over all. Yet, it is the lesser divinities that receive worship—not usually the supreme God!

"A hard day! After morning rounds I helped with a repeat elective C-section. The lady belonged to a prominent family in the city. Apparently—somewhat against the desires of her family—she liked the hospital and chose to have her care here. The surgery went well, but after surgery she continued to bleed and was soon in shock. After pumping lots and lots of fluid and as much blood as we could find into her, we appeared to be fighting a losing battle and ended up taking her back to surgery to try and stop the bleeding; but nothing we could do made any difference. Every needle-stick only caused more holes to bleed from, rather than stopping it with the stitch. We finally closed and continued infusing fluids. Later in the evening, the family met with me and requested that a surgeon they know from the city come in for consultation. (The hospital staff is acquainted with him, since he sometimes fills in at the hospital when no one else is available.) I told them I had no objections to his coming, knowing that we had done everything possible. After seeing her, he decided we must have missed a bleeder inside and wanted to take her back to surgery again. But while there, he learned that, indeed, we had not missed anything and that there was nothing he could do either—a consolation for me, in a sense, but no help for the patient. Sometime after that, we were able to get some fresh blood. Once that was received, the bleeding gradually slowed down and finally stopped. It was late at night by now, and I was relieved but did not expect her to live through the night after all she had been through; I told the family so. I got no calls during the night; I thought that strange. Early in the morning I went to see what had happened and to learn why I had not been called. To my surprise, she had lived through the night and was, actually, doing quite well. My prayers had been answered. In spite of this, the family insisted that she be transferred to the city hospital for the remainder of her care. After she stabilized a bit more—and I was pretty sure she would remain so—I released her to them. (Furthermore, our accessory generator had developed an oil leak and we had lost power again, so I was rather glad to let her go.) Things were finally worked out and the transfer completed. DIC (disseminated intravascular clotting) is a complication in which the platelets in the blood—important agents in the clotting mechanism—are consumed, leaving none to close the wounds. It has a number of origins and, not uncommonly, follows delivery. Even in the States with all of our technology, mortality is significant. That this lady survived, at all, is a miracle in every sense of the word. God does still work miracles!

"The next day went a bit better. Another ruptured appendix (our third—and appendicitis is not supposed to happen in Africa) and two broken legs needing fixation were no challenge after the events of the day before! A thundershower cooled things off a bit, and my walk with *four eyes* in the garden was most refreshing. Lots of pretty birds with sweet-sounding songs were as refreshing as the rain.

"Injuries to the neck are always serious. After seeing a young man who had fallen from a coconut tree and ended up completely paralyzed, I had to tell the family there was nothing we could do to restore function. Just to cover myself, I had a neurosurgeon come in from the city to see him, as well. They weren't ready to hear the news, nor ready to accept that—with the resources available in Nigeria he would be unlikely to even survive.

"Another man—already in the hospital when I arrived—had a gunshot wound injuring a lung and the T-8 vertebra (the portion of the spine in the chest) and has not done well. He remains a paraplegic (paralyzed from the waist down) and continues to have trouble emptying his bladder; but more than that, he has developed a consolidated (solid) lung that is going to require a tracheostomy for breathing and exploratory surgery of the chest to expand the lung. We really do not have the capability to do this here. His outlook is not good!

"Two sets of twins were born today. I was called to the OR to help with a C-section on the first set but, by the time they were set up, the mother delivered them both by the normal route. All were doing fine. Later, another lady with twins was not progressing in labor because of the position of one baby in the womb; we finally had to section her. They too, did well.

"It was late at night by the time I got to see a lady with a dislocated hip. We reduced it the following morning when we could see what we were doing. Another lady has been here for a few days with tetanus—but having no means to give artificial respiration, she died of her disease. About the same time, the boy we had seen about a week ago with the supracondylar fracture of his arm, was readmitted with tetanus. Fortunately, he is doing quite well and, I expect, will survive. None of these patients had any money—not even for necessary meds—an ongoing problem.

"Tetanus is a real problem in much of Africa. Almost no one is immunized against it. The World Health Organization (WHO) has done well in controlling smallpox and some other diseases, but tetanus remains a major killer of newborn babies, and others of all ages.

"On my one and only excursion into the city to meet with the tribal chiefs (more about that later), we visited the historic museum. It was interesting for the many artifacts it contains—some dating back many centuries, I am sure—which tell the story I have already referenced about the Yoruba people. We also stopped for a few minutes to see the markets; I was looking for a doll to take home to Avonne to add to her collection from around the world. While I did not find one, Mrs. Moon remembered my search and, on the day I left, she presented me with a black doll and—though a *Barbie* doll and not a traditional African doll—it filled the bill quite well. I was told that the little girls there do not play with dolls.

"One of the most challenging problems I was faced with, over and over again, was that of men with prostates obstructing their bladders. Unfortunately, I had no experience removing prostates, but it was a real problem. Sometimes we could get a catheter into the bladder—and sometimes not; if not, we were forced to place one—through the skin—in the lower abdomen. Not the best answer, but sometimes lifesaving.

"One would not ordinarily expect an infection to go on for three months without causing a lot of problems, but this 18-year-old man had just that. His thigh had become very swollen. I wasn't sure what was going on but, when we opened it up, the entire thigh was full of pus and necrotic debris. We drained it through multiple incisions, cleaning it as best we could; then placing gauze packing and multiple catheters through which we planned to irrigate with antibiotic solutions. He was doing well when last I saw him.

"After removing the cast from the little boy's amputated leg, I took it to the carpenter shop for them to use as a template for a new leg for him. I was not met with enthusiasm! They claimed they were already overworked, and if word ever got out that they could make limbs, they would be flooded with requests. I thought, 'what an opportunity;' but they still didn't share my vision!

"After I had been in Ife awhile, I discovered that many of the people there knew me already, having watched on television as we broadcast a series of meetings from Kamasi, Ghana, a couple of years earlier. Unfortunately, I do not do well remembering people, their names or faces. Hence, though they seemed to know me, I had trouble remembering their names and where they fit into the whole mission picture. But it was nice to be among friends!

"In the Giebel's large library, I came across a book I hadn't seen before that added a dimension to the knowledge I had already received from a book in my own library entitled, *The Gospel in the Stars.* That book describes the Zodiac with its 12 stations. It notes that—when looking back into ancient history—one discovers that many of the ancient names of the constellations and the stars in those constellations have meanings relating to the war between God and Satan; between good and evil; and outlining the whole plan of God from creation and the fall of Adam and Eve to the return of Jesus. Unfortunately, the book I have does not portray a clear picture of the final judgment described in the Bible; I was disappointed by that. The book I was reading in Nigeria did indeed *see* the concept of the final judgment in the constellations. I have been intrigued by this topic since I first read about it, for it strongly suggests that God explained His entire plan (to rescue man from sin) to Adam and Eve soon after the fall, and He recorded it in the heavens to remind them and their descendants, for all time. Unfortunately, over time, the devil has succeeded in hiding those truths from most people today. As I write this, I am reminded that the same story is told in the ancient Chinese characters. In examining those pictographs from five-thousand years ago, still visible on pottery, etc.—one can, again, read many features of the same plan as described in the Bible and in the signs of the Zodiac.

"One night when the sky was clear, I was walking around the mission and had opportunity to see the constellation of the Southern Cross. I had been told—while on Guam—that it was visible from there, but I was never convinced that I had seen it. Those who have viewed it speak so enthusiastically about it; I was happy to be able to share the joy.

"I was wrong! The carpenters did, indeed, make a wooden leg for the little guy. Now, it was our turn to find a way to attach it to him so he could use it. I was soon to be on my way home, so assigned the residents the task of doing this.

"Once each month, the mission president has been meeting with the tribal chiefs. Ile Efi is the headquarters of the Yoruba tribe and, thus, is the palace of their king and the place of their meetings. They had been impressed with the work of the mission and had requested opportunity to understand the teachings of the Adventists that operated it. Since I was filling in for Dr. Giebel, I was invited to meet with them at the appointed time. I accepted the offer with mixed emotions—a bit fearful of the unknown, I suppose, and uncertain of what to bring to them. Nevertheless, I prepared some things and went to the palace to meet them as scheduled. Unfortunately, they were in deep discussions with the king that day and canceled the meeting. I was both disappointed and relieved—although mostly disappointed—as one might imagine. In considering my presentation, a new thought dawned on me that I had not previously seen. It was this: In God's rescue operation, He had to find a way to replace the love in the human heart that had been stolen away by Satan by his deception in Eden. In order for this to make sense to the chiefs, I knew I had to define love. That, I would tell them, was defined by the Law of the Ten Commandments. For example: The least expression of the commandment 'not to steal' might be to refrain from taking something belonging to another. But if love for that other person were really strong, there is no *upper* limit to what a person might give to another rather than to steal from one. Likewise; the least expression of the seventh commandment 'not commit adultery,' is to avoid sexual intimacy with another woman than one's own wife. But like the command 'not to steal,' there is no *upper* limit as to how much love one could give to one's mate in marriage. Each of the commandments may be looked at in this way. And what if everyone living saw the commandments as *opportunities* to express unlimited love for one another? It would truly be a different world! But just to make this plain, God sent His Son to demonstrate what keeping those commandments would look like—even to the extent of giving His own life to save the very ones who put him to death—a living demonstration of the *ultimate* expression of love! It is something like light; there is a *lower* limit to light—that is, when there is no light at all, we have absolute darkness; but there is no known *upper* limit to how light it may be. Likewise; when things get as cold as possible—what we refer to as *absolute zero*, it can get no colder, but there is no limit as to how hot something can get. I thought these concepts would be appropriate and interesting to the chiefs, but it was not to be.

"Looking through the medical library one day, I happened upon a book written by a physician who practiced in South Africa one hundred years ago. In it he described the kinds of problems he had to deal with and how he treated them. He described his operating theater—a small dark room with a wooden table and a lantern—and his use of common modalities to make his work successful. I was intensely interested, for he was doing things much better than we were, with much less than we had. He did have at least one advantage—he had an abundance of boiling water. We, oftentimes, didn't even have water!

"Other interesting surgical cases before the end of my stay included an unsuccessful attempt to debride an infected, open (compound) fracture of a knee—he will likely end up with an amputation later. Another lady had a life-threatening infection of her amputation stump that we had to surgically excise at a higher level; also did a hysterectomy for huge fibroid tumors; more C-sections; drained an abscess in the abdominal wall of a two-year-old boy, and had another patient with tetanus from a severely infected foot. In addition, he had a stricture of his urethra and was unable to empty his bladder. Elsewhere, attempts to place a catheter resulted in trauma with bleeding; it took me about an hour to finally get a catheter into his bladder to relieve the obstruction and, of course, we had to debride his foot. Another challenge was that of an 11-year-old girl who had swallowed a coin which got stuck in her throat. She had sat in the emergency department of the government hospital all day and wasn't getting anything done, so the family brought her over to us. X-rays confirmed the presence of the coin—located in such a place that it could easily be dislodged and result in suffocation. We scrounged around in the storage-room until we found many parts of old, rigid esophagoscopes and were eventually able to construct one that actually worked! My problem was; I had not used one since my residency training (everything is now done with flexible scopes). However, with an anesthesia nurse to give a dose of Ketamine to put her to sleep, I was able to locate and remove the coin—much to the relief of all of us! Some days, you just know in your heart that God truly does hear and answer prayers for help.

"My last day on duty was a quiet day—no calls—but on rounds I found a few pretty sick patients. I discovered that one had died and another, nearly so, without my being notified. This is one thing that has frustrated me. The house staff have a different view of life—for the cost of western health care is beyond the reach of most—so what do you do when you know what might help but can't, for financial reasons, make it happen! The people here are neat people, but the hospital is so inadequate; in fact, I am told, that at one time there used to be running water—hot and cold, and many nicer things than we now have. After taking all things into consideration, I am amazed that things run as well as they do. (Some of the residents who have spent time in the government hospitals in training, say this is the best hospital in the country!) Still, I hope that the staff learns to be more aggressive at saving life.

"As I said my farewells this morning, many of the house staff spoke of their gratitude for what I had given them. Though not, even yet, knowing some of their names, we have had a good time together. My gift was a Nigerian shirt and pants.

"This has been an enjoyable experience; I really didn't know what to anticipate. But in spite of power and fuel failure; frustrations of quality care, sadness for those who have died and all the rest, I have been blessed. When I realize that Ile Efi is one of the best hospitals in the nation, and that Nigeria is, at least, as well off as most of Africa, it is no wonder that their professional people are drawn to move to the west—for the divide between the wealthy and the poor is, indeed, wide. One must also wonder who Jesus was referring to in telling the story of the Good Samaritan, 'Who is my neighbor?'

"The mission compound would be beautiful if it had a few gardeners instead of so 'many' guards; the trees, flowers, birds and butterflies are all pretty; the weather warm and sticky—haven't had an hour of dry skin since I arrived, I suppose, but one adjusts to the feel! A truly-blue sky I have yet to see; most days are hazy, I'm told, from the fine Sahara dust in the air. The many trees on the compound help to cool the place, I am sure. It would be easy to learn to love Africa. It is too bad there is so much unrest and political strife—so much suffering and pain. One wonders what this continent might have been had the colonialists not exploited it so—perhaps better—perhaps worse—for ancient superstitions and tribalism were not so good either and perhaps, without the colonialists, there would not have been Christianity to help combat those things. The Nigerian society is interesting. The women are the strength of the society—the men the decoration; though chiefs and kings rule, it's quite clear who does much of the work and has the influence.

"The trip back to Lagos was OK. Got stopped by police who discovered a problem with our license plate (and gave us a ticket)! Obtaining fuel was also a problem. Queues are miles long and the wait for fuel—hours. Because of this, the traffic is probably lighter than normal. The country's workers are scheduled to go on strike tomorrow about two weeks prior to elections.

"The mission at Ife is like an oasis, of sorts, as compared to the cities. Since I hadn't really been away from the mission, I haven't had much of a picture of the rest of the country. The rural areas are beautiful with rich farmland and pretty trees, etc., but something about the city of Lagos calls the people from the outlying areas!

"Until today, I hadn't really realized what missionaries sacrifice to serve in a place like this. It is not an easy life, and the rewards are sometimes pretty elusive; yet, there are some real saints, many the products of missions. I discovered, last night, that the lady who has cleaned my house was a convert from our meetings in Ghana!

"As I sit in the airport, the power keeps shutting off! It's still a few hours until flight time so will see what happens in the interim. I thought I had left that problem in Ife!"

Chapter XVII

The World

"... But the cloud kept enlarging as I drove until—all of a sudden—I found myself in the midst of a real downpour; and, after the downpour, the most beautiful full rainbow..."

With rapt attention I listened! The things I was hearing were like music to my ears! Since childhood I had known that one of the signs that must be fulfilled before Jesus could return and bring an end to sin and the evil that is destroying our world was for the gospel to be taken to the *whole* world. A prime component of my daily prayers had been to see that prophecy fulfilled. And here, before my very eyes, was a young man telling of a *vision* whereby this great feat could be accomplished via the medium of satellite television. As he spoke, I could hardly contain myself. I wondered—can this really be true? After the service, I approached the young man to verify if what I had heard was what he had really said. He reassured me it was correct, I volunteered to contribute some stained-glass windows (my hobby at the time) for the production studio that he was planning to build, an offer he accepted.

Danny Shelton was a singing carpenter from southern Illinois. During the week he did carpentry and, on weekends, he and his 11-year-old daughter, Melody, traveled the country singing gospel music (his wife had been killed in an auto accident). One night, while on tour, Danny could not sleep. He had heard—in his mind—the command to build a satellite station to reach the world with the *Undiluted Three Angels Messages, to counter the counterfeit.* There was no vision, no actual voice—only the words in his mind that he could not dispel. As Danny tells the story, he was a carpenter with nothing more than a high school education, poor and barely eking out an existence. "Who was I to even consider such an impossible endeavor," he recalls. But—before the night was over—he had concluded that the *voice* he *heard* must have either been from God or from His archenemy, the devil, and he was convinced the devil would not instruct him to take the gospel of Jesus to the world.

Arriving home Danny began, at once, to find out all he could about what it would take to fulfill his calling—only to see miracle, after undisputed miracle, take place in response to every step he took into the unknown world of the budding satellite television technology. I will not repeat the beginning of that story for it has been recorded elsewhere, but the story and the miracles continue to this day! I, too, began to work; I had made a few stained-glass windows for the little church of my childhood, but I needed help in designing the windows and making the drawings. My son, Greg, a student of commercial art at a school in Chicago at the time, agreed to work with me on the project. By the time the production studio was completed, our project, too, was complete—a picture of a transmitter radiating electromagnetic signals, superimposed upon a large, six-foot-diameter picture of the world, with three *modern* angels encircling overhead. Meanwhile, Danny phoned me, one day and invited me to serve on the Board of Directors of the new *Three Angels Broadcasting Network.*

By divine inspiration, by the example of Jesus, and by my own personal experience, I knew the power of the healing ministry of Jesus in touching hearts and opening them for the reception of the gospel. In sharing this, health programs were incorporated into the lineup of programs from the very beginning.

Not long after this—at a time when I was looking for ways to produce good health programs—*Faith for Today*, one of the first religious programs to be broadcast on television (then going by the title, *Christian Lifestyle Magazine*), was in trouble and looking for new programming ideas and financial backing. I met with the host, Dan Matthews and his staff, in Thousand Oaks, California, spending the better part of a day sharing thoughts and planning ways to impact the hurting world around us with programs focusing on health and lifestyle issues that might benefit both *Faith for Today* and the *3ABN* viewers. I left that meeting, mid-afternoon, with very mixed emotions—liking the concept, but not certain of the format. In my state of frustration, I decided to drive inland to Loma Linda to visit my brother. To avoid driving through the city of Los Angeles, I decided to go out across the high desert where I hoped to find peace and rest, but the farther I went, the more uncomfortable I became. It was hot! It was dry! The way was much longer than I had remembered, and I was not finding the relaxation and peace I had hoped for. All during that time, I had been pleading with God for direction regarding our plans and decisions. At that point—when it seemed like it could get no worse—I noticed a small, dark cloud far to the east ahead of me. *Strange*, I thought, for there to be clouds like that at this time of the year. But the cloud kept enlarging as I drove until, all of a sudden, I found myself in the midst of a real downpour; and, after the downpour, the most beautiful full rainbow, I believe, I have ever seen! For a long time it lingered; I basked in its glory, realizing that God had performed another miracle—this time, just for me. Following the storm, I soon found myself driving over the pass and down into the San Bernardino valley and on into Loma Linda—just as a glorious sun set in the western sky. I knew that our efforts that day had not been in vain!

Back home, a young pastor by the name of Mark Finley from the New England area came to Chicago to develop a center for training ministerial students for public evangelism. He had experienced the benefits of sharing information about health, along with his preaching messages, and was looking for professional people to help teach his students and to provide presentations at his meetings. Roy Wightman, Health Education Director at Hinsdale Hospital and with whom I had worked, introduced me to Mark. We soon began working together—helping people quit smoking, teaching them how to prevent heart disease, cancer and many other maladies. When, a couple of years later, my wife and I had the opportunity to join a tour group to the Holy Land that he and his wife, Ernestine, were leading, we often shared our thoughts and dreams for taking the gospel to the world. Later, when Mark became the Ministerial Director for the Trans-European Division of the Seventh-day Adventist Church and heard the call of God to preach the gospel in Communist Poland, he called and asked if I would join him in that endeavor. I did! A couple of years later, he was called back to Poland and, once again, he invited me to join him. During our exercise walks in the forest preserve, we spoke of an invitation he had received to become Speaker/Director of the television ministry, *It Is Written*. He had reservations about it; he saw himself as an evangelist, believing that personal contact and visitation were necessary for effectively reaching people. However, I had seen the effect of Christian television on viewers and was convinced that one could speak just as effectively through the television screen as in person—and to a vastly greater audience. Mark did accept the opportunity and now, many years later, he still has not lost the thrill of sharing the gospel via this modern-media miracle.

While working with *Lifestyle Magazine*, Glenn Aufderhar, President of the Adventist Media Center, invited me to join an evangelism planning session to be held at the center in Thousand Oaks, California. I accepted the invitation, somewhat reluctantly, but with a burden to share from my experience at *3ABN*. As it turned out, that meeting provided incentive for another to follow, this time on the East Coast. When at that follow-up session at the Church World Headquarters, we discussed the option of broadcasting an entire series of evangelistic lectures over satellite television to the entire world (Billy Graham had, just recently, done something similar for one weekend in Europe)—the general consensus was that it was neither feasible nor cost-effective, but the idea did strike a chord in the heart of a few who soon began to plan and put those plans into action. Since that time, millions and millions of people from all around the world have heard the gospel for the first time and have accepted Jesus as their Savior.

Nor has God forgotten *3ABN*! By His blessing and with the financial support of self-sacrificing, Bible-believing Christians, *3ABN* was the first television network—of any kind—to broadcast its message 24/7 to the entire world. While it is one thing to send a signal out into space, bringing that signal back down to earth for all to hear is an altogether different problem! But that, too, is happening and is now enhanced by the added digital technologies of the Internet, cable networks, direct satellite television, IPTV (Internet protocol television), etc. Viewers from around the world regularly contact *3ABN*, daily expressing excitement in their newfound faith in Jesus—our Creator, Redeemer, Divine Intercessor, Judge and soon-coming Savior—all of this, and better health as well!

God is so good! To Him be all the glory!